# How To Save Free Enterprise*

**\*from bureaucrats,
autocrats, and technocrats**

# How To Save
# Free Enterprise*

WILLIAM McDONALD WALLACE

 1974

DOW JONES-IRWIN, INC.
Homewood, Illinois  60430

\*from bureaucrats, autocrats, and technocrats

First Printing, October 1974

**Library of Congress Cataloging in Publication Data**
Wallace, William McDonald.
    How to save free enterprise from bureaucrats, autocrats, and technocrats.

    Bibliography: p.
    1. Bureaucracy. 2. Management. 3. Job satisfaction. I. Title.
HD38.W33    658.4'02    74–78160
ISBN 0-87094-079-1

*Printed in the United States of America*

*To the memory of my brother*
*Robert Bruce Wallace, Jr.*

# Preface

AMERICA HAS LOST much of its cocksure "can do" faith in less than one decade. No wonder; nothing seems to work any more. Increasingly intractable problems bedevil us as our institutions become ever less responsive to our needs.

This book argues that much of the difficulty lies with the institution of bureaucracy, the taproot of many of our worst problems. Bureaucracy's troubles arise from a coercive social order based on a false view of human motivation in the world of work. Bureaucracy gets the least out of people because it inhibits cooperation and teamwork, and thus it is forced to become coercive to get results. Coercive bureaucracy systematically inhibits teamwork, alienates employees, and inflates costs. This book describes how this loss of efficiency, combined with alienation, leads to unemployment and to widespread demoralization outside the bureaucracy itself.

This book sharply disputes the idea that no useful alternatives to bureaucracy exist for large organizations. It shows that an unbureaucratic alternative does exist and it works. Further, although bureaucracy can damage any culture, "unbureaucracy" can work cross-culturally.

The recent enlightenment of the "new biology" relates the evolution of human psychology to our long history as teamhunters. My interpretation of the new biology argues that a natural social order—fraternity—evolved along with hunting to satisfy five emotional needs. When these five needs are satisfied, they "release" cooperative teamwork in the human species.

This interpretation of the works of the new biologists is my own. I assume full responsibility for my integration of their research with mine. Many of my "biological" conclusions result from deductive reasoning. Much of the evidence simply does not lend itself to proof one way or the other. But enough evidence does exist, I believe, to allow us to make deductions which go well beyond idle conjecture.

The ideas expressed in this book could never have been put in written form without the influence of many people, either through my reading of their works and correspondence or from personal discussion with them. Several people were of great personal help in critical evaluation of numerous drafts of my theme, in either the formative or final stages of its development. I owe special thanks therefore to G. Altman (Col. ret. Israeli Army), Donald Bolme, Thomas F. Comick, Thomas R. Craig, Gerald Dennis, Raymond D. Larson, Kiyoshi Okawa, Glen L. Parker, Dwight Robinson, and Mechai Viravaidya. This does not imply, however, that any of them necessarily agrees with my views.

Bellevue, Washington
*August 1974*

W. M. WALLACE

# Contents

The Five Social Needs. The Identity Crisis. Status and the Job Hierarchy. Role. Prestige. Rewards as Income.

## Part III
### Bureaucracy in Blunderland: Three Case Studies

## Part IV
### Fraternity in Action

# Introduction

Many serious problems face Western civilization today because our enterprises increasingly fail to achieve a real team spirit. Esprit de corps in human enterprise probably arose in the fraternal bands of our ancient ancestors, the teamhunting hominids. It has influenced human endeavor ever since. Patriotism and similar emotional states based on loyalty to family, church, political party, or just one's own friends are all modern manifestations of our ancient fraternal urges.

As large scale industry displaced the family enterprise as the mainstay of the economy, however, a cold, impersonal form of administration known as bureaucracy took hold. Bureaucracy, supposedly the ultimate form of "rationality," regards emotions such as fraternity to be "irrational." It also assumes that fear and greed are the only motives for good work. Bureaucracy thus depends on a coercive social order which tends to inhibit esprit de corps and undermine teamwork.

I contend that the bureaucratic social order is responsible for many of our present difficulties: simultaneous high rates of unemployment and inflation, inexorable expansion of numbers of governmental officials without reference to need, a welfare problem that dominates the state, loss of technical efficiency, and a steadily worsening position in international trade. Hovering over most of these problems lies a gloomy and thickening cloud of employee dissatisfaction with organization life. The resulting alienation, apathy, and psychological distress have extended to the upper reaches of both business and government bureaucracies.

The inhibited teamwork, inflated costs, and alienated employees these problems reflect are directly traceable to the coercion and fear on which the bureaucratic social order is based. If cooperation and teamwork were substituted as motivators, the fraternal social order

1

which would develop would be a viable alternative. This system could revitalize the free enterprise system by working within it rather than seeking to replace or overthrow it.

In tracing the evolution of a system of human enterprise from the natural fraternal system of our forebears, its subsequent devolution into bureaucracy, and its predicted rebirth as the fraternal social order, we will first establish the biological basis of fraternity. The rise of bureaucracy will be traced in the second chapter of Part I.

After discussing why it has been falsely assumed that bureaucracy is the most efficient social order for the workplace, Part II will provide a general diagnosis of bureaucracy's woes. Part III is comprised of three case studies of bureaucracy in action, each devoted to a different purpose and in a different cultural setting.

Part IV gives examples of the team hunter's social order as it has been applied in the modern world, often unwittingly. The major evidence comes from Japan, the only modern country to apply the natural social order to its economy, more or less completely.

In Part V we will examine what life without bureaucracy might be like. Chapter 10 does this in regard to the fraternal enterprise. Chapter 11 looks at fraternal free enterprise from the viewpoint of the economy as a whole and explains how it could help us cope with many of our problems. We could, for example, create an institutional framework for a full-employment, free-market, free enterprise economy devoid of the cost-push inflation inherent in bureaucracy. Many related problems would then become much less difficult to solve.

I have also included two appendices. The first explains the biology of fraternity in greater detail, and the second briefly explores the matrix form of organization a corporation could adopt as a mechanism to shed bureaucracy and convert to fraternity.

# Part I

## THE EVOLUTION AND DEVOLUTION OF HUMAN ENTERPRISE

# 1

# The Evolution of Fraternity

## ORIGINS OF FRATERNITY

The natural social order for human enterprise of whatever size or purpose has its genetic origin in emotional needs and urges predating by far the development of the human intellect. One of the crucial emotions in the social order is a desire for friends and comrades bound by feelings of mutually reciprocated loyalty, trust, and affection. Humans are not just animals who must live in social groups to survive. We are a special kind of social animal, a fraternal creature unlike any of our primate cousins, the monkeys and the apes.

Most primates are social animals out of biological necessity. Banding together for protection of the young and for common defense, social grooming, and infant play typify almost all primates. But only the faintest glimmer of fraternity can be observed among apes and monkeys. The peer group of friendly social equals that is found in all human cultures does not exist elsewhere. Monkeys and apes, in fact, live in an almost friendless society, controlled by a pecking order based on social dominance that is determined in open competition, whereas humans have strong genetic inhibitions which prevent dominance struggles and pecking orders among close friends. In larger, more impersonal groups these inhibitions break down because our fraternal urges have evolved from ancestors who lived only in small face-to-face groups.

Our distant ancestors probably once lived in a social order similar to that of other primates. Fraternity evolved to inhibit dominance struggles because, for reasons we may never know, our prehuman ancestors changed their economic occupation. They gradually gave up the life of individualistic fruit pickers, seed gatherers, and root diggers for the more adventurous and risky business of hunting.

5

As hunters, these ancestors evolved into a distinct and indeed unique branch of primates. Anthropologists call our prehuman hunting ancestors the hominids. The hominids not only hunted, they teamhunted, because they had lost their natural fighting fangs in the process of acquiring omniverous teeth (see Figure 1), and their physical size (about 4 feet tall, 80 pounds) made them ineffective as lone hunters. Unless they cooperated in teams using artificial weapons it is improbable that the hominids could have become hunters. The teamhunting life style made a crucial difference in the course of human evolution. In fact, it has been stated that "The biology, psychology, and customs that separate us from the apes—all these we owe to the hunters of time past."[1]

The chief reason teamhunting inspired innate emotional inhibitions against dominance struggles is because it is not possible to cooperate and compete at the same time. Moreover, the dominance struggle serves social purposes, but it has little economic relevance anywhere in nature. The economics of gathering is almost purely individualistic; each creature fends only for itself. Normally there is plenty of food for all, but order must prevail. Chaos would reign if every monkey tried to reach for the same mango. The dominant monkey or ape, usually a male, has first pick of the fruit. The dominance struggle thus establishes a sort of "chow line," which remains comparatively stable. No. 1 brooks no nonsense, and fear of No. 1 keeps the others in line. But greed makes all the males envious of No. 1 and thus its potential rivals. If No. 1 falters, another status-hungry male makes his play to take over.

Now consider how this system would affect team hunting. No. 1 would have to take the most dangerous risks himself. Why not, since he gets the prime cuts? If No. 1 were injured and out of action, a new dominance struggle would break out, which would hardly be a boon to trust. There would be fights to establish a new rank order. Dominance would disrupt teamwork, and the group would face serious instability both from lack of positive cooperation and a higher exposure to risk.

The psychology of dominance thus makes no provision for the economic cooperation and sharing which teamhunting requires. The motive for dominance is little more than selfishness and greed. Jane Goodall's films of chimps amply attest to their greed and failure to share when given handouts of bananas. The purposes of survival are served in the abundant gathering economy but not in teamhunting.

Teamhunting requires a different psychology. Because members must depend on one another, they must cooperate and trust one another. Hunters must share the spoils with campbound dependents and,

---

[1] S. L. Washburn and C. S. Lancaster, in Richard B. Lee and Irvin DeVore (eds.), *Man the Hunter* (Chicago: Aldine Publishing Co., 1968), p. 303.

**Figure 1**
EVOLUTION OF MODERN MAN

The **chimp**, a modern Great Ape and a vegetarian, may resemble our own early prehunting ancestors. Note his large canines or "fangs." These natural weapons serve mainly defensive purposes.

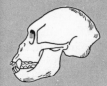

**Ramapithecus**, believed to be the earliest known hominid, shows much smaller canines and the beginnings of omniverous teeth. Evidence from fossil remains of prey and weapons suggests a possible teamhunting existence dependent on artificial weapons. His fossils date from about 15 million years ago.

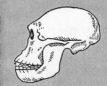

**Australopithecus** was the first fossil to prove the existence of the hominid line of our ancestors. He hunted with crafted weapons in teams. His fangs have almost disappeared. Earliest fossils date from about 4 million years ago.

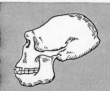

**Homo Erectus**, sometimes called the Java Man, was an early human about half way between the hominids and ourselves in brain case size. He teamhunted and used fire, probably the first to do so. His fossils date from about 700,000 years ago.

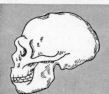

**Neanderthal Man** lived in a highly developed Stone Age hunting culture about 100,000 years ago. He is thought to have invented the bow and arrow and possibly religion. He has a bigger brain case than our own. His disappearance and the emergence of modern man remain something of a mystery.

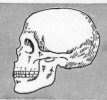

**Homo Sapiens** (modern man) first appears in fossil form about 35,000 years ago. He differs from the Neanderthal largely in anatomical detail. His early innovations include the oldest known cave paintings. He teamhunted until, running out of hunting territory, he began turning to agriculture about 10,000 years ago.

Source: Drawings taken from Bjorn Kurten, *Not from the Apes* (New York: Pantheon Books, Inc., 1972).

perhaps, those who remained behind to protect the camp. They must take risks with their own lives so that others can eat. Humans normally will not take such risks for the privilege of sharing with rivals, but they might do so for friends they trust and for whom they feel affection. Friendships were developed to promote the cooperation and sharing which teamhunting requires. Fraternity thus evolved to serve economic risk-taking purposes, not merely for social companionship.

## THE EFFECTIVE TEAM

In human evolution, survival of the fittest applied to the most effective teams and not to the strongest individuals. Social Darwinism, based on the survival of the "fittest individuals," has been thoroughly discredited. Indeed, it never had much relationship to Darwin's concept of evolution. Darwin's own views went something like this:

> If the contest exists between individuals only, the qualities of mercy and altruism will contribute nothing to a competitor's fortune. But if the contest is between societies, the members of a successful society must have two sets of emotional responses: the many facets of friendship and cooperation reserved for members of his society, and the many facets of hostility and enmity for members of the opposing society.[2]

Thomas Huxley and Herbert Spencer were largely responsible for distorting evolution into a struggle between individuals competing for scarce resources. Ardrey has paraphrased their views as follows:

> Huxley interpreted the evolutionary contest existing in the time of human dawn as one between individuals, not groups. Like Spencer he could not, perhaps, in his passionate advocacy of the theory of evolution, forgo the dramatic appeal of cave-man contest. . . . club against skull, with a shrinking woman in the dim cavern's reaches clutching a wailing babe. The Huxley distortion of individual conflict set back progress in evolutionary thought for sixty or seventy years; together with the Spencer jungle distortion condemned evolution to the milieu of a bar-room brawl in which nice people do not indulge; and so totally blacked out Darwin's true convictions that to this date the observer of human affairs, impressed by man's real capacity for mercy, for charity, and for altruism, can find no principle in the evolutionary process adequately to explain them.[3]

The most effective teams depend on harmonious cooperation between biological unequals. Differences between individuals broaden the team's skill base. And, because many talents are mutually exclusive, different strengths inevitably entail different weaknesses.

---

[2] Darwin paraphrased in Robert Ardrey, *African Genesis* (New York: Atheneum Publishers, 1961), p. 186.

[3] Ibid., pp 185–86.

Fraternity allows us to tolerate the weaknesses we find in others, thus freeing us to applaud their strengths. The friendly peer groups discourages individual dominance because it violates the essence of friendship. Tolerance for weakness, admiration for talent, and muted dominance create the ideal social climate which encourages the individual to build on his strengths instead of defending against his weaknesses, so that he can interact with others in effective teamwork. For example, a football team does not dwell on a good passer's indifferent blocking ability or a good blocker's inability to pass well; rather, each team member is encouraged to develop his natural abilities and to cover others' weaknesses.

The most effective teams, moreover, will not allow status (rank) differences to be attached to different roles. Concern for rank can divert individuals from developing talent into striving for status in a role which may ill suit them. The friendly peer group will inhibit social status distinction except for generalized experience. Nor is social deference to seniority allowed to determine who does what on the team, except where experience counts. When ability alone determines this, unranked team tasks enjoy much greater flexibility and do not suffer from the distortion of status.

It is important to distinguish here between status and prestige. By status I mean formal social rank. Prestige can be defined as the informal reputation and esteem we earn from our fellows by our own achievements. We can all achieve a measure of prestige by developing our own skills, without reference to formal rank. This concept expands the total range of team skills, maintains team harmony, and allows us to enjoy the satisfactions of camaraderie. It also channels our more aggressive urges outward on rivals, as noted below. Bjorn Kurten believes it is probable that encounters between early hominids and hyena packs did much "to promote intra-group cooperation and loyalty, and inter-group aggressiveness, which are such pervading characteristics of man."[4]

## AGGRESSION AND FRATERNITY

The evolution of fraternity sketched above is not meant to imply that man evolved as Jean-Jacques Rousseau's Noble Savages. Rousseau did not sense our fraternal heritage or understand its original predatory purpose in promoting teamhunting. Moreover, as fossil evidence makes reasonably clear, hominids and later human hunters were often practicing cannibals. Peace and goodwill among men had nothing to do with the evolution of fraternity, which had the much narrower purpose of sharpening the competitive thrust of the hunting team.

---

[4] Bjorn Kurten, *Not from the Apes* (New York: Pantheon Books, 1972), p. 137.

Rivals are the other half of the fraternal coin; man needs rivals as much as he needs friends. If he does not have real rivals, he tends to invent them. Team sports has served this purpose for years, allowing males to band and bond together in order to compete with other bonded bands. War also serves the purpose of providing rivals to enhance friendships. In no sense does this mean we have a "warfare gene," however. We do not even have a "killer instinct," despite our predatory past. Beyond question, human warfare, murder, and other forms of mayhem have a genetic basis, but less lethal and even less violent outlets can discharge the genetic urges responsible for war, head hunting, and even animal hunting.

When Robert Ardrey first popularized the documentation of our hunting heritage in 1961 in *African Genesis,* he unnerved many and outraged those who believed man to be a once-perfect specimen who had succumbed to sin and then fallen from grace. And he took the wind out of the sails of those who would blame all human woes on the effects of the environment on a human genetic vacuum. The effectiveness of Ardrey's argument is not diminished by the fact that he used such words as "killer" and "instinct" a bit loosely, as he later admitted in *Territorial Imperative* (1966) and *Social Contract* (1970). Taking Ardrey as a whole, his view was that: Men have an innate but generalized urge to seek adventurous challenge, to take risks; they prefer to do this as teams of friends against rivals. As individuals we lose our courage and taste for risk the more isolated we become.

## BUSINESS AS SUBLIMATED HUNTING

The development of commerce and business in nearly every civilized culture suggests we have found an effective and realistic alternative to violence for expressing the aggressive side of our fraternal urges. Business rivalry can discharge our aggressive urges in the performance of the function in which they were forged—economic survival.

Antony Jay, a British management consultant, says that, "Man's behavior in business springs not from logic and reason, but from ancient survival imperatives such as hunting comradeship."[5] However, Jay often confuses the dominance psychology of the apes with the more fraternal psychology of the hunting hominid, obscuring this difference in his inordinate concern with the size of the face-to-face team derived from the hunting band. I will develop Jay's essential thesis in a somewhat different way which stresses the relationship between the team's social order and the effectiveness of its teamwork.

If fraternity evolved to inhibit dominance struggles, as has been

---

[5] Antony Jay, *Corporation Man* (New York: Random House, 1971).

demonstrated, a number of questions arise. Why have rampant tendencies toward dominance behavior been manifested in most human cultures, and particularly in Big Business? If business is in effect sublimated hunting, why do apelike power struggles routinely break out in the executive suite? Why do alienation and growing apathy seem to typify so many corporate employees? Why, in short, do business and other organizations go bureaucratic (as will be developed in Chapter 2), thus routinely and flagrantly violating the hunter's fraternal social order?

Finally, the question is, if fraternity really is superior to dominance, would not some business have discovered this and run the opposition out of the market? Indeed this is now happening in Japan, where superior fraternal teamwork gives business brotherhoods an advantage over their more bureaucratic rivals, as will be noted in Chapter 8.

## THE FRATERNAL DR. JEKYLL AND THE DOMINEERING MR. HYDE

Our inhibitions against dominance can be broken down, especially in larger, more impersonal groups. The team hunter's fraternal psychology displaced the older dominance psychology, but it did not remove urges toward dominance from our emotional inventory. Thus we retain a dual psychological makeup: a split personality comprised of a fraternal Dr. Jekyll and a domineering Mr. Hyde. Both tendencies can be observed simultaneously in nearly all cultures. Because bewildering combinations are possible, a plausible but false assumption may be made that cultural conditioning, not innate urges, is responsible for a particular cultural result, whereas it in fact reflects the interaction of these urges with the environment.

If we have a dual personality, however, we don't have an equal need to express both sides of it. Overwhelmingly, we prefer to live and work in the fraternal social order of Dr. Jekyll. The Mr. Hyde within us remains content with shared and attenuated dominance within the fraternal setting. Shared and attenuated dominance simply means that peers will defer to one of their brethren who has achieved specialized skill. Since no one can know everything equally well, each peer has the opportunity to achieve a more limited and democratic dominance along a narrower front. You defer to me on some things, I defer to you on others. This keeps Mr. Hyde happy enough, while also driving him to develop his strongest talents, not his weaknesses.

Mr. Hyde also plays another fraternal role. In the occasional genetic exception, fraternity does not inhibit strongly the individual's tendency toward general dominance. When that individual tries to take over, the Mr. Hyde in the rest of us steps right up to the challenge. We put him down. Even among apes the excessively pugnacious animal often winds up No. last because his brashness gets him in over his head; No. 1 rarely looks for fights.

Thus Mr. Hyde plays the positive role of urging us to do our best, as well as the negative role of standing watch over the other Mr. Hydes to see that they do not get pushy. But large size means problems. Because impersonality erodes fraternal inhibitions, specialized dominance is given an opportunity to use institutional means to reexert generalized dominance and to repress any attempted put-down. Typically a high official begins by pleading that his "position" gives him access to more information which justifies his dominance. Then he uses this dominance to put down all challenges to his position by better informed subordinates on other specialized issues. They are no longer peers, but caste inferiors. We have no inhibitions about dominating hierarchical caste inferiors; we tend to repress them and to squelch any sign that their ambition threatens us.

### THE SOCIAL ORDER AS RELEASER

Fraternity "brings out" feelings of friendship in man just as environmental events will bring out or trigger specific types of innate behavior in many animals, man included. Biologists call this process the "innate release mechanism" or identify the stimuli as "behavioral releasers." The scent of blood for example, can "release" a shark's predatory instinct. A cheeping sound releases a mother hen's brood-tending instinct. Sudden movement releases the startle reaction in humans. Environmental stimuli can release a wide range of innate behavior.

The fraternal social order releases fraternal behavior in man. All human social orders, one way or another, deal with five sociopsychological needs: (1) identity, (2) status as social rank, (3) role, (4) prestige as reputation, and (5) reward. The fraternal social order satisfies these five needs, and departures from that order will cause need deprivation relative to the degree and kind of departure. A lack of need satisfaction leads to various maladies such as alienation, apathy, frustration cum outrage, anomie, and power struggles. Such responses more or less obviously and directly erode teamwork. If the needs are satisfied, cooperative team behavior will be released by the social order.

The evolution of the five crucial needs is traced in Appendix A, and brief discussions of how the fraternal social order releases fraternal behavior to meet these needs are given in the paragraphs below.

1. *Identity.* Membership and its accompanying sense of belongingness identifies the individual with the team. Reciprocal loyalty binds the team to the individual and the individual to the team. Because membership cannot be revoked as an expediency, the individual is secure in his identity and has no identity crisis with respect to who he

is, socially. Membership in a family and citizenship of a country meet the fraternal identity criteria.

2. *Status.* A precise social rank tells the individual where he stands socially, relative to all other members. He may stand as an exact social equal to everyone else, but if social rank order enters in it must meet the following criteria:

*a.* Rank must be objective and attach directly to the person.
*b.* Promotion in rank must be guaranteed with experience.
*c.* Tests of merit or skill in promotion, where used to supplement experience, must be objectively applied and measured.

Tribal hunting bands often used initiation rites to test skill and stamina upon entry into the group. Status rose thereafter, with experience. Those who survived the initial tests of entry and further survived the rigors of the hunt (or war) might then retire to join the council of elders. Student classes (freshman, sophomore) approach fraternal criteria, as do the Boy Scouts merit badge program and the military rank system. Rank makes social identity more explicit, but it prescribes only rank, not role.

3. *Role.* Role assignments, which depend on ability, presume flexibility of duties. Role does not impinge on social rank, except possibly for purely ceremonial or ritualistic roles. Role subordination, where necessary, is technical and need not imply status subordination. In the effective fraternal team, all members participate in decisions concerning the team. The team need not have a designated leader, but if it does he functions as a spokesman, not as a policy decision maker, and never as a tyrant. Unpopular roles are rotated. Small groups of friends who decide to do something together almost always approach the problem of role fraternally.

4. *Prestige.* Prestige differs from status as school class differs from course grade: A senior with a C average has more rank but possibly less prestige than a sophomore with an A average. An even closer example is the military system of rank compared to the winning of medals. The private who wins a Congressional Medal of Honor for bravery in combat does not outrank the sargeant who has won no medals. All individuals must be free to strive for prestige, or the esteem of their fellow team members. There can be no systematic barriers to the earning of prestige, but it must be earned; it cannot be conferred. It determines who the individual is within the team.

5. *Reward.* Team performance determines total reward. No individual member has a prior claim on a fixed sum of reward, regardless of total team performance. No catch, no meat . . . for anyone. Relative shares may be exactly equal, or the deviation from equality must be seen as equitable by the team membership as a whole. The commonly

acceptable deviation will be based on social rank, perhaps modified by the number of dependents. As a practical matter, division of reward other than equal shares does not occur unless there is a savable economic surplus. The fraternal team pays the member according to his rank and not according to his job, which will in any event be flexible and not rigorously defined.

Adverse reactions set in by genetic command if there are serious departures from these fraternal ground rules. As with nutritional requirements, we require a reasonable balance in the satisfaction of all of these needs. The order in which I have listed them reflects in general their relative importance. Cut off identity, the first need, and nothing else matters. At the other extreme, no tangible reward may be required (but since we are concerned mainly with teamwork in economic affairs, reward does have importance). Nevertheless, economic reward will mean comparatively little provided we enjoy the social security inherent in the first four needs and the minimum economic needs for survival are being met. We can tolerate wide swings in income if they imply no change in our identity or status. And in the nature of fraternity we ordinarily are very flexible about role, but not if identity, social rank, or reward are attached to it.

## FRIENDLY GROUP FORMATION

To discuss these five needs, however briefly, imparts an unwarranted intellectual aspect to their evolution. Friendly peer groups fall into fraternal patterns of need satisfaction so naturally they scarcely think about them, especially when they embark on a group project.

Years ago I belonged to a neighborhood group of young boys called "the solid five." During May of 1942, the ominous tone of the war news excited us more than the sunny promise of summer vacation. At 13, we took the war very seriously. Bataan and Corregidor had just fallen, and we expected teeming hoards of Japanese invaders at any time off the Washington State coast. The solid five, all Boy Scouts, would "be prepared."

We began our preparations for guerrilla warfare by digging a foxhole in a nearby vacant lot. With mounting enthusiasm, it quickly became a veritable bunker which could be entered only by a long tunnel. We prepared for the worst, but alas, on a single June morning, our Navy's victory at Midway abruptly extinguished the prospects of a Japanese invasion.

Undaunted, we made our bunker into a clubhouse. When the first autumn rain proved it a doubtful one, we surfaced to begin a proper edifice. On and off about 15 boys became active in our clubhouse project. Before long it acquired a plank floor and roof which kept out the heaviest of rains. One room would not do; we started a second, then a third. Before we finished our clubhouse had grown to three floors, five rooms, two coal stoves, eight built-in bunks, and even a head. Though it looked top-heavy and swayed in the wind, three sturdy yellow pines lent firm if slightly lopsided support.

We could take the worst of weather in comfort. Worried neighbors, however, began to talk about our pride and joy in terms of building permits, fire hazards, and sanitation codes. When the city fathers concurred, we had to demolish the finest handmade clubhouse in Spokane.

Still for a time our towering clubhouse was the envy of the south side. We worked very hard to build it. One of the rooms was built around a several hundred pound packing crate we had located some miles away. We managed to push it by hand through the snow all the way to our construction site.

Yet no one was ever the "boss." We had no designated leader. Since my older brother had taken more shop courses than the rest of us we often deferred to his experience, but it never occurred to us to elect a leader. We made decisions by consensus without even knowing the meaning of the word. Some one would have an idea, and the rest of us went for it or we didn't. Nor did we have special "jobs"; we just mucked in together. You might call it teamwork, though we didn't especially think of it as that. But we had taken great pride in our accomplishments and enjoyed immensely the camaraderie which went with it.

Every group of boyhood friends, of course, does not exist without a leader. Where any significant difference in age exists, an older boy will almost inevitably surface as a "leader" to whom younger boys will typically defer. Social cliques and street-corner gangs often form around a charismatic individual whose personality some boys find attractive. (Others, of course, may find his personality unattractive and for that reason avoid him and the group.)

While the charismatic individual no doubt would qualify for the title of "leader," loosely defined, cliques and gangs often deny that they have leaders despite the observable presence of one individual who is clearly most influential. Partly such denials merely reflect confusion because we use the word "leader" to cover a wide range of characteristics. It can mean a formal dictator with arbitrary life-and-death powers over subordinates or a "boss" with the power to hire and fire individuals within the group. At the other extreme, the word may refer merely to the most influential individual in a casual group of social associates. In this case, a charismatic individual might quickly lose his charisma for most of his associates if he started behaving like a "boss." When street-corner gangs deny they have a leader, they probably mean they have no formal or designated boss.

In casual social groups of young males which form around a particular individual, the charismatic individual's main draw might be his appeal to the opposite sex, his athletic prowess, his intellectual achievements, or some combination of these or other attractions. Younger boys, in particular, might "model themselves" in the image of the older boys they admire. These groups hark back to the early gathering stage of primate social groups, not the later hunting bands. The dominant individual becomes a group focal point who tends to maintain order and settle disputes among "subordinates" (often to protect the weakest) but not to coordinate work in the usual sense of the term. Teamwork hardly enters into such groups, whose main purpose is usually simple companionship.

Spontaneous, "bossless," ad hoc work teams, on the other hand, may be formed by strangers with a common interest in the performance of a task, frequently an emergency of some sort. A short time ago I was a passenger on a one-car narrow-gauge "train" in Borneo. A newly built dirt road crossed the tracks at one point, and a heavy rainstorm was washing much of the earth from the roadbed across the rail tracks, so that mud covered them an inch deep. The driver stopped the rail car, fearful he would derail if he tried to push through. There were no tools aboard, but a railway employee got out and, using a slat, started to push mud off one rail. Two of us passengers, complete strangers and of different nationalities, could see that mud was washing down faster than one man could push it away. The other passenger picked up another slat and began removing mud from the second rail. I spotted a place up the road a few yards where a diversion of the mud rushing down was possible and dug a diversion channel with a stick. Within seven or eight minutes the car could ease past the mud slide; we got back aboard and were on our way. Hardly a word had been spoken, and indeed we could barely see each other in the twilight downpour. Not a single command or order was issued by anybody, and we were entirely self-appointed workers. A common interest in getting the job done motivated our teamwork; leadership influence did not come into it. Friendly or small-group teamwork does not necessarily require a *designated boss.*

While small groups of friends usually settle easily in fraternal teamwork, large size can cause devolution to the dominance orders of the lower primates. Humanity has been confronted by the demands of large-scale society for possibly less than one tenth of one percent of its past. We have no reliable genetic social guidance system when dealing with large social groups.

## REASON AND EMOTION: A MATTER OF COMMUNICATION

Our fraternal urges in large-scale society are just as strong as they ever were. They continually seek an outlet, but now cultural constraints can cause serious distortions. The problem lies not so much with large size as such but with a lack of understanding about how we can design our natural social order into large-scale enterprises.

Ironically, our lack of understanding is due in part to the ease with which we skillfully and unthinkingly create fraternity in small, friendly face-to-face groups. Reason and logic play little role in this process because we operate by genetic reflex. When large size confronts us, we are forced to rely on our intellect.

When we think abstractly about society, however, we begin with a serious handicap. Neurological communication between reason and emotion is tenuous at best. Our brain, easily the brightest in the animal kingdom, evolved in three stages. The first two, which contain our emotional urges, evolved very slowly and are well "wired in" to each other. But the third and last stage, the neocortex, evolved rapidly, long after hominid hunting had been well established. The neocortex is poorly related to the older parts of the brain, yet it contains most of our powers of abstract thought. Consequently, we can invent abstract social theories or philosophies that may be at odds with the biology of our emotional and social needs.

Until recently, when searching past experience for social wisdom we ignored the 99.9 percent of the human record that represents our prehistory. Marx's search of the past was made in prehistorical ignorance; thus his discourse on the origins of human dominance struggles was without benefit of the facts. He made no allowance for the predatory basis of the desire for comradeship or for our innate need to engage in rivalry.

## THE EVIDENCE OF THE NEW BIOLOGISTS

Prehistory alone gives clues and evidence, not proof of our fraternal heritage. But in the past ten years the horizon of knowledge of our hunting ancestors has been pushed back by millions of years. Scientists such as Louis and Mary Leakey have discovered older fossil remains of the hunting hominids, their weapons, and their base camp architecture.

In addition to fossils, the evidence comes from expanded knowledge of animal behavior in the wilds. We have no reason to suspect that animal behavior would change very much over a course of time in which little anatomical change occurred. Thus we would not expect the modern ape, for example, to differ from his prehistorical ancestors, and we can assume the modern hyena behaves rather like his Pliocene counterpart.

When, in 1924, Raymond Dart first unearthed an *Australopithecus africanus* skull in a setting suggesting it was the remains of a small-brained prehuman ancestor who hunted with weapons, hardly anyone took him seriously. Biologists then widely believed that no primate hunted in the wild and that man had turned to hunting under pressure of the Ice Age only after he acquired his big brain and became smart enough to invent weapons. The notion of a weapons-wielding, upright primate hunter with a brain 40 percent the size of modern man's outraged prevailing opinion. When mounting fossil evidence discovered thereafter confirmed Dart's hypothesis, a scientific change of opinion was forced in the late 1950s. Skeptics remained, however, into the early 1960s.

Then a different kind of evidence came in. Jane Goodall pioneered study of chimpanzees in their native state in Africa's Gombe Forest. By 1965 she and her husband and photographer Baron Hugo van Lawick had considerable film footage documenting two previously unknown facts. First, chimps routinely made crude tools to grub for insects and sponges to collect water from tree crevices. Second, they occasionally hunted, caught, and killed small game. They did so as individuals. Others at about the same time observed similar hunting behavior among baboons. These facts tended to convince the remaining skeptics. A hunting hominid who used tools and weapons no longer seemed so improbable or outrageous.

Thus it was established that the hominids hunted and used crudely crafted weapons, but how do we know they did not follow the baboon and chimp pattern of individual hunting? On this point we have already mentioned the hominid's diminutive size and the fact that over millions of years his fighting fangs had diminished in size, as depicted in Figure 1. Armed only with sticks and stones, the hominid would have been little improvement over the fang-equipped chimp or baboon as a lone individual. And with mere occasional hunting, meat would not have become enough of a staple to favor the biological change from vegetarian to omnivorous teeth.

Indeed, if the hominids had tried to take to systematic hunting as individuals, it would have proved a self-defeating exercise. Consider the problems in relation to the hunting behavior of baboons. The very rarity of the savanna-dwelling baboon's hunting gives him an opportunity at an occasional tempting target, such as an unguarded infant antelope. Ungulates such as antelopes normally coexist peacefully with baboons, since each depends on different vegetation, and normally neither regards the other as a food source. But if all the males in a baboon troop took to systematic hunting they would promptly scare off their potential prey. They would have to range much more widely, and do so alone. The elaborate baboon security system, in which the whole troop forages while deployed in a highly effective defensive convoy, would collapse. The troop surrounds and protects the fangless mothers and helpless infants by an inner screen of dominant males and an outer screen of aspiring young male adults, an incidental but highly effective consequence of baboon dominance struggles (see Figure 2). Any bab-

**Figure 2**
BABOON DEFENSE CONVOY

Adult males and older juvenile males guard the troop's mothers and infants. This formation could not successfully adapt to systematic hunting. (Source: *The Emergence of Man,* Rev. & Enlarged Edition, by John E. Pfeiffer, Harper & Row, 1972.)

oon troop that tried to take up lone hunting away from the troop would face extinction. The hunter himself would enormously increase his own risks. If the mothers and almost helpless children were left defenseless, any hyena pack or lion pride would make short work of them, especially if they remained at a fixed site to enable the lone hunter to find his way home.

Staying together in a "convoy," however, would scare off all the prey, as we have noted. With the alternative of a fixed base camp protected by some of the males left behind as reserves, two problems would arise. A fixed or semifixed base area would reduce the amount of foraging resources (see Figure 3). The only way to supplement reduced resources is for the individual hunting baboon to share; he must bring his kill back to camp to share with his adult male rivals and the mothers and infants for whom he has no concept of economic responsibility. While most primates have no need to share, and thus no psychology to encourage sharing, we might still argue that, having had his own fill, the successful hunter might turn what remained over to others. The meat won't keep anyway. In fact, this kind of "sharing" can occasionally be observed among chimps and baboons. We could even imagine that satiated sharing might form a convenient base for a more systematic sharing to evolve. We certainly cannot argue that this did not happen with the hominids; we just do not know.

But we do know that a lone hominid hunter, if he tried to return with his kill instead of eating it on the spot, would increase his vulnerability

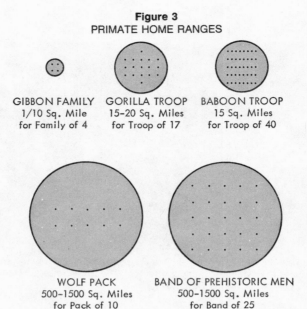

**Figure 3**
PRIMATE HOME RANGES

GIBBON FAMILY
1/10 Sq. Mile
for Family of 4

GORILLA TROOP
15–20 Sq. Miles
for Troop of 17

BABOON TROOP
15 Sq. Miles
for Troop of 40

WOLF PACK
500–1500 Sq. Miles
for Pack of 10

BAND OF PREHISTORIC MEN
500–1500 Sq. Miles
for Band of 25

Hunters require a much greater territorial range than gatherers. These relationships rule out systematic individual hunting by other primates. Note that wolves, armed only with fangs, require 2.5 times as much territory per capita as men using artificial weapons. Both man and wolves teamhunt and share. (Source: "Primate Home Ranges" in *The Emergence of Man,* Rev. & Enlarged Edition, by John E. Pfeiffer, Harper & Row, 1972.)

to other predators. He has lost his fangs and depends on sticks and stones for weapons, and if he carried both his weapons and his catch by himself he would not be prepared to defend himself. To take such risks he would have to be motivated to share in advance, not merely after his fill. Working against such motivation is the fact that individual hunters are much less likely to survive than those who kill, eat, and run back home. Thus the idea of individual hominid hunting from a protected base camp would select rather sharply against a psychology of sharing. In short, based on what we know about primate behavior, we cannot put together a reasonable scenario for the lone hominid hunter which does anything but point him toward extinction. From the time we pick up his unmistakable fossil trail (about four million years ago), only teamhunting makes any sense at all. Of course, we must deal in circumstantial evidence, not proof. But arguments in favor of individualistic hominid hunting must begin with a near void of evidence.

## A DIFFICULT TRANSITION: HUNTING TO AGRICULTURE

The concept of cooperative or teamhunting easily fits the facts of hominid fossil remains and of what we know about later human hunters. We have also mentioned a number of behavioral elements in modern primates which in somewhat different combinations would support teamhunting. We can observe reciprocity in baboons in social grooming, tool making, cooperation in defense, and the beginnings of shared dominance. Goodall and van Lawick have even observed signs of friendly affection among adult chimps which grew up as blood-brother playmates.

It seems probable that in the hominid random mutations and chance events somehow nudged these elements into a recombination which gave rise to teamhunting. No doubt it took millions of years. Long gaps in the fossil record suggest that in the transition from gatherers-hunters to hunters-gatherers, the human line may have been a less than ideal adaptation. Rather, it was an experiment in natural selection which, as it evolved, hovered perilously close to extinction. The delicate job of psychological reprogramming needed to convert a selfish, domineering, individualistic vegetarian into a reliably cooperative teamhunter, willing to take risks and then share with his fellows, probably entailed many false starts and failures. A number of fossils suggest that this happened. Nevertheless, the task seems to have been reasonably complete three or four million years ago, with the development of *Australopithecus africanus*. I suspect nearly the whole inventory of human emotions and innate urges had been laid down by then. Evolution since has concentrated on the development of our intellect and continuing change in anatomical detail.

We can assume that the development of our intellect entailed no major new emotional developments because fossil evidence suggests the life style laid down by the hominid changed very little until the invention of agriculture about 10,000 years ago. The inventory of tools and weapons expanded and craftmanship was improved. Man went after progressively bigger game, including the biggest to be found; indeed, he became nature's master predator. As his ranks swelled, he spread over the whole globe. Only when he ultimately ran out of hunting territory did he turn to agriculture. Whereas it takes square miles of hunting territory per person for men to survive as hunters, mere acres will suffice for farming.

The evidence suggests that man shifted from hunting to farming not out of desire but from a shortage of hunting territory, and he has been rather unhappy ever since. Farming may provide a good living, but it calls for little camaraderie, and adventurous it is not. Nature's risks of flood and drought are impersonal and one-sided, a seeming visitation if we lose and a thief of our sense of personal achievement if we win. Altogether, hunting was much more satisfactory, which is the short answer why we took so long to put our superior brain to other uses. It also suggests that we acquired no new emotional outlook or psychology in the course of becoming the primate with the brain.

Why did nature program our simple hunting ancestors with so much intellectual overkill? Professor Kurten has answered as well as anyone:

> To produce an increase in the available skill of the brain, natural selection had to call forth a vastly greater unrealized capacity, which remains dormant in the savage but can be activated by suitable education.
>
> In a corresponding way, intelligent animals like apes, dogs and dolphins can be taught difficult chores, thus activating brain resources not normally used in the wild.[6]

While agriculture emerged 10,000 years ago, it did not replace hunting everywhere all at once. A few hunting tribes still survive, tucked away in obscure corners of the earth.

Before the North American Indian tribes became overwhelmed by technology, disease for which they had no natural immunity, and hordes of European settlers, many scientists were able to study them in a natural state. Their culture provides a broad glimpse into the situation of man during the transition from hunting to agriculture. Indeed, the observers described a social order similar to the fraternal one we have been discussing. Lewis H. Morgan noted that for the Iroquois, "Liberty, Equality, and Fraternity, though never formulated, were cardinal principles." He also noted that they had no chief as such.[7]

## FOCUS ON THE PRESENT

My thesis that fraternity makes for more efficient enterprise than does bureaucratic dominance must stand or fall on the evidence from the contemporary world. I began with the past in order to put the present into a genetic perspective. One reason it is advisable to do this is because of the mystique surrounding the word "culture" which developed between the two world wars and survives to the present. Now, however, it is on the defensive.

The notion of a "human nature" slipped through in the overriding concern of some social scientists with cultural variation. It became

---

[6] Kurten, *Not from the Apes*, p. 84.

[7] Lewis H. Morgan, *Houses and House Life of American Aborigines* (Chicago: University of Chicago Press, originally 1881, reprinted 1965), p. 14. The role of Indian chiefs is seldom recognized. Such chiefs as Geronimo and Sitting Bull were war chieftains, the military leaders. They did not rule their tribes politically. The war chief had no more political rights than anyone else.

fashionable to think no norms at all existed; our intellect provided the only limitations to the range of possible cultural variations, and it had divorced us, socially speaking, from the biology of innate emotions. This contention has been largely negated by the work of the "new biologists."

In some fields, such as management and economics, however, the word was not gotten around. They remain under the influence of "culturism," with one myth in particular enjoying high fashion. This myth holds that a culture's institutional efficiency faithfully reflects its broader social values. It is considered intellectual bad manners to make critical observations about the culture, particularly its institutions. Rampant inefficiency, for example, must mean the culture respects "spiritual" values more than "materialistic" ones.

By the decade of the 1960s evidence against this proposition was almost universal. Even the most casual observation of institutions around the world reveals multiple gross departures from cultural ideals. Rare is the culture that is not shot through with internal cultural contradictions. This is nothing new; partly it reflects a clash of internal interests, which is easily understood. More broadly, the problem reflects what we might call in the modern idiom "intellectual chauvinism." We have traditionally associated ideology with the intellect and regarded emotions as something to ignore or some "sin" to be overcome, without understanding the purposes our emotions can serve.

This book cannot cope with all the ramifications of this problem. Our focus will be on human enterprise, primarily the business firm. We will point not only to the general prevalence of conflicting internal cultural ideologies but to a remarkably consistent pattern of pathology in a wide range of cultural settings which suffer from self-inflicted bureaucracy. Bureaucracy tends to inhibit teamwork and thus to generate inefficiency wherever it appears. Parkinson's Law[8] and the Peter Principle[9] enjoyed worldwide acceptance because they touched on sensitive problems which infest bureaucracy's social order everywhere.

It could be said that if you've seen one bureaucracy, you've seen them all. Pathologically speaking, however, there are interesting clinical differences in detail between one culture and another. The pathology of bureaucracy bears more than a passing resemblance to cancer—malignant organizational cells expanding regardless of need. Detailed discussion of bureaucracy's pathological character is deferred to Part II. Here, note only that the cross-cultural syndromes of bureaucracy lead to the suspicion that ill health in human organization com-

---

[8] C. Northcote Parkinson, *Parkinson's Law* (Boston: Houghton Mifflin Co., 1957).

[9] Lawrence J. Peter and Raymond Hull, *The Peter Principle* (New York: William Morrow & Co., 1969).

pares to ill health in the human organism. Each case reflects certain biological truths about the human animal (the word "social" no more excludes biology than does the word "physiological"). Though wide cultural differences occur in diet, they all must meet certain innate nutritional needs if the body is to remain healthy. So must the healthy organization give reasonable nourishment to innate social needs if it is to remain healthy.

## UTOPIA

What then would a healthy organization be like? Let me describe how, ideally, a large industrial enterprise might organize itself fraternally; how Big Business could apply the hunter's natural social order to its own society and thus nourish the social needs of its employees.

As an employee, what could you expect of such an enterprise? First, your company would recruit you as a permanent employee, not to fill a particular job vacancy. You would "join," much as you might pledge a college fraternity. You would regard yourself as belonging to a brotherhood that is completely loyal to your interests. This business enterprise is no fair-weather friend that would lay you off in stormy economic weather. You would join with the rank of "freshman" or as a young man, and your pay would be relatively low. As you gained in experience, good times and bad, you would receive regular promotions in rank, along with your fellow "classmates," until you would retire as a "senior."

Your total pay (and everyone else's) would reflect your firm's performance and cash flow. A large part of your pay would come as a bonus tied directly to sales revenue. After all operating expenses were paid, the remainder would be split up as salary and bonus, according to rank. You thus would realize that every dime's worth of supplies or minute of time you waste is a dime less in the payroll kitty. Besides yourself, you must consider your brethren; they consider you.

You might not always find your duties fascinating, but you would never face a dead-end job. You would never be left long in any job with which you could not cope. Indeed, your talents and weaknesses would come to light mainly while you are in "reserve" training to learn a wide variety of different skills. During your entire career you would look forward to regular rotation through reserve training assignments designed to teach new technology or techniques. In hard times relatively large numbers of employees would receive training assignments, because the volume of business would be low; a slump would give more people an opportunity to sharpen up or widen their skills. When the upturn came, fully trained reserves would immediately go to work to meet the resurgent demand.

Your training would assure that you could do well almost any job assignment you draw, for you never would be assigned to jobs for which you have shown little aptitude. If you should see a way to eliminate your job assignment through better procedures, you would let your elder brethren know at once, because this would mean one more person need not be hired in the future, and the payroll kitty for everyone would be that much bigger. You, of course, would draw another assignment, either in operations or in reserve. If by error you should receive an assignment you cannot perform very well, your elder brother would unobtrusively reassign you and hope that no one noticed his placement error. None of these assignment changes, in or out of reserve, would influence your rank or pay one way or the other.

Formal job assignment, however, would be rare. More likely your unit would draw an assignment and your team would decide among yourselves who does what, for how long, and in what order. You would rotate the dirty or monotonous jobs. If things go wrong, the elder brothers would ask your opinion and, of course, the opinions of your fellows about what the trouble can be. You would get together after work and consider the problem until you had figured a better way of getting the job done. You might even call in an industrial engineer to help if the problem were technical.

During your entire career, no one would ever formally evaluate your performance. The chances are rather good you would never be directly criticized for doing poor work. But you would, over the course of your career, accumulate a general reputation. If you were of management rank and you had achieved a very good reputation, you would probably be asked to stay on beyond normal retirement as a "senior" or to join the council of elders. As an elder you would not make decisions but merely offer counsel and help to achieve consensus on important matters. You would participate in decisions mainly by discussing the real nature of the problem. Not until these discussions had gone on for some time would anyone ask "What should we do about this?" You would have learned as a "sophomore" and "junior" that once general agreement about the nature of the problem emerges, the decision of what to do generally appears under the weight of logic.

Throughout your career you would have enjoyed following the sales "score" between your firm and the opposition. Seeing your company win would mean as much to you as seeing your country win, and much more than seeing your old college football team win, for you would be enjoying the thrill of being on the team, not just the vicarious pleasure of being a fan. The camaraderie of your fellows would be one of the greatest pleasures of your career. You would even hate to take vacations and often would have to be forced to do so. Camaraderie would more than make up for the inevitably less pleasant things you would have to do now and then. And, when disappointments and failures occurred, the sense of everyone piling in to put things right would make the extra effort seem worthwhile. Your business brotherhood's almost complete freedom from internal recrimination, faultfinding, and scapegoating would make your career enjoyable. The money would be nice, but you would never rank it higher than the satisfaction your association with your firm would give you.

Your main emotion would be loyalty. At times, true enough, you might feel you would prefer to just go fishing, but this would let your teammates down, and so you would stay in the game. You might sense that reciprocal loyalty is life's toughest taskmaster and sternest disciplinarian, but it would never enter your mind to ask if, given the chance, you would have joined another firm. You would have bonded too strongly with your brethren for that question to make sense; you might as well ask if you would rather have had a different family.

You may feel that this is a hopelessly idealistic, hypothetical case, or you may have detected the fact that it is not hypothetical at all. Rather I have summarized the system of industrial relations that characterizes the economy of Japan, but in real-world practice. For as with the fraternity of the Iroquois and the "solid five," little theory is attached to this practice. Japanese firms do consciously strive for harmony within and competition without, but they take it as a self-evident law of survival. The Western notion that internal strife plus external competition somehow improves teamwork strikes the Japanese as another example of Occidental inscrutability.

I have given you this peek at my "solution" of how to save free enterprise in order to provide a real-world referent before discussing the devolution of human enterprise and the pathology of bureaucracy. We cannot be sure we deal in pathology unless we can point to a standard of reasonable health. As you will see, there is a widely accepted Western myth that bureaucracy's only pathology comes from large size, and otherwise it represents a high point in human organizational achievement.

# 2

# Evolution in Reverse: The Rise of Bureaucracy

## BITCH, BITCH, BITCH

It is popular to bitch about bureaucracy. Its critics, often deadly enemies of one another, can unite in their common antipathy. These critics include the masses as well as the famous. French students who revolted against scholastic bureaucracy in May 1968 promised to persevere "until the last capitalist is hanged by the entrails of the last bureaucrat." Critics have included such diverse personalities as the outspoken observer Admiral Hyman Rickover, the sociologist C. Wright Mills, President Richard Nixon, economist John Kenneth Galbraith, and Joseph Stalin. As early as 1926 Mao Tse-tung identified "bureaucrats" as Enemies of the People (p. 13 of his little red book), and his later Cultural Revolution was a heoric attempt to rid China of them forever. It is reasonably clear he failed.

Many employees of Big Business and not-so-big businesses condemn bureaucracy in chorus with legions of their customers, suppliers, and stockholders. Civil servants in federal, state, and local government, together with much of the public they serve, also give evidence of animosity toward the institution. Probably no other institutional form devised by man has been subjected to as much criticism among its own practitioners. The very mention of the word "bureaucracy" brings to mind a host of discouraging images: the spectre of endless delays; a mass of red tape; wearisome functionaries dodging their responsibilities by passing the buck; thickets of deadwood; a monstrous hulk so obese it cannot get out of its own way; endless duplication and overlapping of functions; institutions so rigid as to suggest rigor mortis. It can be maddeningly frustrating, the more so since it is difficult to get much satisfaction from hating something so impersonal. Indeed, semantically bureaucracy can be both a technical term and a swear word.

Why, with such a wretched reputation, does bureaucracy seem to prosper and expand as an institution? Besides the fact that we have the handicap of a poor wiring job between our reason and our emotions, the principal reason is that no effective alternative forms of organization are available that can do the job as well, some academic scholars falsely assert.

## THE INFLUENCE OF MAX WEBER

Bureaucracy's academic reputation owes much to a German sociologist of the early 20th century, Max Weber. Weber profoundly influenced the American academic community, particularly through two of his translators, C. Wright Mills and Talcott Parsons. While they and many American social scientists challenged Weber on one point or another, hardly anyone disputed his definition of bureaucracy or his central contention that in it mankind had achieved its most technically proficient form of organization. Indeed, he maintained that "The decisive reason for the advance of bureaucratic organization has always been its purely technical superiority over any other form of organization."[1] Moreover, Weber, more than anyone else, extended the definition of bureaucracy beyond government civil service and made it clear that to work at its best, bureaucracy had to be drained of all "humane" values:

> Its specific nature, which is welcomed by capitalism, develops the more perfectly the more bureaucracy is "dehumanized," the more completely it succeeds in eliminating from official business love, hatred, and all purely personal irrational and emotional elements which escape calculation. This is the specific nature of bureaucracy and it is appraised as its special virtue.[2]

Thus Weber made emotion the false enemy of efficiency, rather than the basis upon which organized efficiency fundamentally depends. He succeeded in distorting the "humane organization" into something "irrational." Many who feel that efficiency can only be achieved by cold calculation (and to hell with the human consequences) owe a great debt to Max Weber's influence, even if they have never heard of him.

It might be expected that the evidence of the new biology would trigger a complete rethinking of these Weberian conclusions. That this has not been the case in evidenced by the views of Lionel Tiger and Robin Fox, who have made substantial contributions to the new biology:

---

[1] H. H. Gerth and C. Wright Mills (eds. and trans.), *From Max Weber: Essays in Sociology* (New York: Oxford University Press, 1958), p. 214.

[2] Gerth and Mills, *From Max Weber,* p. 216.

Large-scale bureaucratic organizations are constantly criticized for their inhumanity and impersonality; they are charged with reducing individuals to numbers, computerizing social relationships, overorganizing their conformity-obsessed members, and eventually producing anomie, ulcers, delinquency, anxiety, and wife-swapping. And yet *no other form of organization can cope effectively with the overarching problems of a system that goes beyond the face-to-face.* Bureaucracy stands at the opposite pole to charisma, with hereditary systems hovering between. The bureaucrat owes his dominance position to formal qualifications; it is not his person that is deferred to, but his office. This replacement of person with office is, as Weber saw, the major characteristic of formal organization, *and as inevitable as it is unprimate and inhuman.* Unprimate because primate politics are personal politics; eyeball-to-eyeball politics— literally. There are no primate officeholders, only primate individuals.

The paradox is that in order to survive, the human animal has to employ a mode of social organization that in many ways negates all those features that have brought him into the exalted position of needing such an organization in the first place.[3]

Fortunately for mankind, things really are not all this bad. But given such views, the persistence of bureaucracy in the face of all the bitching becomes more understandable.

The issue of bureaucracy is embraced in many cultures. Just as we can find its critics everywhere, those who support Weber's claim to bureaucracy's "efficiency" also think in global terms. Even the "culturists" seem to regard bureaucracy more as a machine than as a cultural form of organization, and one from which there is no cultural escape. Parkinson's Law and the Peter Principle also imply the entrapment of mankind in bureaucracy's morass.

Weber's study of bureaucracy ranged freely across cultures and through time. He examined the evidence from ancient Egypt, China, and Rome. He also studied the more contemporary circumstances of Germany, France, Great Britain, and the United States. While he noted the technical superiority of bureaucracy, by no means did Weber regard it as man's perfect instrument; he noted, for example, that "The disintegration of the Roman Empire was partly conditioned by the very bureaucratization of its army and official apparatus."[4]

The alternatives which Weber examined were limited to "charismatic" and "hereditary or traditional" organizations. Quite accurately he noted that the charismatic organization, based as it is on the personality of one man, is too unstable. Bureaucracy is indeed a better bet. Weber tended to dismiss the traditional forms a little too readily as being too set in their ways. He does not mention tribal organization in

---

[3] Lionel Tiger and Robin Fox, *The Imperial Animal* (New York: Holt, Rinehart, & Winston, 1971), p. 48 (emphasis mine).

[4] Gerth and Mills, *From Max Weber,* p. 210.

his discussion of bureaucracy, but in other studies he does, and tellingly. He acknowledged that "a tribe normally comprised many, often almost all, of the possible pursuits necessary to it for the gaining of subsistence." He also noted the crucial socioeconomic distinction between a tribe and a caste: " 'caste' and 'way of earning a living' are so firmly linked that a change of occupation is co-related with a division of caste. This is not the case for a tribe. Normally a tribe comprises people of every social rank." Nevertheless, he notes, "by its very nature, caste is inseparably bound up with social ranks within a larger community."[5] A caste is a social ranking system according to economic function, the social stratification of work.

## WEBER'S DEFINITON OF BUREAUCRACY

Weber took several pages to define bureaucracy. The short definition which emerges is: A Bureaucracy socially stratifies specialized work coordinated by a caste system of hierarchically ranked jobs, autocratically ruled.[6] Weber's full definition reflects the fact that bureaucracy, as the word itself suggests, is a form of rule through bureaus. He broke his definition down first according to the characteristics of the institution and then by the position of the officeholders in it.

Institutionally, the first Weberian principle of bureaucracy is that of fixed jurisdictional areas (the formal division of labor) which are controlled by rules or administrative regulations. The activities of each function become official duties. The authority attached to each functional department is limited to whatever "coercive means" is delegated to its officials. "In public and lawful government these . . . elements constitute bureaucratic authority. In private economic domination they constitute bureaucratic management."[7]

The second Weberian principle of bureaucracy is based on the *Führerprinzip,* which establishes the autocratic nature of bureaucratic rule. "The principles of office hierarchy and of levels of graded authority mean a firmly ordered system of super- and subordination in which there is supervision of the lower offices by the higher ones."[8] And "the office hierarchy is monocratically organized," or ruled autocratically.

Weber noted several other "principles," such as the creation and preservation of records and files; prior training for office; bureaucratic duty as a primary, not secondary occupation; and stability of regulations. He also noted a segregation of private life from bureaucratic office.

---

[5] Gerth and Mills, *From Max Weber,* p. 398.

[6] Ibid., pp. 196–204.

[7] Ibid., p. 196.

[8] Ibid., p. 197.

The bureaucrat himself in Weber's definition conforms to the following precepts. First he regards his office as a vocation, not exploitable for prebends (income derived from the powers of office, exclusive of salary); in other words, he should be honest and not take bribes or extort them. He is also supposed to be loyal to his office and to the offices of his superiors, as opposed to being loyal to their persons independently of office.

Second, a bureaucrat's personal position is patterned as follows:

1. He enjoys distinct social esteem over his subordinates and "the ruled." His social position is guaranteed by prescriptive rules of the office's rank order, and he can apply sanctions to subordinates who "insult" him or hold him in "contempt."
2. He is appointed to office by a superior official.
3. Normally, in public office, he presumes life tenure (a rule increasingly honored in the breach).
4. The bureaucrat receives a fixed salary. The salary is not measured in terms of work done but according to the status of his office.
5. He moves from "lower" or "less important" positions to higher positions.

## USEFUL ELEMENTS IN BUREAUCRACY

Weber's definition of bureaucracy can be the basis for examining in what sense he was correct in claiming that a modern government or economy cannot dispense with bureaucracy, on purely technical grounds.

First, you cannot dispense with the division of labor. You can go overboard in specializing areas of effort, and most bureaucracies do so, but specialization is here to stay. Division of labor, however, did not grow out of the Industrial Revolution. It began with hunting, primarily based on sex but not limited to it. The men hunted while the women looked after the kids and gathered food, as they had done in prehunting days. Apes do not practice economic division of labor in their dominance-ordered societies; as division of labor came in, dominance went out.[9] Teamwork builds on division of labor, not on dominance.

Second, you cannot dispense with some form of coordination for the division of labor when successive subfunctions are combined or inte-

---

[9] In her *The Descent of Woman* (New York: Stein and Day, 1972), Elaine Morgan completely missed this point in discussing the hunting society as a "Tarzan dominated society" (me Tarzan, you Jane). Tarzan, Morgan forgot, was "of the apes." Tarzanian dominance went out when hunting came in, and women's status rose, it did not fall. The fall of women's status was more a posthunting phenomenon. It became especially acute with bureaucratic caste systems which socially stratify the work. All caste systems tend to demean household work.

grated toward a useful whole (several pieces to a part, several parts to a component, several components to a subassembly, several subassemblies to a final assembly, etc.). Production of this sort is comparatively new and has taken on added complexity since the Industrial Revolution. A coordinating hierarchy cannot be avoided in large organizations, and coordination obviously requires technical regulations and standard procedures.

But the bureaucratic hierarchy as defined by Weber goes well beyond the technical requirements of coordination. In no sense does a coordinating hierarchy "have to become" a caste system. The ascription of social majesty to the coordination of work as opposed to actually doing the work is wholly gratuitous. Making invidious social comparisons between the different elements of a divided task is like saying a car's timing mechanism performs more noble service than its pistons or crankshaft. Granted the timing mechanism performs a "coordinative function," without "subordinate" functions to coordinate, that function would have no relevance. All necessary functions are interdependent.

It might be assumed (and it is by many) that coordinating the work is more difficult or demanding than doing the work. It might then be argued that coordination "deserves" higher social rank. The trouble is, it is often much easier, more comfortable, and less demanding to coordinate than to actually do the work. Not always, of course, but hierarchical skill inversions occur frequently enough to undermine any general rule to the contrary. In any event, divisive social comparisons between economic functions are what a caste system is all about.

## THE ROLE OF RELIGION IN THE RISE OF AUTOCRACY

Autocracy, the monocratic principle (*Führerprinzip*), does have a place in human enterprise. Most collective effort requires division of labor to succeed; if the effort is large, it will also require a coordinating hierarchy. Autocracy's place is valid when the specialized jobs which need coordinating depend for success on involuntary servitude.

Karl A. Wittfogel has amassed convincing historical evidence that despotism in human affairs developed with the "hydraulic society" built around large-scale irrigation networks.[10] These networks had to be designed, built, and maintained over wide areas serving many farmers. Corvée labor drafted temporarily for such work probably constituted the earliest widespread form of involuntary servitude controlled by a bureaucratic hierarchy. Initially corvée labor may have been voluntary service, a sort of self-imposed labor tax. Japan's experience, at least, suggests this possibility; mountainous terrain limited Japan's irrigation

---

[10] Karl A. Wittfogel, *Oriental Despotism* (New Haven, Conn.: Yale University Press, 1963).

networks to small local systems maintained entirely by voluntary community cooperation. Elsewhere, as in China, broad alluvial plains permitted large-scale networks. If local cooperation broke down, an "irrigation authority" of some sort became necessary. But bigness alone did not necessarily compel autocratic coordination; it merely made despotism more likely.

The precondition to autocracy was not hydraulic agriculture, however, as much as a legitimate theory of dominance. Genetic inhibitions against roughshod dominance of peers make it necessary to invent subpeers, superpeers, or both, if dominance is to succeed in human affairs. Even a slave must cooperate to some residual degree, or the cost of administering the lash becomes uneconomic. Not only must you hire too many slave drivers, but after each lashing the slave's capacity for work drops, while the cost of keeping him alive may increase. You can achieve much greater economy of effort if you can convince the slave that his lot, like yours, is somehow preordained and beyond the influence of either of you.

This was the role of religion, whose part in relegitimatizing primate dominance orders cannot be overestimated. After the hunting economy succumbed to agriculture, it was back to the gathering economy on a more sophisticated level. Religion could provide legitimacy for more sophisticated dominance orders.

This process probably was not instituted cynically, since religion had preceded agriculture by hundreds of thousands of years. Neanderthal fossils indicate there may have been religious practices 100,000 years ago, and it can be assumed religion played a useful role in human survival when we were all hunters-gatherers. Religion seems to have been a part of every culture so far identified; every primitive people had a genesis myth, which helped to maintain social cohesion.

Thus man did not "whistle up" religion to justify renewed dominance orders so much as he stumbled across its utility in this matter. Mankind's first superpeer, the tribal godking, drew his superstatus from supernatural premises long established. Agriculture, however, may have fostered the godking myth. Farming increased tribal size and promoted confederation, while producing an economic surplus large enough to sustain a priesthood, warriors, politicians, and other satellite occupations. The demand for tillable land caused territorial disputes between tribal groups, thus establishing a need for political order and common defense. The functions of warrior chief, political leader and high priest might well merge into a godking, and behold, the superpeer! If the godking role were passed on along blood lines, a closed caste would be formed, based on function. Inheritance of power is a partially successful way to damp down dominance disputes.

Given high caste, it would be necessary to invent low caste. The priesthood, freed from economic toil, could contemplate their superiority and define the inferior caste. Their own superiority would seem to arise from function, and logic would dictate that inferiority reflect function as well. Since other animals had been domesticated in the service of man, it would seem logical that farmers, whose taxes and labor supported so many others, would also take on a subhuman status. It would seem only right that the lower castes should toil in the service of the higher castes who were devoted to the more ethereal functions of the kingdom.

The Hindu caste system, for example, arose from the belief that various parts of the anatomy of the first man (*manu*) gave rise to various human occupations. Priesthood sprang from *manu's* head; rulers and warriors from *manu's* hands; self-employed farmers, merchants, and artisans from *manu's* thighs; and farm workers, and domestic servants from *manu's* feet. The Indian who believed this and found himself a farmer, for example, would not question the caste system too deeply. Besides, he could look forward to a higher caste in his next life if he played the game well in this one. India has formally abolished the caste system, but caste still retains a powerful hold on Indians of the Hindu faith.

As man turned from hunting to farming, mounting economic surplus enabled labor to turn to other tasks, such as the building of monuments to the godking and temples for the priests. Under these conditions, a slave class might seem as natural as life itself, perhaps even to the slaves. Gradually, the process by which our fraternal urges inhibit dominance could be effectively outflanked. Human tyranny, despotism, and autocracy would follow. Godkings would come to accept their own superiority. Their decisions, as the result of divine inspiration, would brook no question. Close subordinates would grow skeptical, then conspiratorial. The godking might be deposed, murdered, or, as in Japan's case, carefully isolated from the levers of actual power. Powerless, the godking's utility would actually improve, for now he could symbolize a people and rise above dominance struggles. In such a role he would become an object more of veneration than of hate, and a less likely target for assassination. His career would illuminate a truth: Dominance struggles will always break out in human affairs wherever dominance orders prevail.

## THE MONOTHEISTIC ETHIC AND THE SPIRIT OF AUTOCRACY

In the recent past man has largely abandoned the notion of a king's divine right to rule. He has not, however, shed the underlying monotheistic ethic. The notion that superior office somehow confers superior wisdom remains in organizational life, primarily in bureaucracy. We no longer invoke the original justification of divine inspiration to defend high office, of course. We merely abide by its implications and leave the premise discreetly hidden.

The monotheistic ethic gives to the holder of high bureaucratic office some of the attributes of an omniscient deity. A supreme deity, by definition, is incapable of wrongdoing and the source of all good. Sin can arise only from among his subjects. Through his creation, they have been equipped with a universal free will undistorted by genetic variation or environmental conditioning. Subjects do good when they obey the deity's commands and regulations; they sin when by their own free will they disobey. Obedience leads to eternal salvation, disobedience to eternal damnation—the carrot and stick writ large. When things go wrong, the deity's subjects are said to have succumbed to the temptations of disobedience. When things go well, however, the deity gets the credit. The subjects disobey (sin) as individuals; team effort has nothing to do with salvation or damnation. Individual obedience to the deity's rules is of paramount importance.

Secular authority has drunk deeply from this philosophical well. While the human enterprise takes on the problem of survival in this world rather than salvation in the next, the ethic of monotheism continues to influence bureaucratic authority. When things go right, authority gets the credit; when things go wrong, subordinates get the blame. Success or failure acquires an individual cast, never a team character. Nowhere in his definition of bureaucracy did Weber hint at teamwork beyond what was mechanically implied in the division of labor. He says nothing about esprit de corps or team spirit as an element of success. His concept is concerned only with individuals occupying individual offices obeying individual rules and regulations and following the individual orders of individual superiors.

The imputation of supercompetence to quite ordinary folk once they acquire high office is implied by Weber in his discussion of training. If by definition the superior is more competent, it must follow that the subordinates have less competence. Consequently, failure must reflect subordinate failure. If things really go to pieces, it is not the superior's fault. Czar Nicholas II could observe in 1917 that the Russian people really did not deserve him. In his final hours, Hitler made much the same comment about the German people. Thus our philosophy of authority encourages superiors to acquire grossly distorted views of self-importance. This is one of the corruptions of power from which no man in a position of power, either public or private, is immune.

Ask any failed business autocrat and he will tell you that either disloyal, ungrateful, or incompetent subordinates or some unforeseen and unpredictable event brought on his ruin; he himself is blameless.

Indeed it would be unrealistic to expect Herbert Hoover to embrace the responsibility for the Great Depression or Franklin Roosevelt to blame himself for Pearl Harbor. No one steps forward to accept the blame for the difficulties of Penn Central, Rolls Royce, or Lockheed. Our theory of authority, particularly as seen by those in authority, would be destroyed. But more importantly, it is psychologically unrealistic to build up the notion of superstatus based on supercompetence and then expect the superchief to admit error. The Germans seem to see quickly to the heart of such matters; General Alfred Jodl put the issue concisely: "A dictator, as a matter of psychological necessity, must never be reminded of his own errors—in order to keep up his self-confidence, the ultimate source of a dictator's force."[11]

Jodl was right, of course. The effective autocrat cannot afford to dwell on his own mistakes nor allow subordinates to remind him of them. Yet a psychological need to hide from the truth of one's own error makes a hash of the supercompetence theory of superstatus.

The idea that superior office automatically establishes supercompetence is an internal view held by bureaucracy. Outside the bureaucracy, we do not cling to this myth. Where we ourselves are not involved we have few compunctions about holding autocrats responsible for failure, and indeed we rather delight in cutting them down. Moreover, in abstract theory, we do hold the chief executive of an enterprise fully responsible for failure. We tend to justify superstatus, superauthority, and superreward with the proposition that the autocrat must be held responsible for corporate performance. The onerous burden he shoulders is seen as justifying his high status and power. Not many men want to assume the burden of being held individually responsible for the collective performance of their subordinates—or so they say. As it turns out, once they acquire the necessary power, they almost always succeed in avoiding personal responsibility for collective failure, save in a rhetorical or legalistic sense.

## INDIVIDUAL RESPONSIBILITY AND COLLECTIVE EFFORT

Superiors justify their power and privileges in terms of their onerous responsibility for others. But once they acquire the power they use it ruthlessly to avoid suffering the penalties which can arise from the consequences of their exercise of responsibility, unless the corporate ship actually sinks.

We hear about the onerous burden most often when things are going well. In the event of failure, we hear more about unpredictable economic trends, sudden shifts in the market, craven trade unions, govern-

---

[11] Alan Clark, *Barbarossa* (New York: Signet, 1966), p. 265.

ment interference, lack of management depth, unscrupulous competition, cheap foreign labor, and the insoluble difficulties inherited from predecessors. The near universality of this behavior is a signal that it represents more than mere hypocrisy or human weakness. It is, in fact, a perfectly normal reaction to an unrealistic concept of authority and responsibility. The lack of realism lies in even trying to hold individuals responsible for collective performance.

If we practiced what we preached about responsibility, the first to go in every layoff would be the chief executive, in recognition of his planning failure. Every time a subordinate failed to perform his superior would resign, either for failure to motivate him or for misjudgment of his ability, or both. We do not practice what we preach about individual responsibility in collective endeavor because we cannot make a healthy adjustment to our notions of either individual authority or responsibility.

Our concept of authority's role in bureaucracy dehumanizes all subordinates as a class. They become sheep in care of the good shepherd, not equal participants in a team effort. Moreover, the chief executive is superhumanized. He can rarely live up to the role of corporate savior which the top job calls for, and he lives under a stern genetic command to grasp at all the power he can get to protect his own political position, even at the expense of his subordinates.

The concept of leadership thus is made hypocritical. In nature, the leader leads. When defenses are breached and things go wrong, he gets it first, not last, and someone else takes over. The system breaks down when team risks must be taken on the offensive. This explains why our ancestors gave up dominance orders, with a strong leader, for the participatory teamwork and decision making needed in team hunting.

Historical analysis illustrates that it is not possible to pin down individual responsibility for collective success or failure. Historians still argue over whether General Grant was a butcher or a great general. The view can also change over time; legends in their own time can be regarded as bums a couple of generations later. In the end all such judgments are speculative. The same holds true of observations about organization. Consider Amitai Etzioni's dictum that "the organization must distribute its rewards and sanctions according to individual performance so that those whose performance is in line with organizational norms will be rewarded and [individuals who] deviate will be penalized."[12] Obviously his statement implies knowledge and not mere conjecture about individual performance. Then, in what may be one of the more regretted footnotes in the literature of organization, Etzioni cites

---

[12] Amitai Etzioni, *Modern Organizations,* © 1964, Prentice-Hall, Inc., Englewood Cliffs, N.J., p. 59.

Japan as a land of ineffective organization because Japanese business firms do not base reward on conjecture about the individual's performance.

Similarly, there are no valid measures of individual performance in a collective endeavor. Corporate or joint effort necessarily draws on the labor of many. The result is synergistic—a sum greater than the total of the parts. The whole cannot be viewed in sufficient detail to unravel the synergism and uncover each individual's contribution to profits or losses. Decades of research into performance evaluation, merit rating, and similar schemes have together yielded little more than academic snake oil. Individual performance judgments remain relentlessly speculative.

The notion that superiors can accurately judge each subordinate's contribution to a group effort is little more than absurd. It makes sense only if we ascribe to those who hold superior bureaucratic office the attributes of wisdom we usually reserve for the Almighty. That so many people believe that superiors can automatically judge subordinates accurately owes much to the influence of the monotheistic ethic on our concept of authority in bureaucracy.

In other frames of reference, we view the problem more realistically. We accept the fact that time must pass before a proper evaluation can be made of any individual's contribution to history, as well as the concept that a judge should not be associated with those upon whom he sits in judgment. In confronting impersonal analytical problems, we recognize that sorting out the separate influence of one variable when many variables interact to produce a result is a statistically tricky business. But somehow, when superiors sit in judgment on subordinates, all such thorny problems disappear in the bureaucratic hierarchy, as if by supernatural intervention.

## WHO WON THE GAME?

It is possible to identify, occasionally, performance in a particularly crucial job in relation to a group endeavor. Certain people can do certain jobs well or ill, sometimes obviously so. Yet even here appearances can be misleading. Consider a football game. The home team is behind, 20 to 21. It's the final quarter, two minutes to go. The visitors have the ball, first down, ten yards to go on our 15-yard line. The visitors decide to ice the game by going for another touchdown. As the play opens, a visitor tackle, slightly off balance, misses his block, and our tackle rushes through the hole so fast he throws their quarterback for a seven-yard loss and a fumble which our center manages to recover. The home crowd roars with delight. A new ball game!

Our ball, first and ten, 1:40 to go in the game. The coach sends in our star offensive QB known for his long bombs, but he has instructions to go on the ground the first time to get a little better field position. The visitors, fearing the long gainer, call for a looser defense. The play works, and our beefy fullback smashes through the visitors' line to gain 14 yards.

So now, first and ten on our own 36, 1:20 to go. Still fearing the long gainer, but now a bit shaken, the visitors tighten up a bit on defense. Another run, a gain of nine yards. Second down, one yard to go on our own 45 with 1:05 in the game. Now our QB calls for the long bomb to the right end. But the visitors come in tight. They suspect a try for the certain first down. He's back, he throws, and the end is running, running, and . . . he nabs the ball on the visitor's 27-yard line. Our end is off for a T.D., but he steps out of bounds on the 19! Time out, which stops the clock.

Time in, :40 to go. Another pass call. This time the visitors have settled down. Their hard-charging line breaks through. Incomplete pass. But our QB just barely got the ball away before being hit, and he's shaken up. Time out. Seems he twisted an ankle trying to shake off the lineman. Now only :25 in the game, second down, ten yards to go. The coach sends in the kicker with the educated toe. The center snaps the ball, the kicker boots it away clean between the uprights. We win, 23–21!

For months after the fans will discuss just who the "main" hero was and what "key" play won the game. But there is no way to pinpoint any particular individual as *the* key player or any act as *the* key play. A combination of particular acts over a period of time converged to win the game, and the convergence, not any particular act, is what won. A difference in *any* one might have changed the result. All we can say for sure is that our team won, theirs lost, and hurray for our side!

Meanwhile the defeated visitors will reflect on which "key" goof lost the game. The butterfingered QB who fumbled just because he got hit a little hard? The tackle who slipped? And who was the jerk calling for the loose pass defense, thus handing over 23 crucial yards on the ground to the opposition—the coach or the QB?

Thus the doctrine of personal, individual responsibility for collective performance leads many to focus on the particulars of convergence, missing the fact of convergence itself, or teamwork. Nothing I have said, however, should be taken to suggest that recognition should not be given to individuals who perform well. But in the home team victory, we could not limit such recognition to the kicker. His kick, true enough, was the only event mentioned which showed up on the score board. Nothing that came before would have mattered if his kick had failed. If we analyze the whole 60 minutes of play in terms of the last 25 seconds, we could say the kicker won the game. Or did the visitor's center lose it in the last 22 seconds when he mistimed his leap to block the kick by a crucial fraction of a second? We could single out the crucial block leading to the fumble, the decision to gain yardage first on the ground, the following two runs, then the long pass and catch with added running yardage, and finally the successful kick as *some* of the outstanding plays which pulled the game out of the fire.

The essence of good team spirit is that no one person can monopolize the glory or has to suffer the sole humiliation of defeat. Our need for individual recognition in no way precludes our fraternal colleagues from also winning personal recognition.

Bureaucracies face a dilemma in judging individual contributions to synergistic results because they must judge individuals largely in terms of following or breaking the "rules." The dilemma is that the rules can become so complex that nothing gets done *unless* they are routinely violated. When the convergence is failure, heads must roll. Anyone who has failed to cover his tracks makes a tempting target for scapegoating. Rare is the sophisticated bureaucrat who does not devote his most creative effort to establishing that he is not the one who lost the game.

## THE HISTORY OF EMPLOYEE SERVITUDE

In affairs of state, the autocrat's tendency to become a tyrant has long been recognized. Democracies have abolished the tyrant's job by various legal constraints (such as constitutions) which a chief executive cannot violate. The citizen acquires certain vested rights; for example, the state cannot separate him from his identity and status without due process, and sometimes not even then. If the citizen is accused of wrongdoing, the state cannot assume the wisdom of the deity but must take on itself the burden of proof. This, of course, is a sharp break from the monotheistic ethic. The chief executive is the servant, not the master, of the citizens.

We have yet to make this break in employer organizations, which remain largely bureaucratic. Anglo-Saxon common law, for all its tradition of individual freedom, tacitly supports the monotheistic ethic as far as employers are concerned. By any reasonable standards the employee has the status of second- or even third-class citizenship in his employer organization. He must often live in it as a resident alien on a visa subject to revocation without warning or need to show cause.

This situation has developed because the employee's legal status traces directly from that of the slave. The master-slave relationship was legally established in ancient Greece and extended by the Romans. Legal slavery came under theoretical attack by the Christians, but only with the collapse of the Roman Empire and the onset of the Dark Ages was the next legal stage reached—master-serf. The serf acquired some rights, mainly tenure, but few freedoms, and the master's word remained almost as binding as the deity's.

When the feudal system broke up, a new class of independent tradesmen, farmers, and other small businessmen evolved. Beneath this independent status there emerged the master-servant concept, which remains the basis for common law relationships between employers and employees, although it has been modified by various labor laws and trade union regulations. As the independent tradesmen, farmers, and other small businessmen became something of a majority in economic life, they became the masters of their servants—employers of employees. Given the legal right to play god (master), few will spurn it. Servants (employees) picked up some rights compared to serfs, but they also lost some security. The servant can quit, the serf cannot. But the servant can be fired, the serf cannot. We call this free labor. If this concept of freedom applied to the citizen, it would grant him the right of emigration in exchange for the government's right to exile him without need to show cause or even due process.

Before the Industrial Revolution, and particularly in the United States, the illogic and potential for abuse of this concept of free labor remained dormant. Almost anyone who wanted to could become self-employed in some capacity and thus could become a master himself. Indeed, many servants or employees were apprentices who expected to become self-employed, and others were family members and were treated as such. Close personal association and small group size favored fair treatment. Custom and common sense constrained the master from capricious exercise of his right to "exile" the help; masters required loyalty from their servants to get reasonable performance, and they could not get loyalty unless they gave it. Thus the de facto relationship tended to become paternalistic, or that of father and child. A need for temporary work was almost always satisfied by hiring the services of independent, often itinerant workers and artisans. Here the relationship was buyer-seller, not master-servant. Incompatibility of personalities was probably the largest cause of firings and quittings, and separations tended to occur early rather than late in the relationship. In these ways the legal handicaps which in theory dehumanize the employee were considerably rehumanized in practice.

With the coming of modern technology and large-scale industry, however, the employee's legal disadvantages became his practical handicaps as well. As the opportunities for self-employment melted away, the employee became increasingly a second-class citizen in every meaningful sense. His political rights viz-à-viz a government might remain in full force, but the "government" over his daily life, which was largely devoted to earning a living, became increasingly despotic. The father figure became a godking in the larger employer organizations, for all not in direct personal contact with the top. Industrial bureaucracy was born.

One of the ironies of this process was that it occurred under the relentlessly anticaste pressure of Calvinism, whose concepts became known as Puritanism, the Protestant ethic, or the work ethic. Even more ironically, it was Max Weber who did much of the early scholarly work on Calvin's work ethic. Calvin's message was: "Follow your calling." This was the way to salvation, provided the individual worked hard and gave his best effort. No social distinctions were permitted among the various callings; all not in conflict with the Ten Commandments were exactly equal in the eyes of God. The notion of social stratification or ranking into a caste system by ascribing higher social worth to some jobs compared to others was in fundamental conflict with the work ethic. Nor was the management of work seen as more worthy than the work itself. Honest toil was great and good.

Bureaucracy has done much to destroy the work ethic by its social stratification of various types of work. Work has little meaning to the individual independent of the social context in which it occurs, and bureaucratic hierarchies stand in fundamental conflict to the social milieu of the work ethic. The work ethic never presumed the work could be done at an enormous social distance from its source of control.

## THE BACKLASH

When the master-servant relationship began to take hold in the United States, it did so in a culture which had conditioned its citizens to oppose autocracy and social caste systems. This was only somewhat less true in Western Europe. Thus the bureaucratic autocracy not only went against the biological grain, it clashed head on with the broader culture as well.

A backlash to the trend to bureaucracy promptly surfaced as Marxism and, later, communism. On another tack, the trade union movement was able to seize some power from the employer.

Unfortunately, these reactions identified the wrong villain. The capitalist and not the bureaucratic autocrat became the symbol of evil. Marxists even promoted the autocrat from his limited economic tyranny to the more comprehensive form of despotism they call the Dictatorship of the Proletariat, a great leap backward to the shepherd-sheep arrangement. Demigods such as Lenin, Stalin, and Mao appeared. For all its theoretical atheism, Marxism remains in the grip of the monotheistic ethic.

Western philosophical and ethical principles suffer from excessive abstract application. We have supported the principle that power corrupts; now we must qualify it. Political power of one adult over another adult truly does corrupt. But physical power or control over materialistic things does not necessarily do so. Money corrupts mainly when translated into political power over other people. Profits corrupt nothing at all in themselves, though greed surely can and does corrupt profits.

The reverse of profit would simply be to pump more resources into a project than can be recovered, a sure path to economic ruin. When the hominids discovered that by investing indirect labor in crafting tools and weapons they enjoyed a greater return in the hunt, their direct source of income; they discovered profit as well. The discovery of such things as pottery and fire also provided a return from the investment of effort. In a sense the human animal might never have evolved were it not for economically profitable returns on investments. This does not mean that any profit is automatically good, but it should caution against its condemnation in the abstract.

The contention that the only purpose of a business is to make a profit for the stockholder distorts the concept of profit, however. An economic return to the stockholder is surely a legitimate concern of the business, but it provides three other equally important things: a secure and healthy livelihood for its employees, useful goods and services for its customers, and markets for its suppliers. If any one of these objectives is seriously eroded, there are distortions in the other three. Any effort to maximize one at the expense of the others will prove self-defeating in the long run—and often in the short run. Profits can play a useful noneconomic role as well by providing a utilitarian means of keeping score among commercial rivals in the great game of business.

The question remains: Why did the owner-capitalist instead of the master-autocrat role of the businessman come in for all the flak? To understand this we must turn to economic principles as divorced from religion. The classical economists invented a new species of animal, superficially of the primate order but psychologically unlike any other creature. In a masterstroke of abiogenesis, economics conjured this creature into being and gave him the name of Economic Man.

## ECONOMIC MAN

Archeologists have never discovered any fossil evidence of Economic Man. Accounts of his existence, however, abound in the texts of classical economists. Only through these records do we know him. Above all else, Economic Man is a consummate social isolate. We have never been able to pin down the existence of a female of the species, and of his sex life we know nothing at all. We do know that he has no fraternal attributes whatsoever; esprit de corps and camaraderie have no relevance for him, and he has no grasp of the concept of loyalty. His only concern is money.

While he always wants more money, he will promptly take less in response to market changes in the demand for his services. He sells his work services as a wandering labor entrepreneur, completely mobile, and in eternal competition with every other member of his species. One customer for his services is the same as any other. He forms no attachments to anyone; in the life of Economic Man, that would be to exhibit irrationality. Economic Man regards himself as a commodity. His great appeal to economists lies in the fact that his behavior can be predicted with mathematical precision.

When capitalists heard accounts of this strange creature they confused him with their own employees, especially in regard to hiring and firing. Thus the hire-fire cycle of labor-cost adjustment was born as a logical response to the commodity theory of labor. Employers did not relinquish the status of masters in charge of servants, although, because commodities are inert, they had to reanimate their employees while on the job back into servant status. Employees tended to get the worst of two worlds in this scheme. They suffered the disadvantages of being a seller with none of the independence or social equality we presume exists between buyers and sellers. As servants, meanwhile, they lost their previous paternal protection, to become domesticated sheep without a shepherd, as it were.

Since the new element in this arrangement was the Economic Man concept, or the commodity theory of labor, it was to this that the employees reacted. Thus their animosities were directed toward their bosses as capitalists more than as masters.

Our cultural values on the subject of industrial relations compose a remarkably confused and conflicting inventory. We now recognize that Economic Man has very little in common with human beings. Nevertheless, "cost-effective experts" have recently begun applying the logic of Economic Man to the lower and middle reaches of management. No longer is management exempt from hire-fire treatment, as it has been for most of our industrial history. Management backlash has begun to appear, with talk of trade unions of their own.

## CATCH 23: IS THERE AN ALTERNATIVE?

Despite all the miseries evidenced by bureaucracy, the experts cling to the myth that it is inevitable because it has no alternatives. Point to the alternatives, and they plead cultural differences. In other words, we accept bureaucracy's assaults on our culture's most treasured values because no other form of organization will work, but we cannot use proven alternatives because they came from different cultures.

If you should get into a discussion with an expert on this, the following Catch 22 type dialogue would likely result:

YOU: Let's quit all the bitching and get rid of bureaucracy!

EXPERT: Oh, we can't do that.

YOU: Why not?

EXPERT: Well, we have to be realistic. Let me assure you I find bureaucracy frustrating too. But there's no better system, no efficient alternative for Big Organization.

YOU: How can you call bureaucracy efficient? I thought red tape, boondoggles, overlapping and duplication of effort, all the political infighting and such caused lots of waste.

EXPERT: Well, of course, but we are dealing with the problem of people —and people, let's face it, aren't perfect.

YOU: You mean the system is okay but the people in it don't measure up?

EXPERT: Something like that—we're dealing with human nature, remember.

YOU: And we can't design a system more in tune with human nature?

EXPERT: Oh in theory we might, but in theory bureaucracy works perfectly. It's in practice that human nature lets us down.

. YOU: So its a question of human nature, not the system?

EXPERT: Precisely.

YOU: Well, what about Japan? They don't use bureaucracy in theory or in practice and whatever it is they do use, they seem to be doing right well by it.

EXPERT: Oh, well now you're talking about a completely different culture. The Japanese are a homogeneous and insular people. They have learned how to work together for centuries. They are hard working and very achievement oriented.

YOU: But I thought we Americans were supposed to be hard-working, achievement-oriented people, sturdy pioneer stock driven by a work ethic.

EXPERT: Well we are—or were—but that was when we were mostly small farmers or businessmen. People in Big Bureaucracy don't have the same incentives.

YOU: Why is that?

EXPERT: Too big, too impersonal, too dehumanized and regimented; you can't have the same sense of participation.

YOU: Then why do they work at all?

EXPERT: Well, unfortunately, it takes the carrot and the stick working on their fear and greed to make them work. That's human nature, sad but true.

YOU: But what about Japan? They *use* participation in Big Organization and people seem highly motivated.

EXPERT: I've explained that already—Japan is a different culture. They are highly motivated and work centered. They don't need the carrot and the stick.

YOU: But whenever the Japanese experiment with Big Bureaucracy they run into the same problems we do—alienation, poor morale, etc. How come?

EXPERT: I've explained that too. Big Bureaucracy is simply too dehumanized, too impersonal. Human beings simply are not as motivated in Big Bureaucracy.

YOU: Then why do we use the bureaucratic system?

EXPERT: Apparently you just don't listen. I've already told you. No effective alternatives can match bureaucracy's efficiency in large organizations. There is no point in carrying this discussion any further if you won't listen.

# Part II

## BUREAUCRATIC
## PATHOLOGY

# 3

# Social Disorders of Bureaucracy

**THE ORGANIZATION MAN REVISITED**

Contemporary thinking about life in bureaucracy owes much to William H. Whyte's 1956 classic, *The Organization Man*. Nearly a generation later, we can review Whyte's "generation of bureaucrats," the bulk of white-collar workers below the top. Whyte pursued his quarry in ideological history, through the pages of fiction, into the classrooms and in suburbia. When discussing the subject actually at work, he focused on the special frustrations of the research scientist.

Whyte feared that if the scientist were to become a "company man," individual excellence would give way to group mediocrity. He saw a fundamental conflict between the individual and his organization, not in economic but in moral terms. Economically, he viewed the corporation as essentially benevolent; what he was worried about was the organization man's soul. Disclaiming any solution to the basic conflict, he nonetheless urged an end to the "company man" and a return to the Calvinistic concept of a "calling." "Why should the scientist be company oriented?" Whyte asked. "It is not to his self-interest, neither is it to that of The Organization." Rather, "It is his work that must be paramount." Whyte maintained it was "not just for the scientist, not just for the brilliant, that the moral should be drawn . . ." and urged all white-collar workers to "fight the organization." They otherwise faced "surrender," no less because the promised benefits of the organization were "offered in benevolence." "That," Whyte concluded, "is the problem."[1]

---

[1] W. H. Whyte, Jr., *The Organization Man* (New York: Simon & Schuster, 1956), concluding chapter.

While benevolence and the company man have largely departed from the scene, hand in hand, incredible mediocrity has ballooned as corporations and individuals follow Whyte's advice. Indeed, in aerospace, the nation's largest employer of manpower and scientists, mediocrity would look pretty good at this writing. Aerospace has engineered a string of technical and financial disasters unrivaled in modern industry, marked by charges of gross mismanagement and even hints of fraud.

Whyte did not foresee the kind of fight awaiting his "generation of bureaucrats" nor the ruthlessness with which bureaucracy would fight back. Brutal treatment by some of the most respected names in American industry of employees who committed the crime of honesty when faced with bureaucratic blunders has been documented. And as Admiral Hyman Rickover has observed, "If you must sin, sin against God, not against the bureaucracy. God may forgive you, but the bureaucracy never will."[2]

Few corporations still try to manipulate group harmony through the various "human relations techniques" which bothered Whyte. Today they are more likely to apply the more straightforward techniques of coercion. Whyte's "social ethic" has given way to the "knuckle under or get out ethic." Even the surrender of his soul may not save the worker from a mass white-collar layoff, an event hardly conceivable in Whyte's mid-50s. Whyte's bureaucrats who entered the corporate world in the mid-50s have suffered a totally unanticipated loss of employment security.

## THE EMBITTERING OF A BUREAUCRAT

Suppose that you, just out of college, had joined your firm in the 1950s. You would have been an aspiring company man through and through, brimming with spontaneous loyalty. A few years as a scrub and your hard work might have paid off; perhaps you made the management team in the branch sales office. You enjoyed your sense of belongingness and camaraderie, took pride in branch achievements. Your loyalty was fully reciprocated, you then believed.

You didn't necessarily like everyone on the team, of course. Take garrulous Joe, the assistant branch manager, a fussbudget and bore. You suspected he no longer earned his salary, but then in his day he had earned a lot more than that.

Then came the merger, bringing consultants whose frustration you could sense, since job definitions lacked tightly defined responsibilities.

---

[2] A. Ernest Fitzgerald, *The High Priests of Waste* (New York: W. W. Norton & Co., Inc., 1972), p. 224.

You had taken over a few things normally part of Joe's job, but he kept that Ajax account when he saw how much you disliked it. To you this was teamwork, but you could see how an outsider might conclude things were a little too loose. Still, three weeks later, it came as a numbing shock when Joe was let out—almost 57, and chop!

A young man from the new head office, John, a Harvard MBA, replaced Joe. He was supposed to "help standardize procedures," but not long after he arrived, he and Fred, the branch manager, announced a new setup to "tighten up the lines of responsibility." Actually you came off rather well, with a "bigger" job and a nice raise as well. Maybe the new setup wouldn't be so bad. Times change and we have to change with them.

Then suddenly, Fred announced his resignation: "a better opportunity." John stepped up to Fred's job. You didn't really feel you were a contender, but it was a jolt when John's job went to Tim, another young MBA from the outside. Tim really knew computers, they said, and many procedures were being computerized.

None of this sat too well with two others, Jim and Bob, each of whom thought Fred's slot should have gone to him. Both became carping critics of the firm. The old esprit definitely disappeared, and office talk became increasingly cynical. You heard that headquarters had shut down the Indiana plant—obsolescent. Jim proclaimed that some of his customers supplied by Indiana were horrified, and he didn't blame them for switching to the competition. The computer setup meanwhile ran into some bugs, and Tim quietly disappeared. As John explained, "Tim just didn't work out." The big reorganization came two years later. The company consolidated your functions with division headquarters. Again, you lucked out with a promotion of sorts at division. Several others were given notice, including Jim and Bob. It was said they had poor attitudes.

Your new colleagues at division complain constantly about this "damned bureaucracy": can't go to the john without authorization. Oh, some of the work has been pretty interesting, despite the red tape. You can't really complain about money, what with two job promotions and a few merit raises. And to be honest you don't work all that hard; always some bottleneck somewhere holding you up.

You soon miss the old days when you felt part of a team. Now you feel more like embodied red tape, a bureaucrat. And, you hate to admit it, but you could probably have saved Tim. You spotted his mistake when he made it, but John insisted on tight job responsibilities and young Tim had a know-it-all streak which put you off. It cost the company a mint, but so what. Look what they had done to Joe, Jim, and Bob.

You find the new chain of command overpowering. You've come up several levels yourself, but the higher you rise the further away the top seems to get. You now report to a unit chief who reports to the assistant manager. The assistant manager reports to the territorial manager who in turn reports to the director of sales for the division, and he reports to the divisional vice president of marketing. The vice president of marketing seems to report to the vice president and divisional general manager, who comes under a new setup called the group vice president. The groups report to the president in New York.

You feel frustrated by this monstrous hierarchy, but you learned quickly that to question it is taboo. You asked questions because you had devised a procedural simplication. Then you found out that procedural change authorization has to come from several levels up and you have no right of direct access. Your unit chief actually agreed with your idea, but he vetoed the matter anyway because the sales director had devised the procedure you were questioning. His rival had tried to use procedural issues in a power play to take over sales. The sales director won, but he remains springloaded on the whole issue of procedure. You know enough to let it drop, although your enthusiasm is completely deflated.

What particularly disturbs you is the knowledge that people you do not know and cannot even contact directly have enormous power over you. And they exert this power in their own personal political interest, not just on behalf of the firm. Had you pushed the new procedure you might have touched a raw nerve and, being none the wiser, found yourself out in the next "economy cut," now an annual routine. Your growing sense of fear galls you. Good work, done without political controversy, may keep you on the payroll. But you note with dismay that this route has its own dangers. How much more useless red tape must you keep quiet about? Then, if a palace revolution occurs, another lot of consultants comes around and suggests a general housecleaning. Out goes the old red tape together with those who dutifully accepted it to avoid the wrath of higher-ups. You lose either way. You know the chill of being at the mercy of forces you are quite helpless to influence, and you know you face these all alone.

## THE FUNCTION OF MANAGEMENT

In the last chapter we pointed out that the division of labor is necessary in any system of human enterprise, and that large enterprise also requires a coordinating apparatus. As management science emerged in America it focused on the best ways to divide up the work into specialized sectors and the problems of coordinating the specialties. Production schedules, cost accounting methods, statistical quality con-

trol, and a host of other impersonal techniques rightly absorb the ener-
gies of management experts. I have no quarrel with these techniques
as such.

You cannot build a steel mill with a group of people who are merely
enthusiastic. The job has to be broken down into many separate operations in a sequence of activities guided by managers working from a
plan of operations. This plan, in effect, dictates what must be done,
when, and by whom. Some leeway can exist, of course, but without a
plan there can be hopeless confusion, and enthusiasm and esprit de
corps will vanish.

A rational plan takes advantage of the division of labor. Scarce resources can be economized, and greater output can be achieved with
less input. These advantages led Max Weber to proclaim bureaucracy's
inherent technical superiority over all other known types of organization. It does not follow, however, that the work plan must dictate the
social order. A rational, impersonal, and specialized approach to work
need not ignore people's social needs, any more than it ignores their
physical needs.

In discussing the social disorders of bureaucracy we will not consider
the best ways to organize the work or the various management techniques. Moreover, we will not discuss how to "manage" people in the
sense of manipulating them. The effort to manipulate people for the
benefit of the enterprise at the expense of the individual's social needs
will inevitably backfire on any enterprise that tries it.

## THE POLITICS OF MANAGEMENT

If we call the power to control work management authority, we can
refer to the power to control people's social lives as political authority.
Management authority thus concentrates on such issues and techniques
as production schedules, investment levels, marketing strategy, and
equipment technology. The only "political" power the manager really
needs to coordinate the work is the power to deploy people. Bureaucracy, by loading all our social needs onto the job, leaves the authority
to manage the work impersonally open to political tyranny. The manager then not only must make technical decisions about the work, he
can hardly avoid making autocratic political decisions involving employee social relations. To deploy people simply to coordinate the work
efficiently would be politically neutral, if it were divorced from other
social issues. If you do not change a person's identity, status, pay, or
prestige when you change his role, you will encounter little resistance.
Of course you cannot require an employee to do something for which
he lacks the skill, and you have to allow for continuity of team relation-

ships. These constraints aside, "deployment" decisions meet little resistance when they are free of the political threat of arbitrary social changes.

The bureaucratic social order makes it remarkably difficult to separate technical management decisions from arbitrary sociopolitical change. Suppose the market drops off and you therefore schedule less production. But less production may trigger a layoff, an event of enormous sociopolitical importance to those affected. Who gets laid off and who stays becomes a highly charged issue. You may have made an entirely "rational" decision from a management viewpoint, but perhaps without intent you have also made a political decision. You have hashed up the identity and status of those laid off, aside from cutting off their income.

It will seem logical and rational to you to lay off "the worst" workers and retain "the best" workers. Subjective judgment must enter into your decisions, and you will be exposed to accusations of favoritism and poor judgment. Perhaps you unwittingly retain a talented conspirator with charismatic appeal, however poor his work seems to you, who organizes the employees into a union and calls a strike. You, a reluctant tyrant at worst, will then discover that the politics of production take precedence over the management of production. "Your" workers will have become your political adversaries.

Thus you cannot make technical management decisions without first laying the political groundwork. To keep political peace, you typically must employ more people than necessary. With your deployment leeway constrained, costs will rise in consequence. You, perhaps, will complain about "irrational" labor. The workers likely will rage against a tyrannical management that is devoid of human feeling and only "out for the buck." Both you and your political adversaries will thus miss the real culprit, the bureaucratic social order (BSO). The theory of bureaucratic rationality has caused the political problem by refusing to separate political authority from managerial coordinating authority. In the fraternal social order, you would merely have deployed some people into temporary reserve training assignments. A layoff would never have occurred to you, any more than a nation faced with a poor crop would consider exile for its "worst citizens" to ease the food shortage.

The clash between the human need for social stability and the organization's need for operational flexibility may of course remain latent. Well staffed and organized, a new bureaucracy may function quite well, with high morale and harmonious human relations. If organized in keeping with the outside environment, it may not need to make many internal adjustments and thus may perform reasonably well for a long time. No real clash may occur between human and organizational needs.

Ultimately, however, conditions change. Competition may force a contraction in operation, or a new technology might require a complete internal reorganization. In such cases, latent difficulties surface quickly. Technical changes that are otherwise perfectly sensible can leave the social order in ruins, and the social needs of many can get badly mangled. Teamwork vanishes as potential victims resist the changes.

## THE FIVE SOCIAL NEEDS

The five social needs all humans have in common (as set forth in Chapter 1 and developed in Appendix A) are identity, status or social rank, role or job, prestige as reputation, and reward or income. The balance of this chapter will discuss these needs, concentrating on the first two, for two reasons. First, they are the most important. Second, bureaucracy's failure to satisfy these two needs in a natural way causes most of its problems, including problems in satisfying the other three.

## THE IDENTITY CRISIS

The bureaucratic social order, as I define it, does not accord any rights of membership to the individual but rather regards him as an impersonal seller of services. The individual acquires an identity through his work, occupation, or profession; in the bureaucracy he is known as an engineer, typist, mechanic, driver, chemist, clerk, or whatever. When occupational labels become job titles, they carry the burden of social identity in addition to role. Having an occupational identity in an enterprise raises no particular problems per se, provided the identity is reasonably broad and provided it is also secondary. Pathology arises when the job title carries the entire identity burden, and it worsens when the enterprise defines the job precisely and narrowly.

In legal terms you work for a bureaucracy as a seller-servant (employee), whereas you belong to a fraternity as a member. If you identify with your work you will "belong" to your work and not with the customer for it. For an independent worker who has many customers for his services, this is fine. For an employer and an employee, however, the buyer-seller relationship is, socially, entirely unnatural for both parties.

### The Buyer-Seller Relationship

Biologically speaking, we can think of the buyer-seller relationship as symbiotic predation, a relationship that may be peculiar to mankind. Symbiosis is a mutually beneficial relationship between two different organisms which occurs frequently in nature. Predators, however, kill for a living; "making a killing in the market" differs little in spirit from bagging a big buck. Reciprocity makes commerce symbiotic, however predatory it may be. Both parties can gain from the transaction, even though their interests fundamentally differ. But if symbiosis is to balance predation, the two sides must be evenly matched. This need for balance is recognized in team sports and other competitive activities. Either side should be able to break off the relationship without undue harm to the other. The ideal relationship between buyer and seller is impersonal under normal circumstances, but no single transaction should be of crucial importance to either's survival.

A sound commercial relationship also requires that the seller manage his own work. A cab driver subjects himself to his customer's instructions as to destination, possibly choice of route, and perhaps, within limits, whether to hurry up or take his time. Beyond that he resents instructions on how to operate his cab. Normally, his identity, status, or prestige do not become involved in his role as cab driver with respect to his customer, who does not expect to interfere with the social aspects of his work. The customer has contracted for the driver's services, impersonally and casually. The driver does not look to him for a promotion in his social rank.

As a bureaucratic employee, however, you enjoy little control over your own work. Even if you furnish your own tools, the bureaucracy may still insist on telling you just how you do your job. The lower your level, the less control you have over your work. The employee enjoys only the weaknesses of being a seller and none of the normal strengths. Severing the employment relationship normally proves traumatic to the individual, but rarely is this so for the bureaucracy. The identity of the "seller" can be destroyed; that of the "buyer" remains unscathed.

When the bureaucracy imposes the master-servant relationship on the lopsided buyer-seller one, the seller must concede all sorts of political and social power to the buyer. Employment in the pure bureaucracy thus becomes a form of servitude. The bureaucracy, however, can successfully coordinate its work only by imposing the master-servant relationship, mainly because it treats an employee as an Economic Man, a seller of labor. The bureaucracy thus "releases" the predatory instinct in employees. As competitive sellers of services, they prey on the bureaucracy, each other, or both, because the system's rewards encourage such behavior. This is hardly conducive to teamwork, and the bureaucracy has little option but to achieve coordination via coercion. Everyone ultimately loses in this game.

Trade unions developed in part to restore balance to the buyer-seller arrangement. By and large they have done so successfully—too successfully, some might argue. Moreover, various laws constrain the bureaucracy's power over individuals in such matters as safety and working conditions. None of these constraints correct the basic pathology of the competitive buyer-seller relationship, however. Often constraints merely induce wasteful practices while avoiding the key issue.

Defenders of the status quo often sniff at the accusations of waste by proclaiming that they put "human values above materialism." No doubt they really think so, but actually they do not. Biologically, man wants to identify with, not against, the enterprise upon which he depends for economic survival. He wants to cooperate and work as a team, and he needs to feel a sense of comradeship with peers and those above and below him in social rank. He wants these things, instinctively, but his basic identity in the BSO does not permit it. Job tenure and job seniority do not cure his identity crisis. The employee's identity still hinges on "the job," his work, not on the enterprise as a whole.

## Job Bonding

Poor matching of job and employee also results in waste through poor performance. Bureaucracies often assign people to jobs arbitrarily. The employee may not enjoy the work involved or even have the right skills. He may fail to form an attachment or "bond" with his job for many reasons, yet his identity will hinge on this job. He therefore may become both defensive and apathetic about his job. He will come alive only in defense of his job, his identity; a poor identity is better than none. In the eyes of others he may appear as "deadwood," an inevitable by-product of bureaucracy.

Yet a good job bond can cause more trouble to a bureaucracy than a poor one, particularly in times of change. Technology, for example, can make jobs obsolete or even worthless. Unfortunately, technology does nothing to "unbond" people from the newly useless or obsolete job. Bonding of any kind involves instinct or emotion, not abstract reason, and it seldom is subject to conscious control.[3] People firmly bonded to obsolete jobs can cause delays in making necessary technical changes.

Bonding to outmoded identities can cause delays in other ways, too. Henry Ford's bond with his brain child, the Model T, caused him to lose first place to General Motors. The American shipbuilders' bond with the clipper ships in the 19th century forced them to give up maritime supremacy to British steamships. Bonded to a job, function, product, or method of doing something, most individuals cannot make objective judgments about alternatives.

## A Military Example of Bonding

There is no point in saying you should not bond with your job or function. If you are identified primarily with a job, and if you enjoy it, the chances are a bond will form. A close job identity, however, often

---

[3] The biology of bonding is discussed in more detail in Appendix A.

hurts the enterprise. The military has a long history of this problem. While the military differs in some crucial ways from bureaucracy, as we shall see later, it also suffers from suboptimal functional identity bonding.

Consider the careers of two famous generals. The first, Douglas Haig, commanded Britain's forces on the Western front for most of World War I. As a cavalry general, Haig strove to achieve rapid mobility; the dashing maneuver was often a key to a quick victory. Haig did a brilliant job of getting the British Army, mostly consisting of raw recruits after the regular forces had been nearly wiped out in 1914–15, organized in France.

Haig saw that to defeat the Germans quickly the Allies had to break through the lines and then thrust deeply to the rear. The newly perfected machine gun, together with barbed wire, trenches, and bunkers, barred the way. Haig was so bonded to a cavalry exploitation of an infantry breakthrough, however, that he virtually ignored the reality of machine guns and trenches. He ordered the British infantry to certain death by the hundreds of thousands in one futile assault after another on German trenches. In one attack at Loos, the British lost 8,000, the Germans not a man. Haig refused to view the carnage and slaughter he had ordered; he never went to the front. He aimed at the entirely sound idea of a decisive breakthrough, but his cavalry bond kept him from making a realistic assessment of the type of problem he faced from the well-entrenched machine guns.

Whereas Haig has been generally regarded as one of military history's flops, General Douglas MacArthur is considered one of its authentic geniuses. The difference may lay far less in basic military intellect than in job bonding. Haig's self-identity was tied up with the cavalry, not the British Army per se. MacArthur chose the Corps of Engineers upon graduation from West Point, and the engineers do not identify with any particular weapon or approach to battle. MacArthur thus could identify with the army as a whole and with all its combat arms and could concentrate on the objective, not the means.

MacArthur made his strategic reputation in World War II in the Pacific. True enough, in the opening phase of the war MacArthur, in command of army forces in the Philippines, was caught off guard. Judged on its own merits, MacArthur's defense of the Philippines was in many respects mismanaged. It looked good at the time mainly in comparison to the string of catastrophes which had befallen Allied forces in the initial Japanese onslaught. On the road back, however, MacArthur proved adept and flexible in his choice of means to achieve his objectives. He used air, naval, and land forces separately and together with genius. Knowing that the Japanese soldier was probably the world's most tenacious in defense, he almost never chose a frontal assault. Haig's identity bonds encouraged him to plan only for a cavalry breakthrough and caused him to ignore the evidence against its success. MacArthur's bonds freed him to consider all the relevant alternatives dispassionately.

### Identity in Government Bureaucracy

From the point of view of any enterprise, job bonding promotes professionalization at the cost of objectivity. By forcing identity onto the job, bureaucracy creates an inbuilt bias toward suboptimization. People strive to do their best by their jobs, not by the enterprise. The two objectives often conflict. By job, of course, I refer either to the individual's particular job or to the larger "job" done by a department or function, for example.

America does not have a single federal civil service but a plethora of fiercely competitive civil services. Each has its own identity which determines the identity of all the individuals within it. Partly for reasons of identity and partly because of other biosocial needs, civil servants are ceaselessly and reflexively concerned with enlarging their bureaucratic territory. Duplication of effort, overlapping of functions, and the dogged preservation of useless units result, as well as overjobbing of all units. Overjobbing occurs everywhere, relative to the amount of useful work done. Reorganization of the work does not solve this problem, and even attrition fails to stop the expansion of fake jobs in the many competing civil services.

Presidents since Franklin Roosevelt have discovered they are more the captives than the masters of the federal bureaucracy. Each agency or bureau becomes more interested in perpetuating the problems it was created to solve than in actually solving them. This results more from a subconscious drive than from a cynical viewpoint. The agency's urge to perpetuate itself stems from the fact that the worker will strive to work himself out of a job only if his identity does not depend on it. As the March of Dimes abruptly discovered, actually solving the problem it was created to solve (a vaccine for polio) can create a supreme identity crisis. It had to turn to other problems, real or invented, or lose its identity. Therefore the agency learns to work the problem without actually solving it or else tries to enlarge the scope of the problem. Under most circumstances, it strives to protect its own identity.

Because the identity of many civil servants is dependent upon federal programs, they dedicate themselves to the perpetuation of these programs. This causes frustration among policy makers in Congress as well as among taxpayers. Government payrolls at all levels will continue to expand as long as a civil servant's career identity depends on a single job and his prospects for promotion depend on a single bureau or department.

## STATUS AND THE JOB HIERARCHY

It is paradoxical that bureaucracy's coordinating hierarchy creates a rank order of jobs, but rank order destroys bureaucracy's aim to view the work impersonally, in purely rational-technical terms. Inevitably the level of the bureaucratic job defines its "social worth," quite apart from its technical importance.

Obviously jobs can and do vary in importance. What could be more fair than ranking individuals according to the importance of the work they do? And what could be more objective? There are four major difficulties standing in the way of both fairness and objectivity.

First, how can we objectively measure the individual contribution of a job to the synergistic whole? We can always guess, of course. We can even make elaborate measurements of the guesswork involved. This is not the same thing, however, as objective measurement.

Second, how do we measure the relative shifts in importance of jobs that are caused by outside changes over time? Such shifts occur unexpectedly and erratically. The changes may be hard to identify, much less measure. How far will they go? What ultimate internal impact will these outside changes have?

Third, what do we do when the market puts a "low price" on a job vital to us but a "high price" on a job of marginal importance? If the market determines the price and hence the social worth of the job, it can upset our job hierarchy. Yet if we ignore the market price we may be unable to fill some jobs.

Fourth, how do we handle the problem of skill inversion, which occurs when lower ranked jobs require greater skills than the higher ranked jobs that coordinate them? By no means does it always require more skill to coordinate work than to actually do the work involved. Moreover, skill discontinuties often become apparent; the good salesman may make a poor sales manager, for example, or the other way around.

Bureaucracy has no very good answers for any of these questions. At best it muddles through. But even if it had the answers and tried to apply them, its social order would take on the character of a yo-yo, clashing with human nature even worse than it now does. To work at all, even incompetently, bureaucracy must violate many of its own social premises.

Jobs therefore serve poorly as vehicles of social worth. Jobholders become inflexible when the job must carry the freight of the other social needs—identity, status, prestige, and reward. The job's only natural function is to spell out the individual's work assignment—his role. It serves poorly any other social function in human enterprise. Nevertheless, in bureaucracy the job upholds status, aside from its function.

## Status as Social Rank

In bureaucracy, the employee's social rank becomes identical with the rank of the job he holds. An exception is the federal civil service, which has a system of personal social rank in its GS grades. Unfortunately, the importance of personal rank has been partially undermined by the introduction of "position classification," which industry normally calls "job evaluation." In most cases now, personal rank depends on the job's position classification, and the civil service thus has lost much of the advantage of a personal rank system.

Just as we strive to protect our identity, we also seek to protect and improve our status. The older we get, the more deference we expect. If the social order fails to accord increasing social rank, frustration sets in, and dominance struggles inevitably follow. When personal social rank is divorced from the job, workplace dominance struggles are lessened. This, of course, is the big advantage of such an approach.

Bureaucracy may decry seniority in theory, but in practice the pressure to base job promotion at least partly on seniority proves nearly irresistible. Meeting status needs through job seniority, however, activates the Peter Priniciple, which holds that bureaucracies tend to promote people "to their level of incompetence."[4] If you do tolerably well in your job, you will likely be promoted to the next higher job, or "level." At some point, depending on the number of levels, you will be promoted into a job you cannot do very well, and thereafter you will not be promoted any higher. Thus everyone in a bureaucracy may ultimately hold down a job for which he is incompetent. Though obviously an exaggeration, the "principle" contains more than a grain of truth.

A much more serious problem, however, arises from job ranking, which inevitably requires merging the promotion ladder with the chain of command. This merger causes serious problems because the effective promotion ladder has six or more rungs, the effective chain of command four links or less. I refer to an autonomous enterprise and not a collection of such enterprises, as in a business conglomerate. Bureaucracy assumes that the more links in the chain of command, the greater the range of skills within the enterprise, top to bottom. The higher you rise, the greater must be your skills. Let us examine this assumption.

---

[4] Laurence J. Peter and Raymond Hull, *The Peter Principle* (New York: William Morrow & Co., 1969).

## The Trees and the Forest

If you want a general idea of a forest, fly over it. If you want some detailed knowledge of its trees, walk through it. Each view gives you a different perspective. Bureaucracy insists that the overflight provides an inherently superior perspective to the walk-through. It would like to give the impression that only the brightest can intelligently evaluate the "big picture" from on high, whereas most any dolt will do down below.

The higher view might require a superior evaluative judgment, of course. Then, again, it might not. Skill inversions occur in all organizations. Bureaucratic skill inversions occur when greater ability is required to do the work than to coordinate it.

In Western culture, after medieval knights gave way to mass infantry and skilled craftsmen gave way to mass production, the hierarchies of skill and coordination roughly matched. Of course it was necessary to drain most of the challenge and skill from the work itself to achieve this match. The unwilling human robot who works on the assembly line no longer typifies the working man. White-collar workers outnumber blue-collar workers; the "knowledge workers" predominate. Even blue-collar work often requires increasing levels of knowledge. The bureaucratic hierarchy also includes many professional workers—engineers, economists, accountants, scientists, and other technicians. Skill inversions are routine in professional work, since coordinating professional work often requires less competence than does professional practice.

The bureaucratic hierarchy does reflect a skill hierarchy of sorts, however, mainly as concerns political skills. Political skills randomly correlate with coordinating skills, but they are not of some higher order than other skills. In fact, it might reasonably be hypothesized that the more politics and politicians are allowed to dominate the enterprise, the worse job it does. Politics, as we have said, concerns itself mainly with social power; management deals with technical and coordinating authority. As a social animal man concerns himself first with social position and only secondly with work. So long as social position depends on political skills, management skills will recede in importance, at the risk of competence for the enterprise.

## Social Distance and the Work Ethic

The erosion of the Puritan work ethic in America since the end of World War II has been the subject of much commentary. Some have attributed this trend to a mysterious "greening process." Earlier, others pointed accusingly at the rise of the "social ethic," the decline of the "inner-directed man," or a loss of our "rugged individualism." Still others have blamed affluence. I believe these arguments miss the truth. Affluence is relative; Americans have always been relatively affluent, and affluence always has been an expected consequence of the work ethic. As to our loss of individualism, Americans have grown less individualistic relative to a model which was always grossly overdrawn. Even before the Civil War, most Americans lived in close-knit communities which stressed mutual cooperation and whose members conformed to group norms.

Much more devastating to the work ethic have been the tyrannization and social status stratification of work that are caused by the bureaucratic social order. Rejection of these effects is the essence of Consciousness III, or the "greening process."[5] When we measure social worth by the kind of work done and the level at which it is performed, this can only erode the dignity of most work. Coordinating hierarchies must conform to the pyramidal shape (see Figure 4). The majority of actual work in most bureaucracies takes place well below the top. Distended social distance thus imparts to work a degree of social degradation.

Social distance comes in two varieties, that of age (seniority) and that of class. Natural selection has designed the human animal to cope easily with the sort of social distance implied by "juniors" and "seniors," and our experience as children makes social distinctions based on age seem natural. Because juniors can gain in experience over time, seniority is refreshingly free of social insult. A strong, healthy, mentally alert young man can give way, socially, to an elderly gentleman without the least sense of having lost a dominance struggle. The young man's ego remains completely intact. In fact, he would suffer loss of esteem from his peers if he did not give way. The demands of social order thus can be fulfilled without the issue of dominance or superiority even arising.

We cope with questions of class superiority much less easily. Successful class distinctions depend in the end on the acceptance of inferiority by the lower class. Otherwise, dominance must be imposed on its members, and dominance struggles will arise. Acceptance of inferiority depends on plausible criteria that can be objectively measured by the lower class itself. Religion, as in the Hindu caste system, has worked effectively on both counts. Caste is plausible to those who believe in the Hindu religion, and, since members are born into their caste, they can expect no more objective measure. The religious significance attached to the Hindu caste system arises in part from its economic function, although it also serves other social purposes.

Education can also serve as an effective means of class separation. As a high school graduate you might ascribe a general social mystique

---

[5] Charles A. Reich, *The Greening of America* (New York: Random House, 1970).

**Figure 4**
SOCIAL DISTANCE AND CASTE IN BUREAUCRACY

Progressive dehumanization is shown in this illustration.

to physicians, apart from their special skills. If you were a graduate engineer, however, even without an advanced degree, you would be less inclined to view physicians with awe. And, knowing how badly your own profession can botch things, you might be less inclined to view the medical profession as infallible. Finally, you might not be prepared to grant social superiority to the medical profession, compared to engineering.

The relation between social classes and education is such that the more education people have, the less they will accept class inferiority. As rule of thumb, with every three levels in a bureaucratic hierarchy, a de facto social class develops. In the modern American bureaucratic hierarchy, however, most everyone is well educated. People even at the bottom are poorly prepared to accept social inferiority. They may find these de facto social classes nearly intolerable.

The bureaucracy usually insists that those on lower levels obtain formal approval in communicating officially with those at higher levels. Sometimes a level exists in name only, and approval is not needed to ignore, or bypass, such levels. Typically, however, the bureaucrat cannot initiate formal contact with an official who supervises his bosses' boss. He must first get approval of the intermediate levels. By the third level above himself he encounters a "superior" social class, a social barrier ignored only at some personal risk. If he is skilled in the ways of bureaucratic politics, he may devise ways around these barriers. Indeed, he may spend a good deal of his time plotting ways of establishing direct personal contact with those in the "upper classes." But he must not appear to violate the most sacrosanct of bureaucratic social codes, going over a superior's head.

Much of the time he may feel no desire to contact his "social betters" in the upper classes. He may even prefer to remain more or less unknown to them, especially if he is young, inexperienced, and unsure of himself. But as he grows older, gains in experience, and develops confidence, he may find the bureaucracy's class system decreasingly tolerable. He may, in fact, find it downright insulting. If he exceeds his "betters" in education or training and equals them in experience, he is likely to discover a particularly penetrating sense of social insult attaching to class inferiority.

If the upper levels institute a sudden reorganization, they can change his situation completely, and without the slightest effort to discover his views. Indeed, he may find that his "betters" regard his views and his problems as irrelevant. Moreover, he may discover that his superiors resent as social impudence any effort on his part to put his views across.

If they change his role without particularly disturbing his other social needs, he may not much care. But the more the reorganization harms his present needs or future prospects, the more deeply he will care. The discovery that he has no right of access to higher authorities which decide his vital interests but do not care to hear his views often triggers outrage. He can come to detest the social class system of bureaucratic hierarchy. Whether he fights the system, becomes apathetic, joins a union, or quits will, of course, vary with his other circumstances.

Differences in education, accent, dress, or manners are unreliable guides in "placing" people in the bureaucratic class structure; only the organization chart tells—how many levels above, how many levels below the individual. Salary and other status symbols may give a class position away, but the most reliable guide to the class structure arises from the number of levels in the structure itself. If more than four levels appear between the work and the autonomous decision-making centers, the problem of social distance arises, which tends to subhumanize employees into animal status.

## Job Evaluation and Position Classification

Man has invented numerous instruments to degrade the social value of work. One of the most effective parades under the banner of "science." Job evaluation (in business) or position classification (in government) purport to measure "scientifically" the relative importance (hence by bureaucratic necessity, the social worth) of various jobs within an enterprise. It is not impossible to come up with a reasonable rank order of job importance. If invidious comparisons among jobs are formally made, however, job content tends to become frozen and much of the work is socially degraded, thus nullifying the work ethic.

At any given time jobs do vary in importance. Some require much skill, some require little. Indeed, many bureaucratic jobs are utterly useless and worse—they cause a good deal of waste. If job evaluation were used to identify fake jobs, a case could be made for the technique. But instead the objective of job evaluation is to compare jobs with one another in order to establish pay grades and thus social status and prestige. By common convention and often as a firm policy, a job analyst must begin by assuming the necessity of the job, however useless it may be.

Once formally evaluated, the job tends to become sacrosanct. An enterprise that is to remain responsive to its mission must make continual adjustments. It must deploy its human resources flexibly and maintain internal mobility. It can never do so if job content becomes a formal and official basis for determining pay and hence status. Because humans instinctively react defensively to change which threatens status, whatever the justification, job defensiveness greatly constrains internal mobility. Many employees also engage in low-grade dominance struggles to get their job ranks boosted.

On a national level this sort of dominance struggle leads to perpetual whipsaw inflationary wage increases. Gidgit makers, noting their "unfair" wage gap compared to widgit makers, strike for an increase to close this gap. Having gotten it, the widgit makers strike to preserve the "traditional" differential between themselves and the lowly gidgit makers. Such an effect can be expected when various lines of work suffer from invidious formal comparisons.

### Distorted Communications

The shorter the chain of command, the faster and more accurate the communication. The more links in the chain, the slower and less accurate the two-way flow of communications needed for effective coordination. It can be proven mathematically that, on the average, with each additional link in the chain of command the time it takes for a communication to go the whole distance is squared.

The coordinating hierarchy, as we have noted, is pyramid shaped, with a broad base of communication sources at the bottom. If all the information they originate were passed directly to the top, it would be innundated. The information has to be screened by a process through which each level filters out information it "thinks" will not contribute to what the next higher level needs to know. As communications go up the pyramid, each filtration center receives information from increasing numbers of subordinate sources. The time required for transmittal is squared with each additional level as the number of filtering centers decreases and the amount of information each must process increases.

One problem in coordinating work through a multileveled communications network is the vertical span of control. The more levels, the greater the control problem. Thus, for entirely mechanical reasons, the chain of command should be short, with decisions made as close to the bottom as possible. The large enterprise needs to be divided into as many semiautonomous units as are feasible for efficient operation.

### Mechanical Distortions

Random communication distortions often occur because of mechanical distance. By honest mistake or accident, vital information gets filtered out in the screening process as it goes up the narrowing pyramid. Misjudgments inevitably occur. If the information rises unfiltered, the possibility of oversight lies at the top. An attempt to cope with this by adding more manpower at the top will simply create more screening levels, as U.S. Presidents have done in creating their huge White House executive staffs.

On any given issue the top can, of course, bypass intermediate levels. Say a crisis arises at an operating level, and top management decides to bypass intermediate levels and make decisions based directly on unfiltered information from the operating level. It can do this, however, only by ignoring other problems that may be passed up along the way. A problem ignored can develop into a crisis for want of a timely decision. Thus bypassing the chain of command in a crisis does not change anything on the average. Punch down here and something else pops up over there.

Such information filtration mistakes have decided the outcome of battles, the course of a war, or the fate of a nation. At Pearl Harbor, for example, radar picked up the incoming Japanese attack, but the officer who got the information decided it was nothing important and failed to sound an alert. Some months earlier, General Claire Chennault, in China, had gotten reasonably good performance data on the Japanese Zero fighter and had devised tactics which would enable the heavier, less maneuverable P–40 to survive. He passed this information on to Washington, but it was either filtered out or unprocessed, and the word never got out to the Philippines. The P–40 pilots in the Philippines had no idea such an airplane as the Zero existed.

Such mistakes happen every day on the more humdrum levels of business and government operation. They also account in part for such multibillion dollar disasters as the TFX and C–5A. In the quagmire of bureaucracy, the problems of social distance can be compounded to preclude timely communication.

## Social Distortions

When social distance arises between the decision-making centers and the work, social distortion also creeps into communications. Because objective truth often clashes with the canons of social respect, reporting objective facts can imply criticism of superiors. Criticism is always distasteful, especially public criticism. The more socially inferior the source, the more devastating does objective criticism, widely disseminated, become. Nothing is so humiliating to the bureaucrat as to have his mistakes and foibles identified and publicized, if only within the bureaucracy, by his social inferiors. If he has the power to do so, he will act swiftly and decisively to still such voices. If he does not, he stands in danger of losing his cherished social position.

Usually "facts" will by themselves expose error only when a situation has deteriorated severely. Before the collapse, facts tend to be ambiguous; they can suggest success, failure, or something in between, depending on how they are interpreted. The interpretation in turn depends on what mix of facts was chosen for selective interpretation.

The man who has an ego investment in, and a command responsibility for, some bureaucratic program will not react kindly toward social inferiors whose selection and interpretation of facts suggest substantive failure. He will expect to receive the benefit of every subordinate doubt, and his readiness to concede failure will depend largely on the face-saving alternatives. Lack of need to concede failure publicly or the presence of extenuating circumstances may help to salvage his reputation. While he may never claim infallibility in general, he will rarely admit fallibility in particular. To varying degrees we all share these reactions in all circumstances, but bureaucracy has a unique capacity to institutionalize fear of subordinate "exposure" into corporate paranoia. It can make truth socially destructive by its pretensions of impersonality in a rational world of work wherein social variables do not intrude.

A social inferior in the bureaucratic social order soon discovers that any tendencies toward blunt statements are carefully edited before being passed upward. He learns the advantages of concentrating on the silver linings, not the clouds. Social respect in communication easily outweighs honesty; in fact, it is rarely possible to disentangle honesty of viewpoint from social disrespect if things seem to be going badly. All upward communication in the bureaucracy becomes systematically distorted with an optimistic bias. Reaction to documentation beyond reasonable doubt that a superior's program or policy has failed differs little from reaction to insubordination.

The clash between truth and respect arises in any autocratic enterprise. Autocrats normally justify themselves on the premise of supercompetence. To point out an autocrat's mistakes calls into question the premise behind his dictatorship, possibly the ultimate social disrespect. Truthful criticism, moreover, may threaten the dictator's self-confidence, causing him to lose his nerve and thus increasing the risk that he will make even more serious mistakes.

We hardly do our best when critics harp upon our mistakes. Self-confidence may not guarantee success, but it does reduce the danger of failure from loss of nerve. Risky ventures put a steady nerve to its greatest test. A corporate president about to risk his company's fate with an unproven product in an already crowded field needs to have his own nerve steadied by the knowledge that his subordinates have confidence in him. Should he learn of subordinates who have documented a case that the proposed course of action could prove disastrous, his self-confidence requires him to suppress them ruthlessly. Successful autocracy requires the whole enterprise to become an obedient extension of the autocrat.

Thus the blind spots and weaknesses of the autocrat become the Achilles' heel of the entire enterprise. For long-term success, autocratic leadership depends on godlike men. Nature has not evolved such creatures; it has only endowed men with the capacity to imagine themselves godlike. A strong primate dominance instinct, an active imagination, a few superior talents, and the absence of fraternal bonding can seduce humans with the illusion of infallibility. This can translate into despotic tyranny under the right circumstances. Bureaucracy frequently produces the right circumstances.

You may have damned your seniors, perhaps accusing them of stupidity in pursuing some wasteful course. Or you may have charged them with political cowardice and dismissed them as hypocrites. Still, in all probability, you would have acted no differently in their position. You are not about to let some junior-grade know-it-all pull the rug out from under you. You automatically dehumanize subordinates more than three levels under you, unless you have formed previous bonds of friendship with them.

You cannot look downward in a bureaucracy without socially looking down *upon*. You impute less competence, less social worth, and other forms of inferiority to all those three levels lower or more. You will not usually know the incumbents of the lower levels personally. Subtly, you classify them by the ascribed attributes of their level relative to your own. Those immediately under you, two levels down, need only be degraded to the extent of different levels of experience. Thereafter the dehumanization process begins. At about six levels beneath you, you deal only with ciphers, objects, or numbers, not with people or even lower animals.

This is not just a flaw in a few individuals, but a human tendency. When we do not know people personally we evaluate them in terms of their status. If their status is inferior to our own, we tend to classify them as subhuman, however subconsiously. If our status depends on our "level" and if that level supposedly reflects our technical competence, it follows that those below us are less competent. Thus if a low-level stranger, by definition less competent than we are, takes it upon himself to criticize us, we are likely to blow our tops. He will in our eyes be guilty of grossly irresponsible behavior, and he must be hushed up, particularly if his "irresponsible criticism" lends itself to "misinterpretation."

Without social respect, there can be no social order, and without internal social order, no enterprise can survive. Yet if there is no objective assessment of operating performance, the enterprise will sooner or later falter or fail. Social distance in the large bureaucracy unfortunately puts social order and objective analysis firmly at odds.

### Redundant Links in the Chain of Command

I have noted that while the chain of command should be short, the promotion ladder should be long. The bureaucratic social order merges the two. Social pressure usually favors the long promotion ladder. The ambitious, frustrated or embittered by excessive social distance, seek release from frustration through promotion. This typically leads to the creation of redundant levels in the hierarchy and more links in the chain of command. Thus begins a vicious circle.

Redundant hierarchical levels abound in most bureaucracies. They distend the chain of command, lengthen social distance, and finally distort communications, both randomly and systematically. One device, a favorite in nearly all bureaucracies, consists of the "one over one" relationship between a department head and his "deputy"—the title might actually be deputy (a favorite in government) or the assistant this or that. The reporting relationship, however, not the title, defines the "one over one" situation. The boss appoints a deputy and requires everyone on the next lower level to report to the deputy, not to himself. Consequently a boss who wants to promote one of his subordinates can "create" the position of deputy, reporting to the boss. Then the boss decrees that all who previously reported directly to him now report to his deputy. He would never admit that he had created the job of deputy merely to insert another rung on the promotion ladder. Instead, he would plead onerous burdens of office whose responsibilities must be shared. He would say he has decided to turn over day-to-day operations to his new deputy, so he is freed to concentrate on long-term problems.

This move almost always meets with disfavor from those beneath the deputy. They see through it. The deputy has not been promoted in the crucial sense of reporting levels; he is as far away from the top as ever. But everyone below the new deputy has been demoted a level. They thus suffer double humiliation; they not only get "passed over" but subtly demoted as well. The social distance has grown between them and the top.

While it must be denied that demotion was intended, too vigorous a protest will open the door to a dominance struggle. Ambitious subordinates will try to bypass the deputy before he can consolidate his position, going directly to the boss for decisions. The subordinate may say the deputy has not had time to become familiar with the subordinate's problem and no time can be spared. If the boss accepts this he has undermined his deputy; the underling will strive to keep open his direct line of communication and to make sure the new deputy never does become familiar enough with his job to intrude as a communications filter. If, on the other hand, the deputy acts quickly to exert his authority and dominance, a nasty scene may result. Such matters call for clever maneuvering. The boss may announce the change while the individual who might object most strongly is gone on a trip or away on vacation, or he may reorganize at the same time. The reorganization catches everyone somewhat off balance. This is known as the churning ploy, an aerospace favorite.

Such problems concern the politics of the work, not the work itself.

Indeed, bureaucrats can become so consumed in political intrigue and maneuvering that the actual work becomes something of a side issue. While it is claimed that the intrigues and maneuvers aim solely to improve the work, they are actually merely monkey business—the old primate dominance struggle.

Fraternity can enter in the struggle, but mainly on the personal level. Bureaucrats seek allies, friends, and fellow conspirators. The rivalries may rage between clique groups which cut through the hierarchy and sometimes across it. The clique may consist of peers or a dominant and his protégés. Cliques often alleviate the frustrations of excessive social distance and distended chains of command and may actually improve communications. Nevertheless, they make a hash of the formal structure, and if they solve some problems, they create others. We often call these cliques the "informal organization." Every bureaucracy has one, and it can even come to dominate the formal organization.

## ROLE

The job has to carry all the social freight in the bureaucratic social order. It has no natural function beyond role specification. Even here bureaucracy botches things. Teamwork calls for jobs to be defined broadly and flexibly, but bureaucracy tends to define them as narrowly and rigidly as possible. For one thing, more jobs can be created this way. More jobs require more coordinators, rules, and red tape, and thus more levels and rungs in the promotional ladder.

In some developing nations, there is enormous social pressure to force the civil service to make jobs available for the educated offspring of the upper social classes. This forces the civil service to define jobs very narrowly, which leads to "overjobbing," sometimes by 1,000 percent and typically by several hundred percent. Civil service effectiveness vanishes with overjobbing on this scale. Overjobbing, as has been noted, is an endemic disease of the bureaucratic social order.

Calvin Coolidge, when asked how many people worked in his White House staff, replied "about half." Coolidge thought he described immutable "laziness" in civil servants. Actually his remark underscores bureaucracy's inherent inability to utilize people effectively. Rarely do more than 50 percent of the people in a bureaucracy "work." Fixed job positions in a rigid "table of organization" usually institutionalize waste. Erratic work loads overburden some jobs, while many others have little or nothing to do.

We can explore hypothetically what might happen to the hunting band if it were placed on a sound business footing, specifically the consequences of adopting some of the advanced techniques of modern personnel administration. Assume you throw the deadliest spear and I swing the mightiest axe, while Ogg does the best job of scouting out the prey. Each of us will glory in doing our jobs well, but we will also be proud of one another. We will have confidence in one another and enjoy a sense of exhilaration at having such outstanding hunting companions as peers and fellows.

Now assume a time machine sends a job evaluation expert to our hunting territory. He will interview us at length on what we do, and he may observe us in action and take notes. He will break our jobs into separate categories and assign points to each based on their "relative importance," as he sees it. He will not presume to tell us how to do our jobs; indeed, he will resist the temptation to suggest improvements. He will rely mainly on what we tell him, perhaps modified somewhat by what he observes.

The job evaluator adds up all his points and computes the score. He arranges our jobs, based on these scores, into a rank order of importance. Say that this particular evaluator believes that unless you first find the prey, you can't very well move in for the kill. Since Ogg finds the prey, he gets the most points. You may come next as spear thrower because you can kill at a distance, which the expert decides is more important than me clubbing at close quarters what you have missed (or only injured).

Ogg will be pleased at first, but lonely later. You will be somewhat upset, and I will be furious. We are now in a pecking order based on the importance of our tightly compartmentalized jobs. Our sense of fraternity will have been badly jeopardized, our esprit de corps will diminish, our mutual loyalties will suffer as our relationships become somewhat impersonal and stiff. We will have become a bureaucracy. At first not too much change in our productivity may occur, since the expert has locked us into the jobs we do best. Out of pride we may still try to do our best.

One day Ogg, having spotted a wild boar, trips while luring it into our trap. The boar rushes Ogg, and we dash to save him. But somehow your timing is just off; you still throw well, but your spear only grazes the boar. I get off on the wrong foot and lose a precious second, but I still do the boar in with a mighty swing of my club. We save Ogg's life, but he might never again be as nimble, and it will be many moons before he recovers.

As No. 2, you must move up the job hierarchy and replace Ogg as scout, though your assets are a magnificent throwing arm, aim, and sense of timing. I also move up, to the spear-throwing slot. I, too, have a good arm, but I don't have your sense of timing and I'm getting a bit myopic. Our ace brush beater, young Ulug, who in a few more years would probably have rivaled Ogg as a scout, moves into my club-swinging slot, although he hasn't much strength in the arm he injured in a fall.

What happens next is obvious. You and I get together and ambush the job evaluation expert, destroy his time machine, celebrate our feat by feasting on his brains, and go back to our efficient fraternal system of unranked job titles. The brush beater takes over as scout, you remain on the spear, and I on the club. We junk the job totem pole and congratulate ourselves on having saved the world from bureaucratic incompetence for another hundred thousand years.

### Jobs and Territoriality

Work loads have inherent fluctuations and cycles which rigid manning tables ignore. Management deals, in fact, with cycles upon cycles, complicated by random shifts and contingencies. When formal, detailed descriptions of job content which delimit territorial boundaries are added to fixed manning schedules, substantial underutilization will result in the best managed bureaucracy. For one thing, enough job positions must be created to meet peak loads. If crossing job boundaries is held to a minimum, it is not possible to create a "team." When work loads fluctuate, rigid job descriptions allow the individual to refuse to help out his overworked neighbor. He may even come to grief with the union, social custom, or enterprise regulations if he tries to do so. The result, often by design, is overjobbing.

Obviously, people should not be doing jobs they do not know how to do. The safety of people and operating capacities of equipment make it sound practice to require proof of competence before allowing people to do some kinds of jobs. Many bureaucracies, however, devise detailed operating manuals which spell out just who can do what and under what conditions. Trade union contracts do the same thing. Where safety is not at stake, rigidly defined job territories aim mainly at creating more jobs by eliminating the economies of teamwork.

The mere designation of a job's territorial content does not automatically bring forth territoriality. Territoriality arises only when the job's content determines the jobholder's pay, identity, and status.

### PRESTIGE

Prestige in a bureaucracy partly depends on job title, but the individual retains a few degrees of freedom in this regard. Engineers typically have more prestige as well as status compared to draftsmen, but an individual draftsman may enjoy a good reputation, an engineer a poor one.

Merit-rating schemes attempt to formalize reputations and to institutionalize them by using the results in promotions. But informal prestige also influences behavior, as people strive to achieve the esteem of their peers or even subordinates. Trouble is, the same act may accord an individual positive prestige by subordinates, neutral prestige from peers, and a negative rating from superiors. Those with a strong need for promotion who also have a sense of detachment from peer-competitors and a tendency to look down on subordinates will aim to maximize their prestige from superiors and merely try to avoid enemies among others.

A number of tactics have proven winners here, in a bureaucratic sense. Those interested in gaining prestige for promotion purposes will be cautious about teaching others their jobs. It helps if your replacement does not look too good compared to you, even after you are promoted. And if you happen to fall ill or leave on vacation, your prestige improves if work piles up while you are gone because no one else knows how to do it. Do not be misled; training a competent replacement rarely enters seriously into the bureaucratic promotion formula. If anyone can pinch-hit for you, your job can even become the target for "elimination" in the next cash-flow crisis or government RIF (reduction in force). Keeping your job a personal trade secret also assists in its territorial defense. You are, after all, in competition for advancement with your colleagues. You "sell" your services, and you can charge more for them only if you and not your colleagues get tapped for promotion. How well your department does will not be nearly so important to your chances for promotion as the personal image you project to your superiors. A good personal image in a failing venture is better than anonymity in a successful one, bureaucratically speaking.

Often it is possible for one bureaucrat to make himself look better merely by making others look worse. He can, for example, call attention to their procedural mistakes. These "mistakes" may actually expedite the department's mission by cutting through red tape, but those who cut through red tape expose the uselessness of those who invent it. The aim is for prestige from the red-tape makers, and hence their personal approval. Those who support the system will be marked for promotion. Those who concentrate on the mission of the enterprise but get impatient with bureaucracy's self-imposed obstacles will be marked as troublemakers and probably ejected.

## Prestige and Responsibility

Prestige is also interrelated with the notion of responsibility for results. In the monotheistic ethic, the individual soul is directly accountable. Salvation cannot be achieved through teamwork. The notion of everlasting life for each saved soul attaches enormous social significance to the individual, although the individual does not necessarily benefit from this theoretical concern for his sanctity.

The concept of salvation as an individual responsibility has been blindly applied to temporal situations such as individual responsibility for collective performance. The Ten Commandments have firm roots in what we might call biological morality, but they tell us nothing about how to get on with our work. The nature of the individual man's moral responsibility before God come Judgment Day can hardly guide us in assessing his responsibility for the collective performance of economic enterprise. Since salvation implies no collective performance, there can be no collective responsibility.

Insistence on individual responsibility for collective performance actually denies the synergism of organized effort. If the whole organization is greater than the sum of its parts, how can you pinpoint individual contributions to the whole, routinely and reliably? You can't, of course. The harder you try to do so, the greater the mess you are apt to make.

Almost every bureaucracy in America claims to "pinpoint individual responsibility." But the bureaucrat means this for others, not himself. He may not find this out, of course, until the accusing finger points his way. When it does, he will exert enormous effort to protect himself; buck-passing is a way of bureaucratic life. He will do anything to side-step the doctrine of individual responsibility. Only a bureaucratic fool fails to take such elemental precautions.

The scientific investigation of disasters such as airline crashes can illuminate responsibility issue. The assessment of the "probable cause" often indicates an improbable convergence of events which produced the disaster. These events may or may not involve individual error, but rarely does some grossly culpable individual misdoing come to light. More often a series of "small" mistakes, the kind we all make every day, converges disastrously. This convergence actually becomes the real cause. To designate some individual as responsible for the event makes sense mostly for purposes of scapegoating.

It might be argued that if people avoided the small mistakes, no convergence would occur, and if everyone did his or her job according to exact procedures, accidents would not happen. This logic lies behind many a checklist and procedural manual. It can also be argued that disciplinary action for procedural violations, however seemingly harmless, will reduce violations and hence accidents. The "crime" is not just an act which does harm, but one which *might* do harm under a combination of circumstances of unknown probabilities. This argument has merit up to a point, but nearly every bureaucracy exceeds this point well into the region of diminishing returns.

British working men have learned how to hoist a bureaucracy by its procedural petard. If they want to strike terror into the hearts of management, they threaten to "work to rule," or follow precisely every procedure that has been specified. They can thus bring operations to a virtual standstill without actually striking.

Any attempt to rely on procedural controls to avoid all error creates an obstacle course. If such controls are followed to the letter, operations become enmeshed in red tape. Few bureaucracies could function without wide connivance in procedural violations. Yet when things go wrong, these violations can be used as a major vehicle for scapegoating. Scapegoats sustain the doctrine of individual personal responsibility for collective failure. Thus the concept induces paranoid defensiveness in bureaucrats.

Concern for procedures rather than for objectives displaces the ends with the means, one of the earliest and most often observed bureaucratic maladies. Many bureaucratic procedural prohibitions concern acts which cause trouble only in convergence with other events. There are so many acts which in proper convergence *might* cause trouble that general prohibition guarantees the works will be jammed. In fact, many prohibited acts may facilitate, not harm, operations under other sets of convergences. This problem can be minimized only in the proper atmosphere: self-motivated people trying to achieve the objectives of the enterprise in a fraternal environment free of scapegoating. When mistakes occur, in such a setting, the question becomes not who is to blame but rather what went wrong.

In abstract terms it is often asserted that whoever heads the enterprise must personally take the responsibility for the results. Indeed, such an onerous responsibility justifies the sometimes enormous sums executives are paid. We honor this code, however, mainly in the breach, except when dealing with helpless subordinates or prisoners of war. We hung General Tomoyuki Yamashita, for example, because he was "in command" of troops who committed atrocities, although they were physically cut off and isolated from his headquarters and disobeying his orders. We actually hanged Japanese generals for a much higher crime—they made fools of the Allied forces. With about 30,000 of his own troops who were nearly out of ammunition, Yamashita underwhelmed 85,000 British troops at Singapore. But since the real motive for the executions might appear unseemly, we cited the doctrine of individual responsibility for collective sins.

As bureaucracy's failures occur with growing frequency, the cry goes out to track down and identify "those responsible." Ironically, bureaucracy's victims, those who decry its incompetence and waste, often make matters worse by demanding retributive, even vindictive "justice." A threat to everyone inside the bureaucracy releases defensive reactions. Among other things, the very rules that most effectively throttle performance are carefully obeyed.

The proper focus for responsibility could hardly be more evident: Hold the individual responsible for those things or actions he personally can do, and hold the group responsible for those only the group as a group can do. It is needless to activate latent paranoid genes by trying to disentangle the particular contribution of one person in an unsuccessful synergistic result. If we forget about individual responsibility in group affairs, we can make use of the most economical form of management known in human enterprise, the innate desire of the individual to contribute to the success of his group. In such a milieu, the lifted eyebrow of a colleague can bring a would-be malingerer back into line. If "higher authority" arrogates the godlike power to unravel the particulars of synergism, self-discipline is cut off and the informal peer group is encouraged to protect subversive elements from the wrath of higher authority.

Within the enterprise, the question of responsibility for results often reduces to a single variable: the surplus (or loss) from operations. Thus we deal with the economic results of the enterprise. Success or failure involves a complex mesh of individual acts, many unseen and unreported. Any attempt to sort the result out by individual efforts will not be just. Collective responsibility boils down to the distribution of collective surplus in the form of rewards.

## REWARDS AS INCOME

The bureaucracy pays the job, not the man. Systems of merit can be built into a job's pay range, but they create difficulties and internal jealousies of their own, and it is not clear they improve the situation. The pure job-based pay rate has an advantage in its very impersonality. No invidious and possibly erroneous comparisons need be made between people holding the same job.

The same advantages apply to personal rank, of course—when everyone of the same rank receives the same reward or income, invidious formal comparisons are avoided. But from the standpoint of balancing the human need for reward or income with the cash-flow needs of the enterprise, the problem is not so much a question of job rank versus personal rank. The more sensitive issue, from a cash-flow point of view, is the question of a fixed wage rate versus one tied to the performance of the enterprise as a whole.

Fixed pay rates do not necessarily hurt the individual's social needs and may even have advantages for the individual. He can budget more closely, at least in theory. But such advantages are hollow if the job itself is insecure and can be abolished at the whim of a superior. And if the fixed pay rate forces the enterprise to engage in the hire-fire cycle, enormous damage can result, both to the individual and the enterprise.

A fixed wage also removes a certain sense of excitement from the game. If the individual has the certainty of employment and status, uncertainty of income will lend adventure and stimulation, a need for all risk-taking creatures. For stockholders, stock ownership may be secure, but the stock's earnings are not. Independent businessmen, family farmers, and hunters-gatherers work under conditions of tenure of relationship but uncertain income. Only if the whole enterprise fails do the individuals involved risk separation from the enterprise.

The notion that an individual should receive a fixed rate of pay from a job within an enterprise regardless of enterprise performance is a peculiarly bureaucratic practice. Until the past few decades, only a tiny percentage of people had even been exposed to such a system. The fixed wage rate thus cannot be defended very well on cultural or traditional grounds, and not at all on biological premises. Up to this decade, the normal expectation was that man enjoyed security of association with his enterprise but an uncertain income from it; his income would depend on how well his enterprise performed, be it a collective or individual effort. The needs of both the individual and the enterprise are poorly served by according certainty of pay but uncertainty of association. We will discuss this problem further in the next chapter, on the economic consequences of the bureaucratic social order.

# 4

# The Economic Consequences of Bureaucracy

## THE VICIOUS CIRCLE OF THE HIRE-FIRE CYCLE

We can only guess at how much harm bureaucracy does. We can, however, describe some of the problems it raises and explain how it damages our economy by socially demoralizing the enterprise.

Among the major economic problems to which bureaucracy contributes are stagflation (combined unemployment and inflation), balance of payments problems and the devalued dollar, excessive deficit government spending, and runaway government in general. Associated problems include declining competence in military procurement and weapons systems design and loss of efficiency in the military. The welfare mess can be attributed in part to bureaucracy, as can a growing public contempt for constituted authority of all types, something well underway before Watergate forced President Nixon to resign.

Many of these problems interact with one another, as well as with the hire-fire cycle which bureaucracy has based on the commodity theory of labor. Figure 5 illustrates this vicious circle of interaction in a simplified form. This diagram shows what can happen within a particular enterprise, given the prevaling notion of Economic Man.

Because the demand for labor depends on the hire-fire cycle, a fear of unemployment is created in much of the bureaucratic labor force. In a bureaucratic social order, with its fixed wage rates, job caste hierarchy, and political autocracy, the fear of unemployment leads to intense pressure to create more jobs than necessary. Redundant management levels are added, followed by distended social distance, a reaction made doubly likely when managers are also subject to layoff. Distended social distance distorts communications and, out of social insult, alienates the

**Figure 5**
THE HIRE-FIRE CYCLE: A VICIOUS CIRCLE

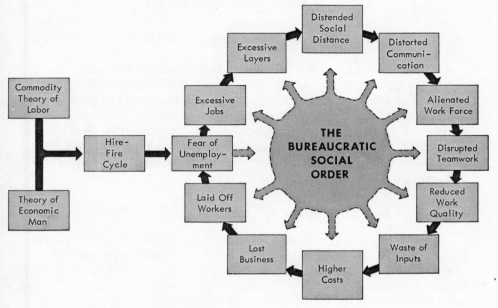

work force. Poor teamwork follows, and the quality of workmanship declines. Poor work causes waste of raw materials, fuel and energy, supplies, capital, plant, and manhours. Waste increases costs. (I refer to this kind of cost increase as cost-push inflation.) Higher costs usually mean lost business, foreign or domestic. Layoffs typically follow, which reinforces the fear of unemployment among the employed.

Thus the loop closes, and another trip around the vicious circle can be expected. Variations on this theme exist, of course, and the timing of the sequence of events depends on how deeply into bureaucracy the enterprise has gone, in terms of the policies which determine its social order. The circle can be entered at any point. Assume a well-run company suffers lost business in an economic recession. If the company cannot reduce its job wage rates to compensate for the lost revenue, it risks bankruptcy, so it resorts to a layoff. This layoff triggers the sequence of forces depicted in the diagram. Attempts to reduce costs in the short run have led directly to a situation which causes longer run cost-push inflation. The process can become self-sustaining and also self-defeating.

Three broad social policies have been identified as the social "guts" of bureaucracy: (1) the fixed wage rate paid to the job, (2) the job caste hierarchy, and (3) the political autocracy which is inherent in bureaucracy. The one that does the most to make the other two almost inevitable is the fixed pay rate which attaches to the job. It forces a resort to layoffs, which in turn makes autocracy highly probable, and the job caste hierarchy based on the fixed wage makes it easier to get around our natural tendency to treat our "teammates" as friends, not economic rivals.

The fixed rate of pay has been subjected to remarkably little attack as a major economic problem because most people would rightly reject the obvious alternative, a pay rate subject to discretionary control by management. Rather than such a solution, I propose a predetermined division of the pie between stockholders and employees, so that if the size of the pie gets bigger or smaller it does so for both, and in a predictable manner. More on the solution later; here the concern is with the problem.

## PLANNING AND FULL EMPLOYMENT

Almost everyone agrees unemployment should be avoided as much as possible. One solution proposed by Keynesian economics was "planning." This solution has largely failed, partly because of the reflexive optimism which marks the planning of the cylical bureaucracy. Fear of the hire-fire cycle itself nurtures optimism. Fearing loss of jobs, and hence of identity, status, and pay, bureaucratic planners look for a brighter tomorrow with grim determination. The planners themselves are hired to plan not for failure, but for success. Dwelling on prospects of failure would hardly improve chances for success once the enterprise is committed, and, in fact, refusal to admit defeat in the face of adversity has saved many a doubtful project. Reflexive optimism, however, induces overoptimistic plans before a commitment is necessary.

In selling themselves and their functions, planners do not promise to reduce the stress of hard times, they claim to avoid them. Planning for adversity becomes a contradiction in terms when long-range planning is seen as the antidote to hard times and unemployment. Thus statistical pipedreams have often replaced realistic forecasts.

Supposedly, planning would solve unemployment problems by smoothing out the fluctuations in demand. Planners would plan the future in a cost-effective way, getting rid of the useless, stressing the useful. Armed with the computer, the planners could mathematically model the future. In fact, they could create many models of the future, then choose the best one.

The failure of planning to prevent unemployment first became apparent in heavily cyclical industries such as aerospace, which are dependent on white-collar employees. The planners themselves became encompassed within the rationale of the hire-fire cycle. It was thought that growth and planning would protect their jobs and multiply their opportunities, but it is hard to justify large numbers of people paid big salaries who can, for example, forecast only declining revenues over the next three to five years. The planner in a cyclical industry who acknowledges its cyclical nature must make his plans for the downswing during the heady days of the upswing.

## "COST CONTROL" WITH THE HIRE-FIRE CYCLE

A cyclical business must vary its costs with the ups and downs of demand or go bankrupt when revenue falls off during the down side of the cycle. Some costs, of course, will rise and fall more or less automatically with demand. Profit and turnover taxes, inventory purchases, and freight costs usually fall into the variable category. Property taxes, interest on borrowed money, and depreciation are usually fixed costs. But the largest single cost for most enterprises consists of wages and salaries.

Unless demand remains reasonably stable, the modern American enterprise usually depends on the hire-fire cycle to keep labor costs variable. With mild fluctuations in demand, most enterprises will adjust by not replacing all those who quit or retire. But when wide fluctuations occur, the practice of paying most employees a fixed wage rate forces the enterprise to hire on the upswing and fire on the downswing.

The employees recruited on the upswing take time to learn new jobs and adjust to new circumstances, a process based on the learning curve. But before the new employees have time to adjust and "come up" the learning curve, another problem called "skill dilution" arises. Skill dilution means that new people dilute preexisting skill levels. Though diluted, the expanded work force turns out more total work, if less efficiently man for man. If they do not turn out enough work, a second wave of recruits arrives to dilute skills even more, although total output still rises. On the average, each new recruit in the second wave "dilutes" the skill pool more than did the first-wave recruits. The first recruits arrive into an experienced, well-trained work force. The second group arrives in a period of some confusion, which they exacerbate. Overmanning results, and people get in each other's way. Planning, scheduling, and administrative difficulties arise. As bottlenecks crop up, more people yet may be hired to help overcome them. All these problems will be even worse if new products as well as new people complicate the learning curve. Even the experienced must then come up a new-product learning curve.

The substitution of manpower quantity for quality inevitably occurs in any rapid buildup or "crash program" heavily dependent on newly recruited people. At some point the first workers start coming up the learning curve, and the work force ceases to decline in average quality and begins to improve its average workmanship. If this turning point happens well before demand peaks, then output can expand rapidly without additional hiring. But, as often happens, the turning point in efficiency comes with a peaking of demand. When demand peaks and begins to decline, given fixed wage rates the enterprise has little option but to "commence firing." It must continue to fire until the sales curve again turns up. When the upturn comes, the cycle repeats itself. Thus the enterprise has hired and fired many extra employees to compensate for skill dilution. Employment levels fluctuate much more widely than actual demand because of skill dilution and consequent overmanning. Cyclical overhiring followed by mass firing will be at its worst when sharp fluctuations occur over a comparatively short time.

Not only does overhiring add to labor costs, but the resultant skill dilution leads to higher material costs. People inevitably make mistakes while learning; scrap rates go up, rework increases, and equipment breaks down more frequently. Man-hours and material consumption both rise in efforts to maintain quality.

## POLLYANNA'S PROGNOSTICATIONS AND CASSANDRA'S REVENGE

Many business enterprises believe that good long-range planning will enable them to even out the peaks and valleys in production. With the development of the computer, sophisticated statistical techniques, and other advanced management practices, they try to forecast demand far enough in advance to smooth out problems of fluctuation. Within reasonable limits, they hope, the enterprise can stabilize employment by offering different products with different peaking periods. Sometimes this does work, but too often such forecasts have gone completely astray. For one thing, planners tend to confuse market forecasts with market control; typically the enterprise has little power to control the cyclical market. Forecasters at best can do little more than predict the timing and size of the fluctuation.

Moreover, the enterprise will corporately resist forecasts of a slump during the cycle's upswing. The jobs of the planners themselves were created to enable the enterprise to navigate around, not up and down, the cyclical swings. There are ethical questions, too, such as whether people should be recruited away from permanent jobs into jobs that are planned for termination. Candor in such matters hardly helps recruiting. With much at stake, top management wants to be very sure before accepting the forecast of a slump; it will demand rigorous "proof" and broad staff consensus before planning on a downturn during a buildup.

No matter how sophisticated the forecasting method, doubt and uncertainty always cloud the future. The accuracy of a forecast can never be proven in advance, regardless of the resources committed to its preparation. The planner always must make assumptions, and then concede his assumptions might be wrong.

It can easily be argued that things which augur well for the future might have been overlooked, whereas current difficulties might be transitory. Many will observe that "planned pessimism" can bring on the very hard times which good planning hopes to avoid. If planning for hard times can help bring them on, perhaps planning for good times will do likewise. Inevitably, an optimistic bias creeps in. Forecasters begin to think in terms of demand rising to meet supply, any supply. In the marketplace of prognostication, fashion will favor the wares of Pollyanna, while the offerings of Cassandra gather dust. During an upswing, the optimistic climate inhibits to the point of preventing any forecast which plans for the hard times of a downturn. The distinction between actual demand and a forecast of demand fades. Fear of mass firings, however, debases the power of positive thinking into reflexive optimism, as we have noted. Instead of damping down fluctuations, "long-range planning" has paradoxically often succeeded in making the swings even wider and more traumatic, when not based on realistic forecasts.

An optimistic forecasting bias can lead not only to "normal" cyclic overhiring but to overinvestment in facilities as well. The enterprise gears up to meet a nonexistent demand, often with borrowed money on which interest accrues and which must be repaid. And, of course, new facilities call for additional hiring to man the new facilities. When this happens the time of reckoning can be traumatic indeed, as many aerospace communities discovered in the early 1970s.

When cries of mismanagement which ironically accuse the enterprise of poor planning begin to be heard, the enterprise can point to "unexpected" difficulties beyond its control or blame another routine fluctuation of the business cycle.

To view reflexive optimism as a triumph of emotion over intellect misses the point. None of us can face a loss of social identity or collapse of status dispassionately. Intellectual capacity has little to do with such innate reactions, as I have stressed. We can, of course, face such losses suffered by others, with varying degrees of dispassion. Thus in the days when business enterprises had tiny, permanent white-collar staffs, when "workers" were often itinerants and most people farmed or were otherwise self-employed, management could in fact view with relative dispassion the ups and downs of demand. Management in no sense identified with labor but instead held to the concept of the commodity theory of labor. As technology and white-collar staff inflation greatly altered the ratio of white-collar to blue-collar employees, the hire-fire cycle had to be applied to white-collar employees as well, or the typical enterprise could not survive a serious downswing in the normally fluctuating market. Yet these white-collar workers, armed with advanced degrees, are making the forecasts. With sophisticated forecasting techniques and electronic data processing, planners statistically search for optimism until they find it. Evidence of coming downturns is dismissed as superficial, but as the evidence mounts a humorless uptight optimism will prevail. Doubters often are regarded as defeatists in a routed army. Such is the nature of reflexive optimism.

We waste emotional energy, however, in berating the planners when their reflexive optimism turns to dust. Clearly, fixed wage rates and the hire-fire cycle are the villians of the piece.

## THE CORRUPTION OF ANALYSIS

The hire-fire cycle took on a new respectability after about 1960, when sacking the "redundant" became the cost-effective thing to do. Since it was claimed that planning would eliminate long-term unemployment, it became acceptable (in theory) to use the cycle in its classical justification: to promote labor mobility between industries. Thus layoffs became "rational" and bureaucracy's theory of impersonal rationality came out from under the cloud that had covered it since the 1930s.

The new element that encouraged this change of view was the computer, which promised a new era of quantitative analysis. As self-anointed high priests of the bureaucratic rationale, computer personnel enjoyed enormous prestige, at least for a while. Staff groups in business and government began preparing the way for perfect rationality expressed in numbers. Brigades of systems analysts, computer programmers, operations researchers, and other esoteric staff were hired, and engineers, economists, accountants, and other traditional business professionals took up the cause. Armed with an array of "advanced management concepts," the crusaders of the computer era foresaw the end of risk and uncertainty in decision making; the computer, they promised, would master the future.

Computers are useful tools when kept in perspective, as are quantitative methods of analysis. But excessive ballyhoo about these techniques brought blunders and boondoggles. Perhaps the most spectacular casualty was the nation's defense. The Vietnam War witnessed the failure of computerized warfare pitted against half-naked guerrillas, as variables such as esprit de corp were summarily dismissed by the quantitative experts of the early 1960s. Defense procurement also proved a disaster. Professional make-work nearly ruined the defense industry, particularly aerospace. Not only did the resulting cost inflation in weapons system procurement defy imagination, but it has apparently become almost impossible to design and build weapons that work or war planes that fly, at any cost.

To a greater or lesser degree, nearly every large enterprise in America, private or government, has succumbed to professional and administrative make-work. The computer does not perform as a sewage treatment plant—garbage in, garbage out. Yet when staff groups explore in enormous detail questions that may be professionally interesting but are largely academic in their relation to enterprise performance, make-work will set in. A small number of such exercises might recover their costs, but mostly they are sheer waste. Well-educated systems analysts and computer programmers operate at their best systematically programming make-work for themselves. But the bureaucrat who suspects that their elaborate mathematical models, decision trees, or probability analyses often are pointless voices such judgments privately. First he will have noticed that these experts command significant starting salaries and that the more they make, the better educated they are, and the more of them that report to him, the more financially rewarding and bureaucratically august the position he himself can command. Second, he learns that they, too, have status drives which urge them to rise in the hierarchy of the system. He also discovers that the majority of them, however well educated, allow the status drive to overcome abstract intellectual honesty. These pragmatists recognize that "principle" won't promote them, but the bureaucracy might. All these facts can become potentially potent weapons in the bureaucrat's own dominance and status battles. Using them, he can document, with weighty computer printouts, whatever preconceived notions his own superiors hold. He discovers a disarmingly simple formula: Start with a superior's "answer" and work backward, analytically.

The computer and its associated software provided enormous new clout in the bureaucracy to that ancient formula for subordinate success: "Tell 'em what they want to hear." Whether in counting bodies in Vietnam, making market projections for new products, figuring cost for new weapons systems, or analyzing the success of a foreign aid project, the computer could do the job. The computer has entrenched the roles of prejudgment and intuitive decisions more than anything since the invention of the godking. A paradox, to be sure; it was supposed to do the reverse. But as the biology of human behavior in defense of status takes control, analytical effort at subordinate levels occurs largely as an exercise in ego defense of superiors, according to the canons of social respect commanded by social distance.

This corruption of analysis often occurs at a subconscious level. Moreover, preconceived notions and intuitive decisions sometimes are correct. Part of the problem is that computer software has been oversold in the field of forecasting. Computers often obscure the fact that forecasts are no better than the assumptions and data which go into them. An assumption is simply a fancy word for "guess." Many executives, confident in their own judgment, conclude that their guess is as good as anyone's; certainly it is better than the guesses of their social inferiors. Knowing the data can be manipulated in support of their guess, they sleep well after making it clear they want support, not critical static, from the computer room.

## PROMOTING THE MOBILITY OF LABOR

There was a heavy turnover in professional staff in the 60s, as people went from one staff group to another trying to get involved in meaningful work. But they discovered it was much the same wherever they went; it did not matter what they did, so long as they looked busy and had an MBA. When hard times come to business, the bureaucratic house of cards may tumble down, as in the 1970–71 cash-flow crisis. In government, however, vertical expansion of bureaucratic territory will continue, along with deficit spending. It is generally agreed that the unneeded project, program, or job should be eliminated, along with the employees in it. Of course, the unneeded project is always the other guy's, never one's own.

While the human cost of unemployment is not ignored, bureaucracy holds that the enterprise should never be the vehicle of social values. Unemployment compensation or the welfare state are looked to to ease the problems the individual faces when his "cost-ineffective" project is discontinued. The promise of good corporate long-range planning and proper fiscal and monetary management of the economy to end the spectre of serious unemployment and smooth out the business cycle breathed new life into the commodity theory of labor. Unnecessary manpower must be treated "rationally" and "impersonally"; chop it out and make it available to other enterprises—make it mobile. The hire-fire cycle thus was justified by cost-effective criteria. The god of growth could not be served if redundant projects and jobs absorbed labor that was needed in more dynamic sectors. Since the trauma of short-term unemployment would be eased by unemployment compensation, and growth and planning would prevent long-term unemployment, the hire-fire cycle justifiably could continue its task of facilitating labor mobility.

Few questioned this until the 1970 recession, when it turned out that human resources were not all that transferable between industries. Many employees had been overspecialized. It also became clear that high job mobility entails a good deal of social demoralization. Even higher rates of physical disease were reported among those who lost their jobs. The effect of changing jobs can be the same as continually uprooting and transplanting a tree. Some do not make it.

In any event, it is possible to have labor mobility between industries without using the "meat ax" on labor forces. Necessary shifts in human resources can take place entirely in differing rates of initial hiring and final retiring. A growth industry hires many, retires few; a declining industry does the opposite. "Meat ax mobility" to balance labor requirements among growth and declining industries is neither necessary nor desirable.

## FULL UTILIZATION VERSUS FULL EMPLOYMENT

Few macroeconomists (or anyone else, for that matter) have faced up to the notion that employment and utilization of manpower need not be synonymous. If you run a restaurant, for example, you do not expect to fill all your seats or tables at all times. If you run a steel mill, you know that always going at 100 percent plant capacity is not feasible. Should you run an airline, you know that once your load factor goes over about 65 percent, depending on your system, you are turning away people. If you are a farmer, you know your work load peaks during planting and harvesting season. You and your equipment and land may lay "idle" (from an economist's viewpoint) much of the rest of the year.

The optimum utilization of any one resource in a complex system will almost never occur at its point of maximum utilization. Work loads, by their nature, peak and valley. Fluctuations occur in nearly everything, including economic demand, and they cannot be planned away. Successful systems have built-in reserve capacity which helps them accommodate to these fluctuations.

Nevertheless, "full employment" is defined as 100 percent effective utilization of the labor force all the time. Economists may hedge by saying that 96 percent employment is effective full employment and the other 4 percent is an irreducible percentage of people going from one job to another. This view implies that no enterprise has any effective reserves of its own. Our full employment equals full utilization formula also implies that our complex economy needs no internal labor reserves. Nowhere except in the civilian labor force do we refuse to recognize the asset value of reserve capacity. Granted, excess reserves can be wasteful, but reserves as such are assets whether we are referring to plant, cash, inventory, or labor. What average percentage of resources should be kept in reserve and what percentage in operations will, of course, vary with the line of work. Generals like to keep at least a third of their combat forces in reserve, sometimes more; so did the hunting band. Athletic teams may keep many more players in reserve than on the field. The airline which aims at the 60 percent load factor keeps 40 percent of its capacity in reserve. The "load factor" of an agricultural economy's labor force will probably average about 50 percent, perhaps less. Systems engineers design all sorts of redundancy (reserve capacity) into their space-age contrivances.

Actually, we do keep much of the labor force in reserve, for the most part in fake jobs doing make-work. No complex economy or enterprise can utilize everybody effectively all the time. It is politically impossible to maintain unemployment rates of 30 to 40 percent, however, and so we turn a blind eye to make-work in order to protect the philosophy of the rational bureaucratic social order. No one knows what the ideal labor force "load factor" should be. Keynesian economics makes no allowances for labor reserves anywhere, except on the dole. The way to full employment is to be managed fiscally. By definition, Keynesian full employment is 100 percent effective labor utilization, month in and month out, year in and year out. Indeed, make-work was sanctified to create employment, so traumatic were the high unemployment rates of the Great Depression. The semantic error of confusing full utilization with full employment has led us into no end of trouble. The economy would be vastly better off if make-work were abolished and employed reserves in training substituted, as in the fraternal social order.

## UNEMPLOYMENT TO DAMP DOWN DEMAND

A subtle new twist to Keynesian economics has appeared in recent years. Postwar inflation has introduced the use of Keynesian economic management to *induce* unemployment. When the economy gets "too hot," it must be "cooled off." Interest rates may be hiked, credit restrictions imposed, government spending cut, all with the object of inducing unemployment by damping down demand.

This strategy is partially self-defeating. Induced unemployment places the burden of damping demand on too narrow a base. A few, say 5 or 6 percent of the work force, are expected to suffer involuntarily a complete loss of wages so that the other 95 percent will not suffer any loss. Since this is somewhat sadistic, unemployment compensation, welfare schemes, and so on are proposed to ease the burden. But this simply defeats the purpose; subsidies of any sort undermine the goal of reducing demand. Even if the unemployed were allowed to starve, however, and they did so without protest, only half the problem would be solved. Starvation would damp down demand, but by the next upswing the labor reserves would have been wiped out. Thus it is grossly inefficient to place the entire burden of reduced spending on the backs of the unemployed.

As long as job wage rates remain fixed and continue to ratchet upward, and as long as we support the economy's manpower reserves (the unemployed) with various kinds of subsidies, we will continue to have both inflation and unemployment. Cyclical enterprises will decrease in efficiency to the point of bankruptcy. Already we are out of the world market in shipbuilding, and aerospace may be next. We need to reform our employment and compensation laws to allow industries to operate without incurring the costly distortions caused by fixed wage rates.

If all wages fluctuated in response to market forces, unemployment would be unnecessary to damp down demand. The burden would fall broadly over the whole labor force, for either the enterprise or the whole economy. Discussion of how this and other reforms might work will be reserved until Chapter 10, however. Briefly, a bonus system applicable to employees could easily be arranged to fluctuate with revenue. And, given our large cross-industry conglomerates, cross-industry mobility of labor could occur by simple intracompany transfer, without resort to hire-fire cycles or intermediate unemployment.

## RIGID WAGE RATES AND INFLATION

Rigid wage rates pose other threats to the economy. The hire-fire cycle itself results from rigid wage rates, since a layoff is the only way a business enterprise can reduce wage costs when it is faced with a business downturn. Wages comprise about 70 percent of all costs, taking the economy as a whole, and fixed wage rates apply to the majority of wage earners.

Trade union pressure, minimum wage rates, and recent custom tend to ratchet rates of pay relentlessly upward. Rarely can the pay rate itself be adjusted to the vagaries of the market. This makes realistic price adjustments to supply and demand difficult and even impossible. "Administered" prices are an attempt to make such adjustments, but what can we expect if the unit price of 70 percent of all costs cannot fluctuate? Only for a few—partners, the self-employed, some salesmen and top managers—does pay fluctuate with enterprise revenue.

When fixed wage rates are attached to particular jobs and most jobs lead nowhere socially, inflation is guaranteed. Genetically driven to seek increasing formal status with advancing years, we will pressure for continuing raises in the job's rate of pay and thus its status. We will also pressure to push the job's relative position in the totem pole upward. Together these social pressures inevitably force wage increases past productivity gains.

The inflation which has taken place since World War II is virtually unprecedented. Much of it comes from bureaucratic "status blockage" (here the reference is to the pressure to increase the rate of pay, not the fake jobs which also increase costs). For years, improving technology allowed us to keep ahead of the pay-productivity game in real wages. But as the service sector increases in relative size and as the public outcry increases about the ecological side effects of technology, it may not continue to bail us out.

Piecework and various other kinds of individual incentives usually fail when teamwork is the basis of the work; maintenance people, for example, feel miffed if production workers get a bonus and they do not. The bonus which tries to measure individual contributions to collective performance always causes internal resentment. Consequently, so-called individual incentive bonuses tend to become some percentage function of salaries, perhaps modified with company performance. They actually work best when they do this and are regarded as bonuses related to company performance rather than "individual merit."

For most bureaucratic employees, the fixed salary or hourly pay rate determines compensation. The fixed rate (hourly, weekly, monthly, annually) of pay not only damps down the individual's personal identification with enterprise performance, it takes some of the fun out of work as well. Provided questions of basic identity and status do not enter in, an element of doubt in future earnings adds zest. This element of doubt cannot be based on favoritism or arbitrariness but must focus on market performance by the whole enterprise. The formula of compensation should be clear, of course. The enterprise which restricts the incentive bonus to the upper levels merely pretends that most employees have no effect on performance.

When the U.S. economy was dominated by the self-employed (farmers, merchants, artisans, etc.), before 1900, we had no wage ratchet. Incomes could fluctuate with the business cycle. We also had little inflation throughout the 19th century, and comparatively little unemployment. *Fortune* magazine notes that "For more than a hundred years U.S. consumer prices tended to decline. Inflation, mostly generated by war, was followed by long deflation that actually brought prices to their all-American low in 1900."[1]

Inflation came into being in the United States when big business became dominant, particularly after World War II. Big business as such did not cause inflation, of course. Indeed, better technology made it possible for many wages to rise while prices fell. Ford's $5 day in 1914 was a good example; the price of a Model T fell to less than $400. Throughout the 1920s prices of many products produced by big businesses fell, their quality improved, and wages tended to rise. Many firms also enjoyed unprecedented growth and thus had to make few serious layoffs in the early phases of growth. This period came to an end in the late 1920s, and the huge layoffs of the early Great Depression triggered the backlash. As the trade unions gained strength, featherbedding, re-

---

[1] *Fortune*, May 1970, p. 155.

strictive practices, and similar wasteful procedures increased rapidly. Later, particularly after the Korean War, white-collar employees began coming into the hire-fire orbit. Management efficiency began to suffer, more or less proportionately.

We have had serious general inflation since. True, technology still lowers the costs of some items, but, in general, from 1900 to 1973 the price level rose about fivefold. Most of this has come since 1940, a three- to fourfold increase. By 1974 double-digit hyperinflation took hold.

There are three kinds of inflation that interact in the hire-fire cycle. The first kind of inflation, discussed above, can be called the wage ratchet. The second kind can be called cost push; this type of inflation is induced by waste, which in turn is caused broadly by poor workmanship. The third is fiscal inflation—government spending more than it gets.

No one knows how much weight should be assigned to each kind of inflation, but my guess is that nearly all the net change in price levels since 1900 can be attributed to these three as a whole. And all three —wage-ratchet, cost-push, and fiscal inflation—arise in somewhat different ways from the vicious circle depicted in Figure 5. A fourth kind, demand pull, arises from growing demand for a limited supply, such as the food price increases of 1973.

I suspect, although of course I have no way of proving, that since 1900 technological cost reduction could well have offset rising prices from constrained supply (for example, downtown real estate in New York, Tokyo, or London). Over the long run, however, wage-ratchet and fiscal inflation could conceivably result merely in changing price tags and pay checks, without disturbing the relationship between them. Presumably you are mainly concerned not with how much a dollar will buy, but how much a unit of your working time will purchase (if you are employed, that is). Cost-push inflation, on the other hand, hits our standard of living and wastes our scarce resources. If it spreads the work to some extent, it does this in an artificial and needlessly wasteful way, both socially and economically.

In the shorter term, of course, wage-ratchet and fiscal inflation do plenty of damage to the economy by pricing us out of world markets. This forces wrenching devaluations of the dollar, either declared or by the float. But these devaluations are of little help to U.S. industries such as transistor radio producers which have priced themselves so far out of the market they no longer exist.

## BUREAUCRACY IN GOVERNMENT

Bureaucracy plays a straightforward role in wage-ratchet and cost-push inflation. In fiscal inflation, it plays a two-part role. First, the problem of unemployment, alienation, and so on, leads to pressure for welfare measures, which do not solve the problem but do provide economic relief of sorts. Second, government employment itself escalates rapidly as the state and federal civil services grow in size, and the cost of wages increases accordingly. Meanwhile government financed make-work measures can add handsomely to deficits. Thus taxes climb while the value of dollars falls.

The growth in government payrolls does not necessarily reflect an increase in government services. All agencies of government expand according to a kind of Parkinsonian logic.[2] The tendency of staff groups to expand vertically (hierarchically) is a worldwide phenomenon. Interagency rivalry also leads to constant intrusions on bureaucratic territory. Each agency or power block struggles to develop its own autonomy without having to depend on other agencies, which always compete with one another for budget if nothing else. This leads to duplication and overlapping of agencies and services.

The Senate Watergate hearings in the summer of 1973 cast much light on how bureaucracy operates in government. President Nixon, long a foe of government bureaucracy, has correctly observed that government agencies sometimes take on missions of their own that are at odds with policies laid down by the elected President. Increasingly, Presidents since Franklin Roosevelt have become frustrated by government bureaucracy. Nixon betrayed his innocence of a real understanding of the problem, however, in the way he ran his White House staff. He committed the classic mistake made by Secretary of Defense Robert McNamara when he created his private staff group in the Pentagon. McNamara's "Whiz Kids" and Nixon's "Palace Guard" both attempted to fight bureaucracy with bureaucracy and thereby added to the overall problem.

Both of these staff groups initially were masked by a myth of superefficiency, and both were later unmasked as masterpieces of mismanagement. The notion of efficiency in either case reflected a mechanistic *appearance* of efficiency. In conventional terms of a logical division of labor, definite lines of authority and responsibility, and all of Max Weber's canons of bureaucracy, they appeared efficient. And loyalty to the chief was all important in both cases.

In both the Palace Guard and the Whiz Kids, the "best and the brightest" were recruited. Most did indeed fit this description, including those in the Palace Guard who got caught up in Watergate. Individually, most of them have to be classed as first rate—intelligent, well educated, young, dedicated, and hard working. The damage they did arose partly from hardnosed application of conventional management wisdom. Indeed, it is often maintained that "efficient" management

---

[2] C. Northcote Parkinson, *Parkinson's Law* (Boston: Houghton Mifflin Co., 1957).

requires inflexible people who demand and get obedience. Subordinates who question a management directive, once it is made, are suspect; if they press too hard they are probably let go. This does not preclude an occasional devil's advocate (especially near the top) nor open discussion or debate before a directive is actually made, again at or near the top. In lower ranks, however, devil's advocacy will be deeply frowned upon. For lower level subordinates to presume sufficient wisdom to probe the judgment of their superiors is a first-order bureaucratic gaffe.

Thus when James McCord claims he had assurances the Watergate break-in had received legal blessings from high up, under a "security" label, his claim is easy to accept. John Ehrlichman's persistent assertion of the "legality" of the break-in at the office of Daniel Ellsberg's psychiatrist by the White House Plumbers is also plausible. It doesn't matter what you do in a government bureaucracy, actually, as long as you label it properly. Had McCord actually insisted on getting the attorney general's or President's personal assurances that the break-in was legal, he would have insulted everyone over him. He would, in fact, have been guilty of insubordination, for no bureaucracy can function without a "presumption of regularity" by subordinates that the orders they receive are proper, even if unusual. I suspect most people would be aghast at the number of laws broken by subordinates on orders by bureaucratic superiors in both government and industry.

The White House created its Plumbers security group out of a sense of real frustration that the FBI and other established agencies had independent ideas on the legality of burglary, with or without a security cover. This is a classic way in which duplication and overlapping occur. When those with independent political clout resist plans or policies they disagree with, the frustrated, at high levels and low, try to "work around" the obstacle. They do so by trying to develop independent capability so that they will be able to avoid dependence on those not under full control.

In the course of the Senate Watergate hearings, many questions were asked of John Ehrlichman and H. R. Haldeman about the staff system in the White House. Both of these former top assistants to President Nixon gave opening statements which together can be taken as a classic, highly articulate case for the bureaucratic staff system they helped organize and obviously believed in. At no time did either gentleman (or for that matter, did many members of the Senate committee) betray much awareness of the inherent weakness in the White House staff system.

For example, it was almost taken for granted that the many "leaks" of secrets such as the Pentagon papers were the work of either "kooks" or foreign agents. It did not occur to anyone to ask the obvious questions: Why so many leaks? Had the whole civil service became treasonous? The reason is that people do not like to have decisions rammed down their throats, even by elected higher officials, particularly if they are cut off from the right to question crucial policy decisions. It does not matter how good a job a staff group does in marshaling various points of view and options in written summaries for a top-level decision on crucial policy matters. If one man alone makes the decision, no matter how great his goodwill or sincerity, subordinates who disagree will many times, in one way or another, sabotage decisions they feel were crammed down their throats, when they think these decisions were wrong.

Intrigue and conspiracy may arise, perhaps by leaking memos to a columnist. Others may resist by quitting, but this is practical for the comparatively few who have independent status and many other options. Those who turn to open resistance typically commit bureaucratic suicide. Those who slump into obscurity by leaving silently accomplish nothing for their sacrifice. Still others resist by "working to rule"—following all regulations and procedures to the letter and thus slowing things down to the point of stopping them.

None of this makes for good government, of course. In my view, a backlash to bureaucratic rule, no matter how well meaning, is inevitable. Bureaucratic government is always excessively secretive and self-protective, and it often is contemptuous of the public it supposedly serves. Lies will be told the public by bureaucratic officials who will later be exposed in some fashion, whether by an Ellsberg, a Fitzgerald, or a Senate Committee. Efforts to suppress leaks will only make matters worse—witness the fate of the Plumbers. If those at the top were really in control, there would be no leaks in the first place. Efforts to suppress those you have no control over are bound to backfire. The real problem arises from the bureaucracy itself, not from the people who pretend to be in control. Actually no one really controls our federal government or ever will, as long as it adheres to its bureaucratic social structure.

The Watergate hearings provided the public with rare, frightful, but fascinating insights into government bureaucracy in action. And while we cannot lay all our problems at bureaucracy's door, we can assert confidently that bureaucracy makes any problem worse.

## THE ETHIC OF INDIVIDUALISM
## AND PROTECTION OF PLACE

In the past, the U.S. economy of self-employed workers operated on principles of fraternity at the community level. The rugged individualist never did settle the West; at best, he explored fraternally. The cooperative community, not the isolated individual, developed

America. Individuals rarely even farmed; the family did this. Most small enterprises normally involved at least a nuclear and often an extended family.

Our romanticized ethic of individualism embraces the notion of the open society in which the individual supposedly finds his own place, depending on his particular abilities and his willingness to work hard. It is fine to advocate finding one's own place if society sees to it that there are enough useful places to go around. It is quite another thing to insist that the individual must find his own place when more people than places exist. And when the number of places is deliberately restricted in order to combat inflation, the dice are loaded. A slot on the welfare roles is not a useful place, but then a dehumanized dead-end job subject to arbitrary elimination hardly qualifies either.

Free land for the taking under the 19th-century Homestead Act worked as an effective policy of full employment, guaranteeing a useful place for everyone. The Homestead Act allowed us to indulge the myth of rugged individualism without much harm. Not everyone wanted to farm, of course, but those who did opened up other places for those who did not. Our reputation as a land of opportunity was based in no small part on giving away choice farmland. In today's terms, the Homestead Act might equate with giving "urban settlers" $100,000 worth of capital assets to start a business, and a title to the assets after a year's evidence that they had actually run it. Something more than "rugged individualism" would be at work—namely $100,000.

Today, of course, something like 90 percent of the work force must rely on employment to secure a place, for better or worse. While the homesteader enjoyed full tenure as long as he worked the property, this protection from economic tyranny no longer applies. Most employees can be deprived of their "place" (employment) on whim. This differs little from arbitrarily depriving the farmer of his land or the artisan of his tools of his trade. The authority which deprives an individual of his place without due process exercises the power of despotism and tyranny.

Compared to the tyranny of the bureaucratic employer, we live our daily lives under a benign government. Except in its own capacity as employer and aside from its fiscal powers, the government rarely touches an individual directly in his daily life. But our employer can uproot us, destroy our status, smash our identity, or the reverse—it can ennoble us, enrich us, and make us famous. The employer might not exercise such power on a whim, but he can. And if he does, the employee has little recourse. One way or another people must find a place. During a "war on inflation," when the government promotes unemployment as a matter of policy, individuals may well be moved to carve out a criminal place, either fraternally or as rugged individualists.

Our official schizophrenia on the issues of unemployment betrays the failure of modern macroeconomic analysis. No country will long put up with stagflation or so called "Phillips curve" capitalism. But then inflation need not be the inevitable consequence of efforts to achieve full employment or the reverse. Optimum utilization of the nonfarm labor force probably falls between 60 and 80 percent, and manpower utilization should fluctuate freely with market demand between those percentages. To translate such utilization rates into employment and unemployment rates, however, would doom any government, because no industrial nation could tolerate unemployment rates fluctuating between 20 and 40 percent. Yet, without substantial reserve manpower, inflation and other economic distortions are inevitable.

No more schizoid policy exists in our economy than the application of various measures which will ultimately raise unemployment and then extend jobless compensation and welfare. Along with his first price freeze, for example, Nixon purportedly aimed to lower taxes in order to create more jobs. Then he proposed to wipe out 150,000 civil service jobs to save money because of lower taxes. The contradiction did not seem to occur to him. When the government hikes interest rates, cuts back on spending, or restricts credit, it frankly aims to increase unemployment. The victims often comprise the economy's most helpless people. The government impersonally drafts them not as "soldiers" but as casualties, the body count in the war against inflation.

This is called "fine tuning the economy." From the end of World War II until the late sixties, the blacks benefited mainly from this practice. Almost by government decree, blacks were "first fired, last hired." Then, as Keynesians fiddled with the economic dials, blacks found they could not permanently join economic enterprises that hire and fire with the economic yo-yo. They had to look elsewhere for an identity. Some found it with the Black Panthers, as Mafia associates, or as independent thugs. Each individual strived in his own way to work his way out of a social dilemma largely due to government fiscal policy.

Reverse discrimination, of course, invites its own backlash. The 1970s recession alienated some of the best trained and most educated of the work force by hitting hard among white-collar groups. Ethnic groups that have gained a modest amount of protection through union seniority will not give it up without a struggle. Anyone nominated for the role of economic patsy to replace the blacks will resist with all the courage biology infuses into the territorial defender. We can, in fact, state the following proposition: A will never sit still if selected by B to absorb damage so that C does not have to. It will not matter if A selects B impersonally or with malice. People react bitterly when selected by others to suffer in place of third parties.

The relative merits of ruination by unemployment versus collapse by inflation lie mainly in the realm of personal preference. Some might prefer to drown, others to freeze to death. Most of us, however, will defend our identity and status against all intruders, even if such defense ruins the economy. The gene which directs us to protect our identity and status is dominant. The enterprise or economy which depends on the hire-fire cycle to balance supply and demand fails to set up a proper community for cooperation, sharing, self-sacrifice, or self-discipline.

Price and income controls suffer from all the disadvantages President Nixon claimed for such economic controls, just before he imposed them in 1971. A superbureaucracy would be necessary to administer them. Red tape, large-scale corruption, black markets, rigidity, and bankruptcy could well result. Such controls can arrest our downhill slide in the short run. But unless the bureaucratic social order is dispensed with, they will break down.

The free market has all the regulatory advantages conservatives claim for it in the determination of the prices of goods and services. This is not true for employee wage rates attached to specific jobs. It is all right to have a market price for jobs, provided the job is defined as some service performed by an enterprise for its customers. The employee job market, however, is something else. Neither the employee, the enterprise, the consumer, nor the public at large benefits from the fiction that the individual "sells" his services *impersonally* to the enterprise as an employee. I am not referring to the self-employed, nor to those who can go in and out of the labor market by choice. Students, housewives, moonlighters, retired people, and others often have perfectly good reasons to prefer temporary employment, and the market can well set the terms of such employment. But the vast majority of people do react adversely to the entirely unnatural institution of a "flesh market" for labor.

When the frontier closed about 1900, several new industries were developing. Automobiles and some others grew so fast that the creation of "new places" for workers more or less kept pace with population growth, including immigration. Not until 1929, in fact, did we suffer our first severe shock of no longer being able to guarantee everyone a place. Wars subsequently spared us the hard truth, until recently. Meanwhile, a steady expansion of fake jobs eroded our institutional effectiveness. The resulting incompetence accounts for cost-push inflation and at the same time increases uncertainty of "place" for everyone.

Some economists have said, in effect, that it is a shame working people will not accept cuts in wages. This is not, strictly speaking, true. Of course neither workers nor anyone else willingly takes a cut in status that is determined by others who enjoy secure status. Nor will we be singled out willingly for a cut in wages as an economy measure to protect others from sacrifice. Further, if no way is provided for regular increments in status, workers will militantly demand some sort of "annual improvement factor," whether or not it is justified by productivity. Enterprises bring this upon themselves, because they fail to provide an orderly way for everyone to improve his status as he acquires seniority, independently of his duties and the business cycle.

The notion of a contractual prior claim by employees on the resources of an enterprise is new in human affairs. It has little to recommend it, because selective layoffs often are the only alternative to bankruptcy. Practical cost adjustments, in other words, must come by the route of selective victimization, which we all resist. If we are to cooperate voluntarily, to become the team player, to impose high standards of self-discipline on ourselves, the enterprise must first meet our social needs in the natural way. Indeed, we need to identify with a human community larger than ourselves for emotional health, but we can do so only when the community satisfies our social needs as individuals. Laws, enterprise policies, or economic theories which fail to account for human social needs will fail us. It is as simple as that.

# PART III.

## BUREAUCRACY IN BLUNDERLAND: THREE CASE STUDIES

# 5

# The English Disease

## TOO MANY COOKS SPOIL THE BROTH

If all the fake blue-collar jobs in Great Britain were abolished, a 40 percent blue-color unemployment rate would ensue. Credit for these fake jobs, which were created to prevent this dismal prospect, is usually taken by the trade unions, and with justification. British trade unions, by historical accident, evolved mainly on a craft basis, or bureaucratically. The initial bureaucratic "job" focus enabled the unions to carve unionized jobs into narrow, undemanding slivers of work. Then the unions enforced the formula that one job equals one man; no one can perform more than one "job." The trade unions call the process by which they create fake jobs "protective practices," but the rest of Britain refers to them as "restrictive practices." Even without the trade union influence, something similar probably would have happened, since no industrial country can stand the prospect of an unemployment rate from 25 to 40 percent. Some sort of job protection technique had to be developed. Fake jobs, or overjobbing, fills this bill in England, as it does in many other countries.

The damage overjobbing does has little to do directly with labor cost. Whether or not an individual company could be crushed by the wage bill for so much "excess" manpower depends on the wage rate. One way or another meanwhile, an economy has to support its entire labor force. Too large a percentage on the dole risks all sorts of disasters. Politically, it is less dangerous to keep "surplus workers" on the payroll, even if in fake jobs.

The average wage paid, of course, must reflect the number of people employed. Such economic forces as currency devaluation will force a

103

nation to keep its real wages in line with productivity relative to other countries. The average shop floor in Britain employs two or three times the people of a normal American equivalent, given similar technology. Since British industry pays only about one third the wage of American industry, it might be expected that things would even out. That they do not is attributable to the *way* in which British surplus workers stay on the payroll, not the fact of *being* on the payroll. In many ways, both subtle and obvious, fake jobs waste material. By material I mean all the physical resources which enter into production, including plant and equipment, raw materials, work in process, fuel, energy, and so forth. In addition, time delays also can cost lost business.

The proverb that too many cooks spoil the broth sums up as well as anything the source of the damage caused by overjobbing. The proverb, please note, bemoans not excessive labor expense but ruined soup. Partly the British spoil their economic soup because of the civil war which passes for industrial relations. Jointly the unions fight management, and separately they wage "territorial" war with one another. Ten or more unions can be found in some enterprises. The union disputes over job territories, the basis of their identity, in practice amount to arguing about who does what.

## THE BACKLASH TO TYRANNY

England, the first nation to industrialize, also was first to feel the backlash of bureaucratic tyranny applied to industrial workers. Once they received legal protection, the trade unions moved quickly to confront the tyranny of arbitrary political rule in the workplace. We have seen that in the bureaucratic enterprise, management control is aligned with political tyranny and have noted how management decisions perfectly "rational" in themselves nevertheless can harm the social order. Britain's idea that "society" exists outside the world of work encouraged management to ignore the social order within the enterprise. Britain also fathered the theory that the buyer-seller relationship should prevail between workers and the enterprise, in preference to concepts of membership or teamwork. Thus the "designated job" came to be seen as the basis for compensation and, by default, as the vehicle of social worth.

British trade unions, too, took their identity from "function" and the designated job. Their first move was to seize political control of job content. For practical purposes, the unions "own the work"; because union rules specify job content and so on, they can specify the selection, placement, and job promotion of workers. This effectively freezes management out of control on the shop floor and deprives it of its political power to deploy manpower. Bureaucracy's power over deployment threatens a worker's identity, status, prestige, and pay, in addition to role. Because British industrial policy refused to acknowledge the social needs of the work force, insisting in theory on management's right of political tyranny within the enterprise, the trade union's reaction stripped it of most of its deployment authority.

By and large the British think that a law-of-nature sort of conflict exists between the interests of management and labor. This conflict can be seen in the bureaucratic social order; the fundamental difference in the interests of buyers and sellers of labor services discourages team-work. But instead of trying to rethink the social order within industrial enterprise, the British have an almost mystical belief that "good-faith collective bargaining" can make the system work.[1] The result has been countless strikes, political dominance struggles, and job territory disputes. Semianarchy best describes the British shop floor; from 40 to 80 percent of an average worker's man-hours consists of "on the job leisure." This receives shocked attention from the press, particularly *The Sunday Times,* but nothing much happens. The two sides exchange accusations of bloody-mindedness and laziness, and third parties attack both "poor management" and "lazy workers." As the semianarchy continues, Britain's economy slides relatively further behind.

The early 60s gave promise of a new negotiating technique, productivity bargaining,[2] by which workers would exchange their restrictive practices for higher wages. Management would gain a bit more coordinating authority if they also promised "no redundancy" (British idiom prefers the term "redundancy" to "layoff"). But by the end of the decade the productivity bargain had proved a disappointment. It did not really cope with the basic flaws in the bureaucratic social order (BSO), and it failed to face up to a serious question: What do you do with the "surplus" workers you agreed not to lay off if they would rationalize their work practices? One of the early promoters of productivity bargaining, the late William Allen, backed by *The Sunday Times,* advocated industrial expansion to absorb the surplus workers.[3] But Allen unrealistically ignored the financial implications of more than doubling capital investment in a very few years, which would determine the possibilities of productivity. Allen offered no useful role for

---

[1] By industrial social order, of course, I do not refer to the largely irrelevant question of property ownership. Poisonous industrial relations typify both the public and private sectors in the British economy.

[2] For a discussion of early productivity bargaining success, see Allan Flanders, *The Fawley Productivity Agreements* (London: Faber and Faber, 1964). For a discussion of its later failings, see E. Owen Smith, *Productivity Bargaining: A Case Study in the Steel Industry* (London: Pan Books Ltd., 1971).

[3] See, for example, W. W. Allen, "Is Britain a Half-Time Country, Getting Half-Pay for Half-Work under Half-Hearted Management?" in *The London Sunday Times,* March 1, 1964.

"surplus workers" while awaiting more capital, lower costs, and increased demand.

In the end the productivity bargains proved inflationary, as even *The Sunday Times* conceded. Workers might give up one restrictive practice only to implement another somewhere else. Under the BSO, they would never give up political control over the shop floor or "ownership" of the work itself. Thus the workers "sold off" restrictive practices about as fast as they could invent others; they knew better than anyone, since they invented them, how many surplus jobs they had larded into operations. Meanwhile, they remain acutely aware that their protective practices insulate them from the massive unemployment of the "bad old days." Avoidance of unemployment, not laziness, lies behind Britain's restrictive-practice-ridden industry. In fraternal association with their brethren, the workers obey the genetic command to defend their identity and status. But they have thoroughly drained most jobs of useful content and normal challenge in order to ensure identities and status for their teammates, and they must look elsewhere for challenge and stimulation. The predatory raid on an adjacent union's territory sometimes serves this purpose. They can also "down tools" at some management slight, real or imagined, or they can always invent another restrictive practice.

## THE WAGE WHIPSAW

The primary challenge to the unions, however, is an opportunity to whipsaw management for a wage increase. A particular local might make pay comparisons with the same union in a different enterprise or a different union in the same enterprise. If the comparison is adverse, the pay difference must, out of "high principle," be rectified to restore "equity," according to the aggrieved union. Upon this rectification, the other union demands restoration of the traditional difference, also using the rhetoric of principle in defense of equity. The application of the equity principle is determined by which side of tradition the union happens to be. Given the proliferation of unions and job territories, unions can always discover "gross inequity." Equity must be resolved on its "own merits" before any other issues, such as productivity, can be discussed. Management may try to counter with a stern "nothing for nothing" ploy, but it caves in when the workers start obeying all management safety and operational rules to the letter, thus ensuring quick paralysis without actually striking, or a quick cost-benefit calculation discloses that a wildcat strike by one of the ten unions in the plant would cost vastly more than giving in "just this once" to a single union's demands.

Britain's attempt to muddle through with its income restraint policy was also ineffective. Income restraints merely postpone things; once the pressure lets up, the unions come in with big "catch up" demands. Thus wages continue to outpace productivity gains. So long as bureaucracy attaches a worker's identity and status to his job content, the whipsaw wage effect will be predictable. Nor will any "social compact" between unions and the government likely succeed in keeping wages in line.

## UP AND DOWN THE PROMOTION LADDER

While wage inflation hurts the British economy, material waste does the most serious damage. Wasted material, of course, contains "embodied labor." The most potent source of bad workmanship in Britain arises from the manpower deployment "system." If you are a British production worker you will likely hire into a job at the bottom of a prearranged pecking order, or promotion ladder. This ladder might lead upward within the confines of a single process, but it could wander around the entire plant. The ladder might be quite short and end with a low-paying job, or it might be quite long and end with a fairly decent wage.

Each job on this ladder will pay a unique wage, arrived at through collective bargaining. The ladder itself was developed in negotiations in the distant past. Occasionally the jobs on the ladder will bear some relationship to each other, but you may discover that they have no logical relationship whatever. The chances are the job at the top will be more demanding than those at the bottom, but skill inversions also occur. Normally you will find that the various rungs on this promotion ladder make quite different demands on you. Some will call merely for a tolerance of the boredom of gross underutilization; you may actually "work" for less than an hour a day. Other jobs make various demands on your physical aptitudes: eyesight, coordination, attention span, and so on. Such jobs will likely involve operating a machine on the production line or moving the product from place to place.

Once inserted into the system, you discover that your personal attributes, skills, and likes or dislikes have little relevance to the jobs you do. You simply embody job seniority. Your seniority governs every assignment you draw and will do so until you leave. You do not simply progress gradually up your particular promotion ladder; you shuffle up and down unpredictably with the vagaries of illness, holidays, quits, death, or the retirement of others. In theory you might go all the way up and down again within a week. Your wages move accordingly.

You will learn each job on your promotion ladder largely by being flung into it temporarily, as a result of someone's illness, for example. Should one of the slots require aptitudes you do not have, that is more or less too bad. If you make a fair hash of things every time you draw some job, you can plead inability and opt out of further promotion.

Those below you then simply jump around you, and you will have reached the end of the line. Normally, therefore, you try to muddle through despite your disabilities.

Whatever latent pride in good work you brought with you will soon atrophy, for your particular contribution to production will often be obscured by the mistakes of others above and below you. Far from trying to give you a hard time, your foreman will tend to overlook any errors you commit. Indeed, if you do goof, you and your foreman together can point an accusing finger at the slovenly job the maintenance people did on the equipment. Above all, you quickly learn, the foreman wants to avoid trouble with your union. He fears the shop steward more than the managing director. He can blame maintenance for production error, and his own production superiors will support him. But if the foreman angers a shop steward who then calls a quicky strike more than once or twice, things can go hard for the foreman.

You also learn how, as a worker, you can get into trouble. You are not likely to do so with management, short of announcing in the company newspaper your intention to sabotage the works. Rather, you must avoid trouble with your workmates and your union. One of the worst things would be to do more than one job at a time. If you are an assistant operator and the operator fails to show up, you must never simply cover for him. You do nothing until you have officially been moved on the promotion ladder. You move into the operator's slot if that happens to be the next rung, but your move must await another assistant operator's arrival. You must at all costs guard your union's protective practices against a predatory management, or your teammates risk the sack. Management can sometimes rid itself of a useless job by proving that things went along just fine with that job unmanned. If you let down your mates by allowing management to discover a dispensable job, you could draw a stiff fine, besides a cold shoulder.

As a production worker, you would commit nearly as great an error if you made some minor correction on your equipment. The job of tightening a nut calls for a "fitter" and his mate, and it is up to mechanical maintenance, not you, to detect loose nuts. Moreover, you have better friends if you do not call attention to equipment faults. Tightening the nut would take no time at all, and letting the equipment break down may take several hours to fix. But this gives your underemployed mates a breather; it is hard to do nothing while pretending to be working. If the equipment breaks down, they can make tea, figure out racing forms, or play checkers.

Say an electric motor needs changing. You tell your foreman; he tells the electrical foreman and the mechanical foreman. After some minutes to chase them down, an electrician comes over to turn off the electrical switch and disconnect the wires; his mate comes along to carry the toolbox. They depart, and after another wait, the fitter (mechanic) and his mate show up. The mate hands a spanner (wrench) to the fitter, who loosens the four bolts on the baseplate. Now the foreman rounds up a rigger, who hails a crane. The rigger slips the crane's hook into the eyebolt at the top of the motor. He must also wait for the replacement motor and slip the hook into the new motor's eyebolt. After the new motor is in place, the sequence is reversed; the fitter and his mate are relocated to tighten the bolts on the baseplate, and the electrical people are found to hook up the wiring and open the switch. With luck a 20-minute job has taken two or three hours, tied up production and equipment, and given the production crew a change to break the monotony of doing nothing.

If your production line happens to be on a "tonnage bonus," however, you learn to play the game a little differently. With the connivance of your mates, you may correct minor faults yourself (on the sly, of course) or announce the need before an actual breakdown. You do this on those occasions when you have "easy" orders to run and can make a killing on a particular shift. Indeed you may work flat out, never mind quality, just put out the tonnage. If some "tough" orders come along and you see that this shift will be a dead loss bonuswise, you can get very rigid with the work and safety rules and push the tough orders on the next shift.

## RESTRICTIVE PRACTICES, WORKMANSHIP, AND WASTE

The scenario above would vary in intensity from plant to plant, of course. Fewer problems occur in a new plant. Management can negotiate better work rules for new equipment when there is no previous manning tradition. Greater restrictiveness occurs in larger, older, more impersonal works with a long history of bitterness between management and labor. But generally management cannot intrude into the placement process, in many cases not even by aptitude screening tests. Examples of what lengths this can go to include the following:

• In a large works with its own fleet of railroad locomotives, locomotive operators successfully refused color blindness tests to differentiate the red and green signals.

• In a rolling mill, crane drivers successfully refused eyesight tests. They carried coils of steel weighing up to 20 tons overhead across the plant.

• In a hot strip mill, production workers refused hand-eye cordination tests for the job of downcoiler operator. Without excellent coordination of hand and eye movements, whole strips of steel, up to 15 tons or more, could be "cobbled" (turned into twisted scrap) by failing to enter the downcoiling mechanism properly. Various other types of damage could also occur, to both plant and product.

Of course, the locomotive driver who discovers he is color blind after a derailment or collision may learn to make compensations. The myopic crane driver, after dropping his coil the two feet he thought was half an inch, may well get eyeglasses on the National Health. And I know of one case where a man cobbled so many coils he opted out of the downcoiler job. Such adjustments prevent total collapse, but not serious damage.

The consumer is generally spared direct knowledge of the waste resulting from the effects of restrictive trade union practices on workmanship. Scrap and faulty pieces can often be recycled, even if at a cost, and inspection does intercept much of the bad work. Some of the waste is unseen, such as poor equipment utilization, excessive consumption of fuel and energy, and lost time, but it all shows up in the cost column. Given British wage rates, the British consumer pays through the nose for this waste.

Except for the waste of embodied labor, however, the wages bill is not what does the damage. Despite all the criticism of overmanning, this is not the problem. Rather it is *overjobbing* and the blind use of seniority to dictate deployment which improverish workmanship, causing excessive inputs. The difference between "overjobbing" and "overmanning" is crucial. Surplus manpower, like cash, can be an asset if properly deployed in reserve, assuming wage rates are not excessive (and British wages are low by American and even other European standards). Proper deployment requires manpower reserves engaged in training who can rotate between reserves and operations. Overjobbing, on the other hand, ironically causes routine labor shortages of "proper skills." At holiday time, especially, shortages of special skills can have bizarre consequences, such as entire production lines filled with inexperienced people all at once.

Suppose, for example, the head of a production line of eight job slots retires. The seven people below each move up and a new man comes in at the bottom. A single retirement has caused not one change of jobs, but eight. This is only the beginning; when the new head of this line goes on holiday, everyone does a job two rungs ahead of his normal position. If the No. 3 man gets sick, everyone moves up three rungs from his previous position, and inexperienced hands with or without the necessary aptitudes control production.

British foremen with whom I have discussed this problem refer to holiday time as "the silly season." A foreman or more senior manager can do nothing about such problems, because seniority has complete control in the selection of individuals for job placement. Degradation of workmanship and needless waste of resources inevitably follow the blind application of seniority in job placement. As a criterion for promotion in social rank, seniority is perfectly sound, but it causes enormous damage when used as the criterion for job promotion. The difficulty, of course, arises from the bureaucratic practice of making a change in job a requirement for promotion in rank.

## LEARNING TO LIVE WITH WASTE

British trade unions have largely succeeded in pulling the coercive teeth from the jaws of the once tyrannical British industrial bureaucracy. The British worker need no longer "touch the forelock" when the foreman passes by. In a larger enterprise not headed for extinction, the worker with only a few years service virtually has life tenure if he wants it. He must, of course, continue to man the defensive barricades of restrictive practices. He has achieved almost complete immunity from arbitrary and capricious abuse by management. The British industrial worker enjoys a better life, socially and economically, than he did before World War II or at any time earlier. The brutish, tyrannized, and miserable old ways live mostly in the memories of workers nearing retirement. Moreover, few British managers begrudge these gains, despite the frustrations they suffer in consequence.

Yet despite the gains, British industrial relations have probably never been more poisonous. By no means have British workers entered into an industrial nirvana. In eliminating enterprise tyranny, they did not gain enterprise fraternity. They do enjoy fraternal association within their respective unions, but against, not for, the enterprise.

British workers for the most part detest the mess and the waste their restrictive practices cause. More than one used the term "soul destroying" to describe it to me. When first introduced to the shocking waste which occurs on many a shop floor, most workers experience a period of depression which may last as little as a few weeks to a year or more. Ultimately most workers learn to live with waste, largely by ignoring it. Or they project their hate for what they do onto management, claiming, with some logic, that management forces wasteful tactics on them. If to preserve their identity and status they must waste, very well, then, waste they shall. But they will not enjoy it.

Laziness has little to do with it. Indeed, it takes a good deal of careful and well-thought-out tactical planning to bring it all off. Given their employment goal, workers do not behave "irrationally," despite the overall economic damage done the British economy. Within their objective, in fact, the workers behave with clearsighted rationality. Irrationality arises from the notion that the bureaucratic social order should prevail within industrial enterprise, public or private.

## INEFFICIENCY IN THE "HUMANE" BUREAUCRACY

The evidence suggests that without tyranny, the bureaucratic social order also would degenerate into slovenly performance. If you insist on bureaucracy then you either run it despotically or else, it runs you, as in the British situation. Rarely does a "humane bureaucracy" work very effectively, because such an enterprise would have to use rigid deployment practices. Humaneness, remember, means protecting the individual's identity and status, which in turn requires the preservation of jobs whether they are useful or not. The bureaucracy, which exercises flexible control over deployment, must behave tyrannically. If human social needs are properly satisfied, the bureaucratic enterprise is deprived of its flexibility.

Neither good management nor superior leadership makes any essential impact on this dilemma. A flexible bureaucracy must make its adjustments tyranically. A "humane" bureaucracy grows rigid and thus performs incompetently. The calibre of the leadership may partly determine where an enterprise falls between these two poles, but the bureaucratic social order itself sets up the inherent clash between humanness and efficiency.

The buyer-seller relationship, as we have stressed, is unnatural for human cooperative enterprise. British trade unions nevertheless accept it unquestioningly because this relationship gives the trade union its own identity. Given the buyer-seller assumption, the unions logically insist on controlling the work themselves, work control being a normal seller's right. Unions thus virtually ban management from the shop floor. But they do not substitute an effective coordinative alternative, because they control only the content of the jobs in isolation from one another. Unions aim at the security of the worker's identity, status, and pay which are all, of course, tied to the job. They deny all responsibility for the coordination of the jobs, claiming this is a management problem. Inevitably sloppy performance erodes the competence of the enterprise and causes waste. Pride in workmanship, in fact, could well undermine the social aims of the unions.

## CULTURAL SHOCK IN BRITISH INDUSTRY

Many students of organization believe that the broader culture's values and traditions shape the character of the human enterprise within it. Of course it may, but British experience certainly indicates the reverse can also occur. In a broad cultural sense, the British abhor waste. They often look askance at the American practice of demolishing a perfectly good 30-year-old building to make way for something newer. Even at comparable levels of affluence, British consumers, by and large, waste much less than their American cousins. "Waste not, want not" is a British more than an American proverb.

The cultural shock many British workers and junior managers experience on entering their industrial wasteland underscores the lack of cultural continuity between a broad society and the enterprises within it. So does the broad connivance in covering it all up. Each for its own reasons, both management and labor discourage publicity on the problem. Complaints about overmanning and restrictive labor practices are tolerated, but the conventional wisdom that the economic cost of overmanning begins and ends with excessive labor expense must be accepted. Arguments that restrictive practices do the most damage by eroding the quality of workmanship are met with angry outbursts and denials from all sides. Those removed by some distance, social or other, from the problem often make the most heated denials.

The argument of excessive labor cost sustains the myth of the inherent clash between "industrial efficiency" and "worker security" in economic enterprise. This myth in turn allows the British to hide from the waste which slowly strangles their economy, and they must hide because of a high cultural regard for frugality. It is okay to wink at "inefficiency" (defined merely as hiring more workers than you really need) if this promotes some humane value such as worker "security." This rationale leaves the theory of the bureaucratic social order largely intact. If enterprise efficiency and worker security inherently are in conflict, then tyranny and not teamwork will achieve whatever level of efficiency the enterprise reaches. But the broader British culture abhors tyranny as much as it abhors physical waste and admires efficiency. The British are less troubled if they define inefficiency as higher labor costs incurred in the interests of damping down tyranny and improving worker security. This bland view allows them to avoid the discomforting notion that the whole system needs an overhaul and encourages them to strive to achieve a balance between what they can regard as "immutably conflicting ideals."

To admit to gross physical waste upsets this neatly balanced adjustment to clashing cultural values. When the element of poor workmanship intrudes, it is hard on a culture which once prided itself on good workmanship and still advertises "skilled British craftsmanship." In a home of the Protestant work ethic, the accusation of poor workmanship cuts deep. Even management (higher management in particular) hides from the issue of waste. To acknowledge the fact of waste as the result of poor workmanship (hence "poor" workers) would "insult" the workers. Tactically, of course, management cannot afford to make such an accusation. Industrial relations are poor enough already. Moreover, the accusation, if true, suggests "bad management" beyond the "acceptable" concessions to worker job security, which in turn forces management to admit the awkward fact that they are largely helpless in this respect. It is one thing to tolerate "overmanning" in the humane interests of the workers. To put up with bad workmanship which promotes no humane interests but instead damages the whole economy is something else.

If it admitted shop floor impotency to stop waste, top management would lay itself open to a serious question: Why should management wages be paid to those without management power? Top managers live under genetic command to protect their own social position first and get on with the job second. If you accept the BSO, the refusal to acknowledge waste as a function of restrictive practices clearly is management's best short-run strategy. It must decry the failure of first line-supervision to lead adequately. The failures of the system must be laid at the door of subordinate social classes or political adversaries.

Yet management does not actually tolerate overjobbing. Rather, the trade unions impose overjobbing upon management by their political power. Labor war would follow any serious nationwide management effort to "deman," and the overwhelming chances are that management would lose any such struggle. Tactics which produce overmanning also produce overjobbing, which in turn causes the waste and bad workmanship. Waste and restrictive practices are so completely interwoven within the BSO they cannot be separated. We shall see later in Part III that this fact holds not only in Britain but elsewhere, regardless of culture.

A determined culturist could argue that the "English disease" grows out of English culture. Britain bequeathed industrial bureaucracy to the world, and it can accurately be claimed that "teamwork" never has been a tradition in British industry. But all cultures share the same biology, and teamwork requires the biological releaser I have called fraternity. True, the fraternal social order has not appeared widely in British industry, and no tradition of cooperative industrial teamwork thus could develop. Instead bureaucracy has inhibited industrial teamwork for decades.

## OTHER BRITISH ENTERPRISES

Fraternity, however, has appeared widely elsewhere in British culture, with predictably efficient results. Britain's unions themselves organize fraternally. The aristocracy enjoys some technical features of the fraternal social order, such as personal social rank divorced from function. Titles such as baron, earl, or duke do not specify function; they are purely social ranks. And the British armed forces have more or less retained the personal rank system, in preference to job rank. Indeed,

Britain's Calvinistic work ethic never imputed superior social worth to some kinds of work compared to others.

The British working-class man who enters the military will entertain no notion of weaving a web of restrictive work practices, but upon entering industry he will participate widely in restrictionism. It might be argued that the military has "greater discipline" which surely it does. But industry once had such discipline, and then lost it. Nothing in the broader British culture explains this differing reaction by people from the same social class. Military tyranny certainly does not explain why working-class boys make reasonable adjustments to the military. They often like their officers but in industry they come to hate their bosses, even though officers and bosses share similar class backgrounds.

Only because the military comes much closer than industry to meeting human social needs naturally can it get away with its authoritarianism. A boy "joins" the army and then belongs to it. He has tenure of an agreed duration. His identity thus becomes very clear and unambiguous, and he needs no restrictive practices to protect it. His personal rank also accords him a social status which rises over time. Improved weapons technology does not threaten his identity or status, no matter how many "jobs" in theory might be "wiped out" by a better weapon. (But like bureaucracy, the military digs in if a whole combat arm such as cavalry, aircraft carriers, or battleships comes under a technological cloud. Such clouds do threaten identity.)

Compared to the bureaucratic social order, military authoritarianism is more managerial in the sense of technical coordination of the work and less political in the sense of manipulation of social needs other than role changes. Direct superiors usually have no political authority whatever over the individual soldier; they cannot arbitrarily change his identity, status, pay, or prestige. The military greatly limits the amount of political authority delegated to officers without formal due process. Thus it strengthens management coordinating authority by eliminating subordinate backlash to political tyranny.

The military has its problems, of course. In peacetime, underemployment prevails outside the confines of housekeeping, training, and maintenance, and these tasks must often be supplemented with garrison make-work. Contrived activity does not appeal to most people. Underemployed, the imaginative human animal easily gets into trouble, as all armies have recognized. Peacetime underemployment in garrison duty, not the requirements of battle discipline, is the basis for most of the military emphasis on authoritarianism. The Israeli army (a cousin of the British army) has found grass-roots participation in battle decisions to be highly effective, and it has successfully junked the elaborate social protocol and authoritarianism of peacetime garrison duty.

The Israeli army, however, does not keep hoards of underemployed soldiers in uniform when no fighting occurs; the geography of their nation allows them to limit duty to the actual needs of training. Fraternity, not wizardry, accords the Israeli army much of its combat prowess.

Thus the "culture" of the particular enterprise determines its behavior independently of the boarder culture. Moreover, as British experience suggests, enterprises can develop internal social orders widely at odds with the broader culture.

## THE COST

The suggestion that Britain's blue-collar bureaucratic social order results in poor workmanship and resultant waste was confirmed by my personal observations over and over. I developed some statistical evidence by comparing the published annual reports of two companies of similar product lines, one British, the other American, for which economies of scale decisively favored the British firm. The British firm used twice the man-hours of the American firm per unit of product, yet British unit labor costs were only 80 percent of the American firm's, with wages in the British firm slightly more than one third the American level. But the British firm consumed about one third more material per unit than its American counterpart, mostly as waste, and it therefore had to charge a higher unit price by about 20 percent. This could be thought of as a consumer tax to finance industrial waste, which in turn supports on-the-job unemployment compensation.

Comparing annual reports, of course, can be risky. Different accounting rules might apply. Moreover, accountants often draft such reports with the objective of confusing rather than clarifying the facts. Broadly, however, the same picture emerged in other comparisons of companies.

In a three-way comparison of the total economic output of the United States, Sweden, and the United Kingdom, I found that Britain and Sweden invested about the same amount of capital per worker, the United States roughly 70 percent more. America and Sweden produced about the same gross national product per unit of invested capital; Britain produced about 20 percent less. This I take as the measure of wasted physical input for the British economy as a whole.[4]

"The English disease" will afflict Britain so long as the bureaucratic social order dominates the shop floor. Moreover, the situation will slowly and progressively deteriorate. American firms also depend on the bureaucratic social order, but much of the potential for physical waste remains latent so long as the bureaucracy can avoid overjobbing.

---

[4] These data applied to the early 1960s.

America for years had a labor shortage and hence there was little social pressure to overjob industry, British style. We shall see later that the overjobbed American bureaucracy will behave much the same as its British counterpart. Britain spoils about 20 percent more material input per capita than Sweden or America. But America is catching up fast with the "mother country" and in some areas is ascending to new heights of incompetence, as we shall see.

# 6

# The Aerospace Debacle

## FORECASTS AND FANTASIES

The U.S. aerospace industry in the decade of the 60s suffered technical failures and financial disasters which resulted in loss of jobs for
millions of specialists. Nevertheless, reflexive optimism (see Chapter 4)
placed aerospace forecasts firmly in Pollyanna's grip, as can be illustrated with a study of the Boeing Company's commercial experience.
In defense contracting the politics of defense and foreign policy caused
even more distortions in market demand, as we shall see.

After a spectacular upswing lasting several years, U.S. airline traffic
growth slowed sharply in 1969 and virtually ceased in 1970 and 1971.
The domestic airlines thus abruptly quit buying new equipment. As
Boeing's sales backlog dried up, the company had to jettison nearly two
thirds of its work force or face bankruptcy.

When the crunch came, more or less in association with the economic slump of 1970, Boeing pointed to the recession as the major
source of its woe. Boeing has little control over the economy, of course.
Blaming the recession was plausible enough on the face of it, and it
appeared to get management off the hook. Had not President Nixon's
economic advisors been predicting a bright economic outlook? If the
government, which has some actual control over the economy, failed
to predict the recession accurately, why should Boeing's management
be held accountable for failure to anticipate and then plan for the
slump? (Lockheed made essentially the same point during the congressional hearings over its proposed bailout.) In short, Boeing argued that
completely unexpected and indeed unforeseeable economic events
caused the sudden ceasation of growth in airline traffic. The slump did
catch Boeing by surprise, but we cannot accept the company's explana-

**Figure 6**
AIR AND AUTO TRAFFIC TRENDS
(growth and maturity)

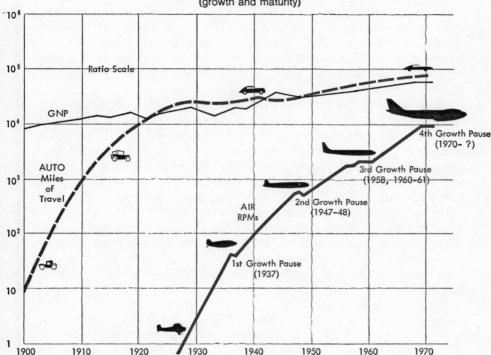

Air travel has followed the classic innovational growth curve. At first technological improvements lower costs and improve quality. Lower costs times better quality times general economic growth equal very high growth rates. Later improvements tend to raise unit costs. This signals maturity for the industry, which then expands at about the same rate as the economy.

For auto travel maturity occurred by 1928. Since then auto travel has moved almost precisely at the rate of the GNP measured in constant dollars. If airlines raise fares at the rate of inflation, as one carrier suggested, traffic will only grow at the rate of the GNP, indicating technical maturity.

In the period beginning in 1970, for the first time domestic air traffic ceased to grow, coincident with higher fares during the introduction of a new generation of aircraft. All the other pauses in air traffic growth forced some manufacturers to the commercial sidelines.

The current pause was forecast in the early 1960s, when the trend became clear. Widely noted at the time, the trend was ignored by carriers and manufacturers as its time approached. The industry never plans on these growth pauses, for to do so requires a plan to fire the very people manufacturers recruit in a buildup. Thus they planned (hoped?) for uninterrupted growth throughout the 1970s, which led to gross excess capacity when the anticipated pause came. (Source: Auto travel: Department of Commerce, *Historical Statistics of the U.S.* Air travel: C.A.B., *Handbook of Airline Statistics.* Interpretation is largely the author's.)

tion of what went wrong. Boeing has repeatedly failed to anticipate turns in the commercial market because of its proclivities to substitute fantasy for forecasts.

Consider some facts. First, 1970 was not the first time an air travel growth pause dried up aircraft sales. As Figure 6 shows, it was the fourth since the industry's inception in 1926.[1] Second, these pauses fit a definite pattern, coming every eight to ten years. Third, Boeing has been badly burned by every one of these pauses, particularly the last three, and it planned for none of them. Fourth, these pauses only partly reflect the state of the economy. The causes of interrupted growth also reflect technical and cost changes within the industry itself which have long lead times and thus can signal a coming pause, independent of the eight- or ten-year trend.

More specifically, air travel has grown smartly through a number of recessions, big and little, but growth *has always ceased* with the simultaneous introduction of a new generation of equipment and airline fare increases. Each time, with the advent of the DC–3 in 1937, four-engined pressurized planes in 1947, the first-generation jets in 1958, and the wide-bodied jumbo jets, traffic ceased to grow. Each pause lasted one year longer than the preceding one: it was one year in 1937, two years in 1947–48, three years in the period 1958–61 (traffic did grow in 1959). If this trend continues, this fourth pause might last four years, already beginning to split with a period of some growth, as was the third pause.

With each new equipment cycle the airlines raise air fares, partly to help finance the equipment. Airline costs historically go up, at least temporarily, when converting to a new generation of aircraft and fall rapidly as the new planes are integrated into the system and the old ones are dispensed with.[2] As the new aircraft begin to age, costs start to rise again just before the next generation of aircraft is introduced. Airline fares follow this cost trend; they go up and stifle growth, then later drop (in constant dollars) and expand the market once again, in part because the lower fares apply to better quality equipment. Each generation of aircraft has only so much potential to lower costs and improve quality, however. So far it has taken about eight to ten years for each new generation of equipment to exploit its market-expanding potential.

Many historical trends suggest that the economy by itself exerts about a one-for-one influence on traffic growth. If the gross national product (GNP) grows by 5 percent, for example, the amount of airline travel will also grow by 5 percent, other things equal. Not only air travel history suggests this, but also the record of nearly every other transportation industry since 1865. Other factors, mainly cost and quality changes, can account for higher or lower growth rates relative to the GNP. Indeed, a growth pause in airline traffic is defined as growth at

---

[1] Aside from 1942, when the Air Corps took over many airline transports.

[2] What with spreading bureaucracy in the airlines, it is not clear they can continue to gain the cost savings they achieved earlier.

or less than the rate of the GNP. A mature industry's market typically moves with the GNP.

Boeing ignored all these trends in their exuberant 1966 forecast. Its brighter tomorrow foresaw no pause at all, all the way to 1990 in some forecasts related to the SST. Apparently even the business cycle would suspend its fluctuations on Boeing's behalf, despite a history of recessions every five years or so. The high economic growth rate which prevailed under the artificial stimulus of the Vietnam War would continue indefinitely, in Boeing's official view. No longer would airline costs rise with the introduction of new equipment, which would have zero defects. No transitional problems were anticipated for the forthcoming new generation of aircraft. The inflationary wage increases the airlines had granted in 1966 and again later, and the fare increases the airlines asked in return, were forgotten, and all the classic signals of a coming slump in the airline growth rate were ignored. Nothing was expected to disturb the growth of airline traffic upon which Boeing's airplane sales forecasts, and in turn company business and manpower recruiting plans, essentially depended. The big employment cutbacks of 1949–50 and 1959–60 were never expected to reoccur.

It might be argued that these trends only became apparent to Boeing with the 1970–71 traffic pause, except that their essential outlines had been identified by the company in early 1961 and incorporated in its official forecast in August of that year.[3] Boeing's "innovation cycle" analysis was made public, distributed widely in the trade, and written up in the trade press at the time. The document was designated TSR–747, coincidently the same number as Boeing's 747 jumbo jet whose introduction coincided with the forecasted pause in air traffic growth.

In 1961 interest in the innovation cycle centered not on the next pause, forecast for the late sixties, but on the prospects of good growth following the 1958–61 pause. The jets then entering service promised to stimulate air travel to new heights after introductory difficulties had been resolved. As the time for the growth pause of the late sixties entered the planning horizon, however, the innovation cycle analysis was quietly shelved, along with its subsequent refinements. The new forecast that emerged in 1966 exhibited the same exuberance that had characterized Boeing's forecasts in 1949 and 1958, just prior to other sudden halts in airline traffic growth. The late sixties' pause in airline traffic growth nonetheless arrived, roughly as it had been outlined in 1961, with the second generation of jets headed by Boeing's 747. Aircraft sales promptly dried up again, for the fourth time under similar circumstances. Completely unprepared, Boeing and the rest of the

---

[3] W. M. Wallace and Thomas F. Comick, *Forecast of United States Domestic Airline Traffic, 1961–1975*, Document TSR–747 (Renton, Wash.: The Boeing Company, August 1961, reprinted November 1963).

industry had once more more or less marched over the cliff to Pollyana's tune.

Boeing's 1966 retreat into fantasy illustrates a classic case of "planners" being unable to plan ahead objectively when the hire-fire cycle comes into play. If aerospace and other cyclical industries insist on adjusting to changes in market demand with the hire-fire cycle, they can hardly expect realistic planning and forecasts. As we have noted, forecasters do not enjoy being the bearers of sad tidings, and they realize that if they push a pessimistic forecast too zealously they brand themselves as "defeatist," a high crime in any risk-taking enterprise. Forecasters are also vulnerable because their forecasts are only projections, which can always be wrong. They must defend these projections against the criticism of superiors whose own judgment may be put in doubt by the forecast. If projected pessimism means the sacking of many people, serious pressures arise to substitute fantasy for forecasts. Such pressure comes not alone from superiors but from the forecaster himself, who prefers to plan for good rather than for bad times, perhaps including his own. If he is right when he projects optimism, he becomes a hero of sorts; if wrong, he will likely be forgiven.

## MANAGEMENT BY BELLOWS AND MEAT AXE

Peter Drucker in effect described the hire-fire cycle as "management by bellows and meat axe." He called such a procedure "a sure sign of confusion . . . an admission of incompetence."[4] Confusion and incompetence surely abound in the aerospace industry, as program after program has gone out of control in the past few years. The statistics of Drucker's bellows (hire) and meat axe (fire) indicate the dimensions of this confusion. Boeing's Seattle payroll stood at about 60,000 in 1964, and by 1968 it had passed 100,000. At the end of 1971 less than 38,000 people remained. Yet by early 1974 Boeing's payroll had climbed again, to about 50,000. Most of the industry experiences similar gyrations in employment.

Aerospace has had a history of indiscriminate use of the hire-fire cycle. As a result, except for top management, employment security has almost vanished. Teamwork and employee loyalty have predictably disappeared. The industry has also had a recent series of technical failures and financial disasters, some of which will be discussed later. The layoffs of the late 50s set the stage for the disasters which followed in the late 60s. Aerospace has yet to pay the price for its more recent massive cutbacks.

---

[4] Peter Drucker, *The Practice of Management* (New York: Harper Brothers, 1954), p. 128.

White-collar workers, including those in management and professional ranks, have suffered more than blue-collar workers. For the most part, they had no seniority protection; traditionally, they had taken substantial employment security for granted. This customary security evaporated in aerospace as companies changed these policies without formal announcement. Often, in fact, they denied the changes, and it was possible that no formal change of policy occurred. With the onset of bureaucracy, top management ignored the issue of employment security for those a social class or two beneath them. Over the years the hierarchy distended to enormous social distance. As bureaucratic layers piled onto one another, dehumanization inevitably followed. Meanwhile, the span of vertical control had grown past top management's ability to coordinate effectively. By degrees ever larger segments of the white-collar staff came under the influence of the hire-fire cycle.

The government felt no responsibility for employees suddenly eliminated in a program cancellation. This was a "company matter." It did not occur to government planners that a ruthless hire-fire policy in industry would have serious delayed cost consequences for government aerospace requirements. Yet nearly every firm which had a big layoff in 1958–62 would later encounter grave cost problems or technical failures after 1965.

## TRUTH IN RECRUITING

Government and industry were a good deal less than candid in their hire-fire employment policies for aerospace contracts. By tradition, contractors hire employees for the duration of some project. A dam or a highway, for example, is usually built by people hired expressly for the project. Workers understand from the outset that they have employment only until the completion of the project, with the exception of a small permanent staff. Wages and other benefits usually reflect the temporary nature of the job. A small but significant percent of the work force (including engineers and other professionals) even enjoy the nomadic life such a policy necessitates.

In practice, aerospace contractors had exactly the same type of employment security to offer. But instead of saying so, they pretended otherwise. They stressed "career opportunities" in their particular company, pretending that the traditional framework of white-collar job security still existed. By and large, the industry had no compunctions about recruiting people out of permanent jobs into projects which they knew had a doubtful future or even a definite terminal date. Indeed, some firms recruited the world around, and none stressed the temporary aspects of the work.

Until the late 50s, a college degree normally promised a "permanent job." For professional and management employees, permanent employment was largely taken for granted; indeed, employment security was a big argument for foregoing several years' income in order to get a degree. Accounting terminology supported the notion of employment security for management and professional people with its concepts of fixed and variable costs. As related to wages, "fixed" referred to white-collar and "variable" to blue-collar jobs. College training had come roughly to signify the difference.

Aerospace engineers who had graduated from college discovered with dismay that they often had less job security than blue-collar workers, despite their degrees. One acquaintance of mine had listened to an aerospace vice president in the early 60s declaim on the security of management and professional jobs, only to get laid off a few weeks later.

It became routine in the aerospace industry to make "overhead" cutbacks, aside from the layoffs which resulted from completion or cancellation of a project. For some years management's upper echelons deluded themselves into thinking they could count on the traditional teamwork and loyalty of white-collar workers without providing the employment security which "released" those attributes. The hypocrisy had become pretty clear by the early 60s, as the vicious circle of the hire-fire cycle took hold. Blood flowing from the meat axe fertilizes the growth of fake jobs. Overjobbing of overhead ranks began with a vengance, and overhead costs skyrocketed. Another cut in the ranks was followed by more overjobbing. In my experience, the 10 percent cutbacks usually triggered a subsequent 20 to 50 percent splurge of new hires. The groundwork for future disasters had been firmly laid.

The victims did not damage the companies that fired them as much as the survivors did. As the survivors began thinking of the "fire next time," loyalty quickly disappeared, to be replaced by a defensive me-first approach. In professional and lower management ranks, the "company man" increasingly became an object of derision. Continued survival came to require political skills more than professional ones. Talented politicians of good professional reputations would stay, and often would go on to do some of the greatest damage.

As in Britain, overjobbing badly damaged the product itself; costs increased and quality fell. But unlike Britain, where damage goes on piece by piece, in aerospace failures came in a program-by-program pattern. Hardly any major aerospace program has escaped in recent years. The costly moon exploration program avoided technical disaster, to be sure, but the astronauts reached the moon before NASA's first major layoffs. In other programs the rot had already far advanced by the time our successful moon landing seemed to confirm unchallenged American technical competence.

## PROGRAM FAILURES

Not since the Boeing B–52, which first flew in 1952, has a successful bomber been designed by the U.S. aerospace industry. The B–70 flopped; the B–58 flew, but so unreliably the Air Force finally junked it. The infamous TFX failed to perform any of its missions successfully, and the Navy scrapped its version (F–111B). The Navy's replacement (F–14) appears in deep difficulties of its own. The replacement for the B–70 (which in turn supposedly would replace the B–52), designated the B–1, also appears in serious cost difficulties while still on paper.

The decade 1961–71 saw an unprecedented string of program failures. Lockheed started off with its commercial flop, the L–188 Electra. The C–5 fiasco which followed, together with the commercially shaky Tristar program, actually bankrupted Lockheed. Congress bailed the failing firm out with a loan guarantee, which assures only the postponement of bankruptcy. Should the air travel market slump continue, the "saving" of Lockheed may only trigger the subsequent bankruptcy of Boeing and McDonnell-Douglas; you can't pour a quart of supply into a pint pot of demand. Lockheed would probably then fail as well. Douglas, in fact, almost perished during a time of strong demand for its products, avoiding bankruptcy in 1967 only by merging with McDonnell. Sales and deliveries of the DC–9 and DC–8 were very good, but costs had gone out of control, for reasons no one seemed much willing to discuss.

General Dynamics avoided bankruptcy as prime contractor on the TFX (F–111A). As producer of the crash-prone B–58 and the lumbering B–36, it had capped what was a less than luminous product line with its ill-fated 880–990 commercial program of the early 60s, on which it lost nearly a half billion dollars. With the TFX, General Dynamics reached new pinnacles of incompetence. Besides being a technical flop, the F–111A cost more than three times as much as its original "cost estimate." Something like $10 billion, or twice the GNP of Thailand, has been squandered on this program.

Aerospace, of course, explores the frontiers of technology, and therefore it has inherent risks of failures. Some problems only come to light after the product enters service. New technology grows ever more complex. It might be possible to write off any one failure, but when nearly everything fails, suspicions arise. Outside of the moon landing, practically nothing else in the entire industry, the largest industrial employer in America, could be declared successful. If the product did not prove an out-and-out technical flop like the B–70 or F–111B, it had serious technical difficulties, often combined with enormous cost overruns, such as on the C–5A, Cheyenne, F–14, and F–111A. Where design problems were corrected before flight, enormous cost overruns were likely, as with the 747 or 737. The DC–10 and Tristar have also had their share of trouble. Hundreds of millions of dollars, many times the cost of the 707 prototype, had been squandered on the SST merely as a paper airplane before its richly deserved cancellation.

The string of fiascos of American aerospace during the decade 1961–71 is unmatched in industry. Such successes as occurred had their design origins in the 1950s, notably the 707–727 series and the DC–8. The DC–9 might qualify had not Douglas nearly gone bankrupt with it. And we do not know that Lockheed's "rescue" will be permanent.

## FITZGERALD'S COMPLAINT

The bureaucratic social order has gone to great lengths to protect the aerospace industry from its failings. A. Ernest Fitzgerald was sacked by the Air Force because he committed the sin of honesty in testifying under oath before the U.S. Senate on the actual cost of the C–5A. In *The High Priests of Waste,* Fitzgerald charged that the Pentagon had a deliberate policy of propping up bloated defense contractors at whatever level of inefficiency they achieved. Trained as an industrial engineer, he observed in dismay the evolution of one aerospace technical flop and cost overrun after another.[5]

Fitzgerald documented the enormous buildup of contractors' overhead staffs and the resulting inefficiency and skyrocketing costs. He rated manpower efficiency at as low as 5 percent in some defense programs, for example giving a 12.5 percent efficiency rating to the Minuteman missile program. At one point, according to Fitzgerald, about 40 percent of the nation's installed Minuteman capacity was inoperational because of production defects.

Fitzgerald admits his crusade to fight waste achieved little. The Pentagon insisted on a policy of "historical costing" which effectively blessed any inefficiencies contractors had built into their operations. Spiraling cost trends were assumed to be the result of "inexorable economic forces" of mysterious origin. Thus Fitzgerald's plea for substituting a "should cost" analysis based on established industrial engineering criteria was squelched time and again by military and civilian officials, often with malice and vindictiveness. They also tried to "reason" with him, directly or indirectly, by telling him that waste in defense procurement was a national policy, a Keynesian effort to maintain a high level of employment and capacity in the aerospace industry. It was strongly implied that Fitzgerald should quit being difficult and overzealous about saving the taxpayers' money or revealing how much

---

[5] A. Ernest Fitzgerald, *The High Priests of Waste* (New York: W. W. Norton & Co., 1972).

was going down the drain. It was not the civilian and military brass, however, but the Keynesian economists who won Fitzgerald's accolade as the "high priests of waste."

Much of the problem Fitzgerald fought so hard to correct could be attributed to a comparatively modest application of the surgery he prescribed. The Pentagon had indeed cancelled many programs, sometimes resulting in mass unemployment. Among the major contracts cancelled shortly before or during Fitzgerald's unsuccessful crusade was the North American Navajo missile, the Douglas Skybolt missile, Boeing's Dynasoar, Martin's big jet seaplane, and, by degrees, North American's B–70. Each of these cancellations triggered secondary job losses among subcontractors. Meanwhile, every serious contender for new defense contracts faced an employment crisis if its bid were rejected because they had to hire enough engineers before the award was made to prove they could perform if they won it. This process was called "stockpiling engineers," a term which owes much to the commodity theory of labor. The losers then had to dump a portion of their "inventory" of engineers. Fitzgerald betrays scant awareness that these policies caused virtually the whole technostructure to maintain excessive overhead staff, a process which got completely out of the control of either top management in industry or the Pentagon. Overjobbing was indeed an "inexorable trend," but of bureaucracy, not economics.

From Fitzgerald's viewpoint it looked as if the government deliberately encouraged aerospace to pad its payrolls. But from the point of view of many aerospace engineers and other employees, the Pentagon was a capricious customer indeed. Reacting to Russia's launch of Sputnik in 1957, the government had urged, even semibribed, young people to study engineering and to undertake careers in the aerospace industry. But career opportunities proved hollow, since most engineers were tied to projects which meant their jobs were lost if the project was cancelled. Some were recruited into projects just before cancellation. Many bewildered victims of such fast shuffles felt as if they had been treated as so much civilian cannon fodder.

In short, government policy achieved the worst of two worlds. On the one hand the Pentagon procurement policy encouraged padded payrolls and all the resultant varieties of waste. Military and civilian defense officials supported a policy of Keynesian make-work, and the Pentagon resisted serious efforts to bring aerospace costs under control. On the other hand, the only cost-reduction alternative the Pentagon would consider was the meat axe. Indeed, the hire-fire cycle was de facto extended well into management ranks. As cost overruns routinely exceeded even the most generous allowances for inefficiency, expenditures continually threatened to exceed the budget. Thus the Pentagon had to swing the axe, even if reluctantly, against programs that became hopelessly bogged down or politically vulnerable, but with each swing the mechanism to hire more staff received an additional shot of adrenalin. Thus institutionalized incompetence eventually strangled the aerospace industry.

## A MEASURE OF COST INFLATION

A good measure of cost inflation for airplanes which actually fly more or less as designed comes from Boeing. In 1952, Boeing took a highly publicized gamble. The company spent $15 million of its own money to design and build the prototype 707, often called the "dash 80." Boeing's pamphlet entitled "The Plane That Jack Built" extolled the glories of risk capital and private enterprise as a creator of "more jobs" and "better living" ("Jack," of course, refers to money). Boeing put together a small team of engineers which designed the 707 prototype that was to fly two years later.

By 1967, 15 years later, Boeing's engineering staff had undergone enormous distension. Out of curiosity, a Boeing financial analyst computed the cost of designing and building exactly the same 707 prototype. Applying standard cost estimating procedures then in use, he concluded it would cost $500 million to design and build the 707 prototype at that time. Not a better airplane, mind you, but exactly the same one.

Of course, some inflation of costs could be expected between 1952 and 1967. It can also be argued that the initial $15 million at risk did not fully reflect actual costs, since Boeing used some Air Force-owned facilities, and other overhead costs may have been "creatively" charged to the B-52 program, then in full swing. Indeed, expressed in 1967 dollars and with due allowance for bookkeeping derring-do, perhaps $50 million, not $15 million, would be a better figure for the prototype 707. At that, Boeing's constant-dollar costs would have inflated ten times, a full order of magnitude, as they say in aerospace. Of course, all this cost increase could not be attributed solely to Boeing, since the company subcontracts much of its work. Forces at large in the aerospace industry generally also influenced Boeing. Boeing was no worse, and perhaps not so bad, as the industry average.

Embittered blue-collar workers played a relatively minor role in these cost increases. Embittered they may have been, but they also were not very well organized in terms of trade union political strength. Boeing had broken a major strike in the early postwar period. Management, to its credit, had firmly resisted the incursion of damaging restrictive practices on the shop floor. It was management's own restrictive practices that were overlooked.

## THE ANATOMY OF OVERJOBBING

In 1963, when the SST began to receive government funding, it became clear that the cost of fuel would be extremely important. The price of jet fuel at the time was about 12 cents a gallon. If the cost of jet fuel declined in the future, SST operating costs would not look quite so bad.

In no way can one "prove" anything at all about fuel costs 10 years hence. One could, however, say without too much danger that the constant-dollar price will not change much, assuming this happens and that does not. Or you can bureaucratically observe that fuel cost forecasts involve some tricky economic questions. All sorts of variables, such as the supply of crude, the demand for other fuels and the state of future production technology, influence fuel costs. You can suggest that with a group of econometricians, statisticians, a computer programmer or two, and perhaps a specialist on fuel prices you could, in six months or so, reach a "definitive answer" to the question of fuel costs in ten years. With voluminous documentation, you could then show that, assuming this does and that does not happen, jet fuel ten years hence will have the same constant price as today. With the aid of perhaps hundreds of thousands of dollars spent on staff and equipment, you would reach the same conclusion you could have arrived at alone.

The go-ahead to "staff up" might have been on the premise that "a definitive study could well support an 11-cent instead of a 12-cent price." (This is hardly likely in the light of developments in foreign oil sources, however.) Such a contention could easily be documented by burying a crucial, if perhaps sporty, assumption to this effect somewhere deep in the footnotes. The bureaucrat in charge of this program would have succeeded in spending several hundred times as much money as necessary to "support" a shaky assumption. He will gain status as a group leader and probably merit a promotion. He will acquire a reputation for coming up with the right answers, and until the bubble bursts, he will do well.

The staff member who would avoid such activities in order to economize on human resources threatens the innards of the organization or technostructure. He spoils everybody's game and threatens people's social needs. Much "surplus" manpower exists, and things must be found for them to do or they have to be fired. If they are fired, their superiors can command a less exalted job rank. Everybody but the enterprise itself loses by economizing on human resources.

As part of the bureaucratic social order, the aerospace industry is subject to bureaucracy's insistence on the buyer-seller relationship for labor, which establishes the predatory relationship between seniors and subordinates. The junior staff "sells" the superior staff on the notion that "we need more people." Everybody sells everybody else on the vast complexities of every problem. In presentations to management the staff prepares elaborate "viewgraph shows" (a high aerospace art form). These presentations normally raise more questions than they answer. The "fine grain research" they call for requires even "more people," and the more exotic their education the higher their salary.

The motive is simple enough. To be promoted, the BSO insists, you must prove "more management responsibility." Freely translated, more responsibility means a greater subordinate headcount. The more educated the headcount, the greater the responsibility implied. Those swings of the meat axe can slice uncomfortably close, so the more "fat" you layer in between yourself and the meat axe, the safer you are.

In playing this game, you must keep the law of diminishing returns locked in your desk. Diminishing returns works this way. With an expenditure, say, of ten units of man-hours you can acquire a 50 percent answer. If you go to 20 units you may come up with a 60 percent answer. A 50-unit input may buy you a 70 percent answer, and 500 units a 75 percent answer. The answer improves very slowly, while the man-hour investment rises so rapidly that more man-hours gain little. Indeed, more man-hours may even decrease the quality of your answer. The curve could start bending backward and often does.

## PREDATORS AND PREY

If you are selling airplanes to a customer, you obviously do not enlarge on your uncertainty of the future. Instead, as your predatory instincts come to the fore, you attempt to convince your "prey" that he must have your airplanes if he does not want to run short of capacity in the future. You bait your trap with every argument you can think of. You need not actually lie, since neither you nor your customer has any way of proving what the future will bring. All the computers and all the statisticians together can prove nothing about future demand. They can marshal evidence and make assumptions, compute trends in clever ways, and perform all sorts of statistical tricks which purport to show this or that, but no one knows the future. You *can* say, to some extent, "if this, then that."

Like your hominid ancestors, you try for the "kill," you go for the sale. You marshal all the arguments of analysis to show your customer why he will need your planes. Your "prey," meanwhile, exercises his own predatory talents trying to beat down your price, get extra engineering effort for nothing, or perhaps gain a more favorable delivery position than his competitor.

Just as overanalysis can be useful in baiting customer-prey, subordinates use overanalysis in baiting their superior prey. The skilled bureaucratic politician can invent fake jobs and phony units at the drop of a casual question. He must be clever of course, and wait for the upswing. In aerospace, an important social better, perhaps a vice president, might ask a subordinate "What effect do you suppose the government's. proposal to cut back on airport expenditures will have on our airplane sales?" The subordinate might answer, "That's sure a good question and one we'd better look into." He does not say then and there that to look into airport expenditures would require hiring some more people. Instead he dragoons every spare body into his office and announces a crisis. "The V.P. has to know as soon as possible what the effect on our sales will be if the government cuts back on airport expenditures. Important meeting in Washington. The company has to take a position."

The staff is pumped up and plunges into the project. For the next week it does little else but exercise the airport problem. An impressive viewgraph show is produced under pressure. Bleary-eyed, the subordinate gives his pitch to the vice president. He reviews reams of charts and graphs, noting that the available data are only suggestive of the problem. The answer that could survive congressional scrutiny and convince the Bureau of the Budget, he says, requires a complex methodology. He "needs" an input-output matrix model of the economy. The V.P., an engineer, has never heard of such a model, but he's impressed. The subordinate clearly has shown initiative and drive. So the V.P. asks, "What's required to explore this further?" The subordinate answers that he can keep this project on a "back burner," but other things piled up while his staff was preparing this "quick and dirty" answer and it would be some time before he could free anyone to do much more. "We don't have many people to spare since the last cutback," he says. Then he baits his hook: "I'm not really in a position to decide priority on this. I know some of our customers are worried, but maybe the "fine-grain" look really wouldn't be worth our while. It would cost quite a bit, and frankly we don't have all the right professional skills for this project. Besides, maybe the airport funds will be restored by Congress if enough airlines complain. On the other hand. . . ."

Pity the poor vice president. He knows the subordinate has explained to some of the customers what he was up to because he got some of his data from them. They may think the company is going to produce some first-class support for their position. Thus the V.P. has to consider customer goodwill. He also must remember that he himself initiated the study and that the preliminary findings suggest a problem. Yet the subordinate does not appear to be pushing anything, just doing a fine job. He doesn't even appear too eager to go farther. Word of his efforts has gotten around, however, and the problem has received "visibility."

If the V.P. does not order further study and something happens later, his explanation that it did not seem worthwhile will sound pretty shallow.

The subordinate gently sets the hook by casually noting that the V.P. might be able to use some of the subroutines from the new methodology in his customer operations group. ("One of the ops analysis boys is really quite enthusiastic, but I have not really had time to check this out.") The V.P. thinks positively: "If it could help our sales effort and customer goodwill both, why not?" So he says, "Look here, why don't you put together a plan explaining just what this will involve, manpower-wise, how long it will take, and the fallout benefits to us. Can you do it by next Monday?" The subordinate promises to do his best. He has such a plan all drawn up, but he has a nice weekend and waits until Monday to deliver it.

In drawing up his plan the subordinate carefully designated each type of specialist as narrowly as possible, deciding he has places for a couple of macroeconomists, an econometrician, two statisticians, a pure mathematician, a computer programmer, and a cost accountant. He leaves out the clerks, to keep his headcount down. He has more than made up for the two people he lost in the last cutback, and the vice president "ordered" it.

The subordinate need not admit, even to himself, that he has already learned as much about airports as can do the company any good. He need not acknowledge that the end calculation, even honestly computed, will be swamped by the estimating error in the basic data. He has only followed his predatory instincts to ensure his own survival; the company has not only invited him to prey on it, it virtually commanded him to do so. The company activated the predator versus prey relationship when it used the meat axe. As some recent victims learned, a pat on the back is only inches from a kick out the door. Maneuvering his headcount up not only helps insulate the subordinate from the meat axe next time, it also helps in getting him a promotion.

In a large corporation the above instance by itself might be trivial. But multiply this instance (a composite of several I've observed) many times, as in the aerospace industry, and overhead costs go wild. The new employees, no matter how talented, come to be described as "fat" and "deadwood." But note who hired them. A V.P. who was not stupid, but was maneuvered by a talented, even brilliant subordinate. Note also that the acquisition of "fat" did not come from getting soft. The brainy subordinate had to work hard and exercise good judgment in terms of his goals in order to increase his headcount and thus his prestige. The enterprise's own policies created a senseless conflict between employee ambitions and its own financial health.

## TRAPPED IN THE BOONDOGGLES

Maneuvers such as those described above are rarely conducted with cold-blooded cynicism. As anyone trapped in a boondoggle often discovers, somebody can always identify with it and thus come to believe in it. Boondoggles do not preclude professionally interesting questions. What might be a boondoggle in one context could be a brilliant piece of staff work in another. But once identity and status attach to an activity, be it a useful project, questionable study, or outright boondoggle, people will defend them indiscriminately. An iron law of nature precludes complete objectivity about our own identity and status. If a boondoggle comprises our status "territory," our defense of it may be no different than if it were a clearly useful project. The greater our responsibility for the success of any project, the less likely are we to evaluate it objectively.

As we have noted, a rigorous law of diminishing returns applies to staff work. After a point each additional unit of staff work, even if of uniform brilliance, will cost more and render less utility. Later, each additional unit of work may even reduce net utility. The study in the file cabinet thus becomes the needle in the haystack. In yonder mountain of staff studies, who knows where lies the key study that would be both useful and timely?

Moreover, bureaucratic layers cut the working-level analyst off from direct personal knowledge of what the decision makers really need to know. Lack of personal contact lends an "ivory tower" character to staff studies. In a crisis, top management routinely violates its chain of command to cut through these levels and deal directly with ad hoc study teams. This often leaves the rest of the staff conducting exercises in futility, politicking, or even conducting a second business from their desks. I have often witnessed flourishing part-time consulting businesses, real estate operations, free-lance writing, investment pools, and so on occupying the time of underemployed staff. But these underemployed were not robbing the company; it could not effectively use them all the time. Their alternative would be to grind out more unread documents and thus decrease further the average utility of staff output by enlarging the haystack.

Social distance decreases the quality of staff work. The more administrative layers that separate the analyst from the decision-maker, the more will controversial material be suppressed to protect the interests of the intermediate administrative officials. Extreme social distance can devastate morale at the working level. Social insult based on social inferiority is often made worse with an inversion of both education and professional experience. Experienced Ph.D.'s might have to have their professional output "approved" or "vetoed" by several "senior" levels occupied by those with less professional education or experience. To understand the reaction this can produce, imagine a physician whose diagnosis of a patient must be approved by both the hospital accountant and food service manager. Furthermore, all his dealings with the patient must occur through these two intermediaries (and perhaps others). All have "authority" to force him to change his diagnosis. The physician's diagnosis must fit whatever medical notions the accountant might harbor and what he regards as a diagnosis acceptable to the patient. This may sound bizarre, but in aerospace this sort of filtering happens all the time.

Why don't people in such a situation just quit? They often do. In late 1971, Boeing's then president, T. A. Wilson, complained on television that the company had to hire 66,000 people in the 1966 buildup just to keep 25,000, most of whom were fired not many months later. One business magazine even described such nonsense as "superb management."

I once worked in a staff unit of about 150 people organized along these "advanced management" lines. Virtually everyone had a college degree and perhaps half or more had advanced degrees, including several doctorates. Our group had been structured into a seven-layered bureaucracy. (A World War II American Army division, never known as a model of streamlined administration, managed with the same number of administrative levels for 18,000 men.) Our group had an "input" of about 300,000 man-hours per year, which cost something over $2,000,000 in wages alone. If the company got $250,000 worth of useful work out of this group, it did well. Possibly half the man-hour input went down the drain on projects started and then cancelled, due to one internal reorganization after another. The reorganizations never reduced the number of levels, however. Another quarter of the input spun off as internal political intrigue, as people kept trying to maneuver themselves to a higher level in the hierarchy. They wanted to catch an occasional breath of professional fresh air. Perhaps a quarter of the man-hour input consisted of useful output or unavoidable slack time. Thus can bureaucracy absorb internally most of the resources committed to it.

## THE PITFALLS OF PROFESSIONALIZATION

In the early 60s recruiting ads for the aerospace industry stressed the dominance of engineers and engineering. The profession had arrived and gained full control, and the professional development of the new engineer was expected to count for much. His work would be safe from lay interference. Engineers would decide engineering matters top to bottom; indeed, they would decide everything, inside the profession and out. What's more, engineers would do just about everything. The profession was subdivided much beyond its usual components, such as civil, chemical, mechanical, electrical, and aeronautical, into esoteric subspecialties. As engineers took over many functions, such titles as purchasing engineer, personnel engineer, sales engineer, marketing engineer, facilities engineer, planning engineer, cost engineer, and schedules engineer sprung up.

The day of the engineer had truly arrived. But the profession promptly began engineering enormous social distance between its own top and bottom ranks. As the majesty of management enobled some, it separated them from those grubbing at the bottom. Social inferiors thus did the actual professional work, which seriously undermined professional judgment. Systematically the professional work was unenriched and narrowed. Complex-sounding sub-subspecialties did not actually involve more skills; these engineers merely fell into the trap of knowing more and more about less and less. Sometimes such narrowing sorted out important problems and expanded the state of the art, but typically narrowing the scope of the job merely created dull routinization of work. Learning everything about the head of a pin may challenge the intellect more than learning about the solar system, but this will largely depend on what you need for the purposes at hand. Engineering philosophy in the American aerospace industry took the view that you should know practically everything about something, never mind the purpose. Few people would concede that they already knew as much as was needed, and further effort would cost too much money.

This philosophy triggered severe cost inflation, as the cost of engineering design changes became almost prohibitive. Now, as some engineers never tire of stating, an airplane or a missile is a "system." Systems have several properties, and a change in one part of the system has consequences for all other parts. A new profession, called systems analysis, has arisen to deal with this fact. In truth, the principle holds for birch bark canoes, an outboard boat, a horse and rider, or an Eskimo dogsled team. All are "systems," as much as a B–70 or TFX. A change in any part has consequences for every other part throughout the system.

But then, some changes have practical effects, whereas many do not. The systems analyst in the aerospace tradition will caution that unless you make the necessary calculations, you cannot be sure about the effects of changes. Neither can you know the impact on No. 4 dog if you add an extra inch of frozen mud runner to the left side of your dogsled unless you make all the engineering calculations. But the question of whether such calculations are worth making leaves a good deal of room for professional common sense. If making such calculations improves your job security and promotion prospects, however, you will always go ahead and make them. Social needs take precedence over common sense. The engineer can always effectively silence the lay critic by the casual observation that "he's not an engineer" and thus chase off a territorial intruder.

Engineers soon discovered the job-expansion potential of the systems concept. Under the systems approach, when an airplane is designed all the engineering calculations are made. Whenever an engineering change is suggested, all the same calculations are made again. Common sense is suspended in the policy of recalculating the whole design to accommodate even minor changes. The twin claims of "systems reliability" and "safety" silence the skeptics. This type of systems approach explains much of the enormous cost inflation in new aircraft designs.

We taxpayers can thank the Pentagon for this "systems" breakthrough. The systems approach promised a new level of weapons reliability. It might be more costly, granted, but the extra margin of reliability would be worth it. What has happened to bomber reliability since the bureaucratization of the systems concept? The first coup was the WS–110A, Weapons Systems 110A, known today as the B–70. After billions of dollars, two were built, one crashed, and the other was grounded. Next came the TFX—enough said. Now the North American B–1 aims to "replace" all these. Success seems as distant today for a workable B–52 replacement as it was in 1957, when the WS–110A contract first went to North American.

In principle, a systems approach to a design problem is perfectly sound. I do not disparage the principle itself but the corruption of the concept to create bureaucratic incentives for overjobbing, which grossly inflates costs. And as the history of the bomber seems to attest, systems reliability is also lost. The day of the bomber may well have passed; I leave that argument to others. But in 20 years we have been unable to design a reliable alternative to the B–52, though we spent untold billions in the effort.

When sales are high, profits are washing in, and the company is enjoying enormous prestige, the one who criticizes overjobbing appears to be a malcontent and troublemaker. Even critics find it hard to resist the notion that complexity somehow obscures the payoff. Surely higher management, in its wisdom, must know what it is doing. How can you quarrel with success? But the success is sometimes ephemeral. About 75 percent of the aerospace management and professional staff man-hours I witnessed was avoidable waste. Waste varies with the circumstances, of course. In aerospace, the wasted efforts could be classified as (1) unusable effort, (2) unnecessary effort in whole or part, (3) internal politics, and (4) make-work or busy work.

This judgment is reinforced by Dassault's expressed policy of using engineering generalists rather than specialists. Jonathan Randal notes that Dassault "uses few engineers in any given process—a few dozen compared to hundreds employed by American firms."[6] Dassault's Mystere and Mirage series have compared favorably with the world's best jet fighters.

When the bubbles finally began to burst in the U.S. aerospace industry, hundreds of thousands of people lost their jobs. The lives of many were ruined. Many aerospace engineers, overly specialized, may never find engineering work again.

## ASSESSING THE BLAME

Attempting to assess individual responsibility for aerospace catastrophes accomplishes nothing but to deflect attention from a dreadful systems problem. I also suspect that we waste time dwelling too much on such factors as Pentagon purchasing procedures and control mechanisms which need reform but are mainly offshoots of the bureaucratic social order. As we have noted, the BSO thrives on proceduralistic red tape for its job spawning. Such operational techniques as PERT, PACE, PPB, and CPM will help or hurt, depending on the social order. None substitute for teamwork. Where individual and group incentives line up "naturally" to achieve optimum enterprise performance, such procedures can be useful, but they fail if enterprise incentives discourage teamwork.

The number and distribution of the aerospace fiascos, large and small, of new technology and old, clearly suggest problems far beyond individual incompetence. I must admit that in the early days my favorite devil was Robert McNamara, particularly for his personal, disastrous intervention in the TFX program and his heroic unwillingness to concede the human factor as relevant in human enterprise. But McNamara was merely a famous advocate of a philosophy he did not invent.

The decline of the "humans relations school" in business reflected its failure to get past initial insights. The famous Hawthorne Works experiments at Western Electric's bank wiring room first developed experimental evidence of the importance to productivity of small work groups. Human relations experts thereafter occupied a prominent place for over 20 years, yet they went little beyond the "case study" method, seeming to resist useful rules, policies, or principles. They discovered fraternity at the Hawthorne Works, but they never articulated its principles.

Because the human relations school failed to differentiate between bureaucracy and fraternity in the social order, it acquired a reputation

---

[6] Jonathan C. Randal, "By Hard Work to the Skies," *The Washington Post,* April 1970.

for unworkable "do-goodism." Its advocates did not challenge bureaucracy's social order or suggest alternatives. It does little good to urge managers to be "people-minded" without a set of workable guidelines, and we should not be surprised that in the computer era the BSO's emphasis on the impersonal-rational-technical side of the enterprise acquired new respectability.

The human relations school fell back on a "mystique" of insights reached by studying "deeply" each "complex" case on its own. I have since concluded these were code words meaning "I don't know what is happening." The closest anyone in the human relations school came to articulating human relations principles was Douglas McGregor, who postulated two types of organizations, Theory X and Theory Y.[7] Theory Y, the employee-centered model, roughly describes fraternity, while Theory X, the work-centered model, approximates bureaucracy. Had he not met an untimely death I suspect McGregor might have tied in his Theory Y humanism with the new biology. Unfortunately, McGregor had no way to relate Theory Y with the evidence that teamwork evolved biologically to promote cooperative hunting.

## INDIVIDUAL PERFORMANCE

Any enterprise must judge the competence of individuals to perform assigned tasks. Inevitably placement judgments will be made, yet the individual commits no sin if he is misplaced. He cannot help it if his abilities do not match the demands of a particular job. The bureaucratic social order, punishes the individual for its own mistake in job placement. ("Sorry, John, but you've just not measured up to our expectations. We've had a number of bad reports on your work. Frankly we've got to let you go. . . .")

If a person performs poorly on a job he should be taken off it. Nothing can seize up an enterprise more quickly than safeguards of due process and a presumption of competence until "proven" incompetent. Reasonable suspicion of inability alone should suffice for removal from a job. But this does not hold for employment. ("General Patton, that slapping incident has caused us great embarrassment. You are hereby relieved of command. You will report to London for reassignment.")

Reasonable doubt exists that Patton should have been relieved of command, but if a mistake was made it was not compounded by banishment. Eisenhower merely relieved Patton of one assignment; he was not "fired" from the Army. Sometimes bureaucracies do the same thing, in which case they violate their own tenets and behave less

---

[7] Douglas McGregor, *The Human Side of Enterprise* (New York: McGraw-Hill Book Co., 1960).

bureaucratically. Indeed, when a bureaucracy performs well it usually does so by violating or ignoring the premises of its own social order. ("Look, John, we goofed in putting you where we did. I don't think that slot is your cup of tea. What would you say if we transferred you to scheduling? Same money, of course.") This more paternalistic approach typifies many enterprises. But in the fraternal organization it would not even have to come to a formal acknowledgment of error. ("Say, John, scheduling needs some beefing up next week, so could you and George go over and help out for a while?") More likely, though, in the fraternal enterprise structured around hunting-band-sized work teams, John would never have been misplaced in the first instance.

In aerospace the misplaced individual was hardly the most serious problem. Far worse were the system effects: overstaffing, suppression of information about technical difficulties, overoptimistic forecasts, wage rigidity which prevented the use of reserves, the firing of well-trained people on the downswing only to hire untrained people on the upswing. Reverse synergism characterized aerospace—the B-70 was a good deal less than the sum of its parts, for example. But in the end talent, energy, and brains were required to engineer the multiple aerospace catastrophes. Indolence, sloth, and stupidity could never have brought off such master-pieces of mismanagement.

## THE CULTURAL HERITAGE OF U.S. ENTERPRISE

Probably no country has deeper Calvinist roots than Scotland. Yet the work-minded, frugal Scots can turn into the most profligate wasters of production in Europe under the immediate influence of the bureaucratic social order. Similarly, America, a culture dedicated to efficiency and with a history of engineering genius, can likewise see much of what it values destroyed by the BSO. Like the British, Americans have had to develop a sort of schizoid view in order to rationalize the tyrannical features of bureaucracy with our broader cultural ideals of "liberty, equality, and fraternity."

Americans tend to rationalize bureaucratic tyranny in terms of our cultural ideals of efficiency and hard work, which we regard as ends in themselves. Our pioneering heritage gave these values an added practical utility. But Americans no longer comprise a nation of small farmers, merchants, and artisans. The rise of big business and government at first could draw on our values of efficiency and our love of new technology. With the spread of bureaucracy came the clash with our humane values.

One myth imposed by the "experts" is that bureaucratization is necessary to coordinate large-scale enterprises. Sustaining this was another myth, that social values do not intrude into the impersonal-rational-technical world of work. Hardly anyone now argues this, but the legacy remains. We instead argue that the social values should not intrude, because they threaten rationality. While admitting the existence of social forces in the world of work, we tend to think of them as irrational and hence bad. We love efficiency, and efficiency demands rationality. Since only the BSO can be rational, bureaucratic tyranny has become a "cultural value." We play down the fact that the BSO tramples liberty, equality, and fraternity and stress instead "consumer sovereignty."

To suggest fraternity in American enterprise often triggers a conditioned reflex: "But that won't work, it would be contrary to our cultural values." Thus we confront a paradox. Having fought the Revolutionary War to escape from largely economic tyranny, our bloody Civil War to eliminate slavery (another form of economic tyranny), and several foreign wars to stop the spread of tyranny (at least we thought so at the time), we now argue that we *must* impose economic tyranny on ourselves. The BSO has driven us to the brink of economic ruin in the name of an efficiency which it does not have and never has had. Such is the power of a myth.

The example of the nearly bankrupt aerospace industry highlights our problem. Aerospace bureaucracy has abused its consumers as badly as its employees, and the American taxpayer has been had. We would face an agonizing dilemma if our interests as employees and consumers were really in serious conflict.

We can, however, strike an entirely satisfactory balance between the demands of production and consumption. The self-imposed, short-run conflicts between "efficiency" and "security" within the BSO arise largely from semantic confusion. We muddle the concepts of "employment" and "utilitization," thus inhibiting the formation of manpower reserves which belong to the enterprise. Both in our hunting and our more recent agricultural past we allowed for manpower reserves. No army that failed to distinguish the difference between "employment" and "utilization" by creating rotational reserve forces would survive combat. With enterprise reserves, the income of all would fluctuate with the revenue of the enterprise on some prearranged basis. Bureaucracy fails to tie individual income to collective revenue. Rather, it gives individuals a prior claim on the resources of the enterprise, independent of its performances in acquiring resources.

The notion that our fortunes should rise or fall with our particular enterprise, individual or collective, is well entrenched. I do not refer to the entire economy of a nation-state as an enterprise, but to the particular enterprise which collects the revenue and issues paychecks. Nor do I mean profit sharing. It is useful to separate the returns to capital (private or social) from returns to labor (all employees) in an enterprise. Wages should fluctuate with revenue, not profits. For one thing, profits are subject to arbitrary definition and bookkeeping manipulation. Revenue enjoys a much more clear-cut status. Of course, nonlabor costs must enter the formulation in determining labor's share of revenue, depending on the nature of the enterprise. I have included an example of how such a formula might work in Chapter 10.

The point is that the financial fortunes of the individual and his enterprise should be linked. A wage-revenue link centers individual attention on the whole, not the parts. It takes no equity interest to forge a bond of identity between the enterprise and the individual. Workers can do without equity in the enterprise if they participate fraternally (which does not necessarily mean equally) in a share of revenue. But a prior claim on revenue based on the importance of their particular jobs will shift identity from the whole enterprise to the particular job. Teamwork then falters.

Failing to link the individual's income with that of the enterprise encourages use of the hire-fire cycle as a cost control device. It would be difficult to devise a more cruel device for the victims, or one more damaging to the enterprise's long-run chance for survival. Fixed wage rates leave little option in the short run. Given a downturn, the bureaucracy has little choice but to "commence firing." This is a system-imposed requirement for the hire-fire cycle reflecting neither genetic needs nor cultural values. The hire-fire cycle is a "tradition" that is justified by false premises. As farmers and small businessmen have always known, when times get rough, you do not toss out the kids; everyone tightens their belts.

The aerospace industry inherited the unworkable propositions of the bureaucratic social order. In the decade of the 60s U.S. aerospace was part of a massive defense industry that spawned more technical debacles and financial disasters than in any similar period in history. Yet this industry was the largest, most lavishly financed defense industry that has ever existed. It employed more highly educated scientists, engineers, and other college graduates than any other industry ever has. Indeed, a significant proportion of all the graduate engineers to this point worked in the U.S. defense industry during the 60s. Yet, with all these human and financial inputs, the industry failed to design and build a single successful new bomber, fighter, tank, or even naval destroyer. Such is the awesome power of bureaucracy.

# 7

# The Civil Service of
# Los Dineros Campos

## THE BSO IN THE THIRD WORLD

No portion of the earth suffers more from bureaucracy than the Third World of developing nations. In many such countries the civil service, in the grip of bureaucracy, strangles economic development. The terminal symptoms of bureaucracy will be explored in discussing the civil service of "Los Dineros Campos," a composite of several countries whose Latin name reflects only ease in using the letters LDC, the common abbreviation for less developed countries. I will relate situations that are accurate in themselves but in which the circumstances have been disguised. I could also use a single actual country as a case study, but this would draw attention to that nation's leaders and particular circumstances and deflect it from the pathology of the bureaucratic social order. Thus I will use examples from several developing nations, largely drawn from personal observations, as I did with the British shop floor and American aerospace.

Not every less developed country suffers from a hopeless civil service, but most do. Generally bureaucracy's debilities are getting worse, not better, in these nations. Some, such as India, Pakistan, and the Philippines, started out with reasonably effective civil services only to see them slowly decay. The most obvious symptom of terminal bureaucratic illness in a civil service is rampant corruption.

## THE KEYNESIAN MYSTIQUE OF PUBLIC WORKS

A good deal of damage has been done to development economic theory by Keynesian economics. Though John Maynard Keynes died before Third World development problems had become an economic issue, he fathered modern macroeconomic analysis. To look at the "big picture" (usually an entire economy), a macroeconomist must make many assumptions about it. A crucial macroeconomic assumption has drifted into the land of unreality in the past few decades—the assumption of a high average efficiency in the human enterprises which do the world's work. It is assumed that institutions perform about as efficiently as technology and capital investment allow. As this book attempts to show, in the bureaucratic institution or enterprise efficiency cannot safely be assumed. The analysis and answers the macroeconomists offer systematically lead us astray.[1]

This same false assumption led to President Nixon's delay in revising his economic policies until events forced him to impose a wage and price freeze to introduce his "new economic plan." Neither has Britain solved her institutional problems with macroeconomic advice. But if the results in Britain and America have been bad, such false assumptions have been disastrous in the Third World.

Keynes correctly identified the importance of new investment in recovery from a slump of the business cycle. A dollar of new investment turns over more often and passes through more hands than does ordinary consumer spending. This insight accorded enormous importance to a government as the manager of an economy. In theory, by spending (investing in public works for practical purposes) in a downswing, the government could moderate the effect of a slump.

The damage done to the Third World came from the mystique which public works thus acquired. The notion spread that a nation could spend its way out of any problem, economic or social. Thrift acquired something of a bad name. It was maintained that once new roads, dams, ports, schools, hospitals, public housing projects, and so on had built up a base of "social overhead capital," economic growth, as measured by per capita GNP, would automatically zoom upward.

The human factor in enterprise efficiency was lost sight of, and only dollars counted. Development economists were annoyed if it was pointed out that the institutions which managed these investments systematically wasted their resources. They hid behind the multiplier effect, the number of times the money turns over. If Keynes could advocate digging up gold from the ground, then digging a new hole and burying it again, why complain about financing a road which washed away in the next year's rain from lack of maintenance?

Evidence of systematic institutional inefficiency makes the macro-

---

[1] This argument has been earlier developed in a series of three articles from *Bangkok World:* "Myrdal's Missing Message, Part I," October 8, 1969; "Part II, Teamwork, Japan's Secret Economic Weapon," October 15, 1969; and "Part III Zaibatsu, Engine of Japanese Industrial Expansion," October 22, 1969.

144

economist nervous when it threatens his job. This is particularly true of government enterprise, since the government is by all odds the most important customer for the statistical services and analysis the Keynesian macroeconomist merchandises. Therefore, the macroeconomist will have social inhibitions about facing the institutional world squarely, though he may privately deplore the waste he sees. If outsiders criticize his statistical projections, he becomes the territorial animal in defense of his status as he reinforces his pretensions of "rational economic planning." In truth, his formidable array of analytical tools for determining the goings-on in the big picture proves nearly worthless in sorting out institutional problems.

Confronted with a dilemma of intellectual honesty versus innate social needs, it takes considerable ingenuity to rationalize away so much evidence of waste. The macroeconomists toil relentlessly at a statistical methodology with no chance of useful application. Still a vigorous market for their output exists in the Third World. Almost in direct proportion to the failures of public works investments, the demand grows for economic feasibility studies to justify them. The greater the failure rate, the more clever must be the method which "finds" such waste economically feasible. I knew a chap who was discouraged that field observations made for many months could detect almost no actual traffic over a vast network of new roads. He contrived a statistical explanation "proving" the traffic "might" exist, thus justifying the road network. His thesis was that if the actual observers were systematically in all the wrong places at all the wrong times, traffic really might be substantial.

Thus part of the economic problems of the Third World stems from years of systematically bad advice from the developed nations, European and American. Gunnar Myrdal first noted this in 1968 in *Asian Drama,* a tome of 2,222 pages.[2] Myrdal made a plea for economists to revive institutional analysis with a convincing argument that pending institutional reform, most of the less developed countries would continue to deteriorate.

## THE CIVIL SERVICE AS A POLITICAL POWER

The civil service which governs LDC differs little structurally from America's. It does, however, have a number of government-owned operations, such as ports, railroads, an oil monopoly, and public utilities. Once profitable, they now mostly lose money or just break even. One turns a slight surplus of less than 1 percent on invested capital.

Three things become instantly apparent to the official visitor to LDC. First, every government office will be vastly overstaffed, and there will

---

[2] Gunnar Myrdal, *Asian Drama* (New York: Pantheon Books, 1968).

be an elaborate network of red tape to give everyone the facade of a job. Second, nothing gets processed through this obstacle course without a bribe, and almost any regulation can be violated if an appropriate bribe is paid. Third, civil service salaries are the functional equivalent of nothing.

The only political force in LDC which counts for much is the civil service itself, the result of a "bureaucratic polity," in the words of F. W. Riggs.[3] But the military actually dominates the civil service. Most of the important jobs in the civil service go to military leaders. Within the civil service competitive political factions usually divide along departmental lines. Political parties do not represent political power outside the government; the party in control of the government has all the power. But the government party frequently splits into factions feuding over power: the budget, functions, and foreign aid.

The government can be fairly described as a government of the bureaucracy, by the bureaucracy, and for the bureaucracy. The public serves the bureaucracy as a legitimizing facade. In the name of serving the public, the civil service actually does a fairly efficient job of plundering it. The plunder comes from many sources: bribes for services rendered, perhaps for the recovery of stolen property, putting out a fire, admission to a school, spotting a railroad boxcar, clearing goods through customs, or issuing a driver's license. With bribes, it is possible to overload trucks, smuggle goods in, cut timber illegally, and avoid normal taxes (a percentage of the tax is paid as a bribe). Construction and other government contracts are impossible without a substantial kickback, but the bribe can be recovered without too much trouble by using inferior materials. Inferior quality also finances the comparatively modest bribes paid to construction inspectors.

## PREDATORS AND PREY: CIVIL SERVANTS AND PEASANTS

Some of this plunder does include an element of exchange, or symbiosis. The bribe payer gets his goods out of customs, his driver's license, the contract, and so on. Graft can be thought of as a sort of tip. But if you are a peasant in the land of LDC (which is likely, since the country is still 70 percent agricultural), corruption acquires a coercive flavor. The police periodically relieve you of any burdensome excess of cattle, pigs, or chickens, in their view. You cannot prove the police actually did the stealing, but when you report the theft to the police nothing happens. If you offer a reward in exchange for "special" service, you may recover your stolen animals that very day, perhaps on the spot.

---

[3] F. W. Riggs, *Thailand—The Modernization of a Bureaucratic Polity* (Honolulu: East-West Press, 1966).

Come harvest season, the "gift" of a share of your harvest to the local province administrator saves you no end of petty harassment throughout the year. A small army of "civil servants" lives in the nearby provincial capital. They come from departments such as agriculture, irrigation, health, education, welfare, highways, and even labor to extend the benevolent hand of government services. But, alas, it is you who seems always to serve them. Whether they simply show up at meal time and expect to be fed, walk off with a chicken, or take liberties with your daughter, you do the serving.

You don't even understand the term "civil servant." Translated literally, the title is like calling the jailer a prisoner. Your own slang expression for police and government officials is "land eater." Traditionally officials are just another of nature's predators. You do not see them often, but like jackals they strike swiftly and make off with your property.

When the communists showed up, they said corruption was wrong and claimed to offer a better way of life. They said civil servants should serve the people, not steal from them. Some of your friends went along with the communists, but you have your doubts; the communists seem always to make trouble. You prefer to be left alone.

Soon after the communists arrived your own government officials came around. Often they had foreigners with them, usually Americans or Europeans but sometimes Japanese or Indians. Your government's officials made many speeches about the "communist menace." They said you should support your government, claiming that it planned to do marvelous things for you and your village—it would build roads, dams, new schools, health centers, post offices, training centers, agricultural experiment stations, water works, and even community development centers.

At first you are really impressed. Soon great large bulldozers and other equipment have transformed the rutted road to the provincial capital into a smooth, hard surface. Buses come to the village; you can ride many miles to see your brother in just a few hours. The merchants in the village now stock all sorts of things, and you don't have to pay as much for many of them as you used to.

But you also discover that the police, who used to drop by only every couple of months, now come around at least once a week. They drive big cars with red lights on the top and radios inside. The Americans have given these cars to the police, along with the fierce-looking submachine guns they carry. You are quick to show the police your hospitality when they come to visit. You are also quick to hide anything of value.

One day another official speech informs you that the main roads are not enough; the government plans to build a network of feeder roads, just for the peasants. These officials, who come from RAID (Rapid

Agricultural Industrial Development), stress the importance of feeder roads to improve agricultural markets and provide better police "protection." They claim that with the new roads the value of your land will increase more than the value of the part they have expropriated as right-of-way for the feeder road. You will get a certificate of merit in exchange for about one sixth of your farm. Since your farm lies about four kilometers from the village where you live, maybe the new road will help you get to it faster, but you can walk about the same speed on the road as on the ox-cart trails. RAID officials also promise to provide expert advice that will show you how to raise three times as much as you now do. They tell you of big new irrigation plans which will enable you to plant a second crop during the dry season.

When construction on the feeder road begins, RAID brings in shiny new American equipment, but it sits idle most of the time. Sometimes you see RAID tractors at work on land the governor farsightedly purchased just before RAID announced the location of the new road. The governor later sold the land to the Ministry of Agriculture for an experimental farm the Americans financed.

An American who has learned your language surprisingly well (although he speaks the uppity dialect of the capitol) comes around to teach you how to triple your crop. He explains about new seed, fertilizer, improved irrigation, pesticides, fungicides, and the necessary equipment. Trouble is, your investment in all this would come to about three times your net worth. Moreover, the irrigation canals have not been built, although the dam was completed years ago. The American explains that the canals are the responsibility of another department. You ask who will buy all your extra harvest, and at what price? The American explains that these questions also must be answered by other departments; his function is purely technical and advisory.

The American was more helpful than the young government officials he was assisting. They had never lived on a farm; their fathers were officials in the capitol. They spoke to you in the idiom applied to beggars, domestic servants, and others of inferior class, and they appeared bored by the whole business of farming.

You discover that you can borrow the money you need for all the fertilizer and other things you need at 30 percent interest, but no one will offer you a price guarantee on what you produce. You do not want to repeat your brother's misfortune; everyone in his province was advised last year to grow watermelons as a second crop. At the price of 15 cents a watermelon, they could make extra money, so they took the government advice and all grew watermelons. When the price of watermelons fell to under 5 cents, some of them lost their farms. You decide to play it safe and continue to grow your crop of corn and beans in the old way. You can raise enough to eat for the year and have enough left for seed, a little bartering, and the required "gifts." This only costs you about 100 days' labor a year. Of course, since the RAID road took its share of your land, you can only grow five-sixths as much.

Still you feel fortunate. Other peasants lived in the good bottom land the government dam flooded out. They had to relocate on a hillside, where they get only about half the yield they used to, and they still can't irrigate. They are quite bitter, and the communists have made many converts among them.

The communists claim that the Americans and other foreigners are "enemies of people." Americans give the police submachine guns, jeeps, automobiles, radios, and even helicopters, and the police use them to steal more from the people. Once your bus was stopped by a group of soldiers who made everyone pay 25 cents before the bus could proceed. The soldiers, who had American guns, said it was a "fine" for riding a bus which didn't have the right kind of license. But the general in the army post said "bandits" sometimes wear army uniforms when they rob people. You don't know what to think; you just pay your 25 cents.

## BEYOND BUREAUCRACY

The civil servants have problems too. In LDC, a civil servant earns virtually nothing as an official salary, perhaps $100 per month if he is reasonably high up. His minimum living costs to support his social position as a government official exceeds his official salary by three times. If he must deal with the foreign community, his needs are about ten times his salary. Salary increases would be out of the question; the sheer size of the civil service relative to the tax base makes livable wages for them impossible. Hopeless inflation would follow a significant wage increase. The civil service, therefore, "lives off the land."

For one thing, LDC has no income taxes and only modest land taxes. Most of the government's revenue comes from sales taxes, import duties, and export duties. LDC has traditionally exported agricultural products and raw materials, and the owners of these operations are taxed on exports, not on income. The national bank, favors this system because it acknowledges that LDC could not successfully collect income taxes. Those with the highest incomes would be in charge of enforcing income tax collection. The bank's pragmatism has succeeded in keeping the dinero, the currency of LDC, on a rough par with the dollar.

The formal structure of the government is largely a facade. Large chunks of the structure, particularly the planning organizations, were created only to please foreign lenders or aid givers. The generals have withheld power from the planning groups, which serve mainly as convenient dumping grounds for officials' offspring educated abroad in economics or statistics.

A network of family loyalties and alliances prevails, broken down into various clique groups. The networks are held rather uncomfortably together by the president, who is the least objectionable personage to all factions and gets on well with foreigners. For the president to keep peace, he must allocate civil service plundering possibilities according to the bureaucratic political realities. For example, though the police have independent power, the president urges them to take it easy on the peasants. The interior ministry responds that reports of police misdoings are exaggerated, but "as long as chickens get into cornfields there will be corrupt men."

Every bureaucracy spawns an informal organization which can partially offset the damage done by social distance, overjobbing and other problems of the bureaucratic social order. The informal organization sometimes enables a bureaucracy to work less rigidly, but in LDC the informal organization has simply taken over. The rational-technical nonsense fools nobody; the informal organization is anything but impersonal. Rather, it operates more or less paternalistically. At the head of the typical clique stands a prestigious father figure, a high official, whose subordinates in effect take personal vows of loyalty. The father figure reciprocates the loyalty and assumes obligations to those who subordinate themselves to him. Should a subordinate die, the father figure will look after his family and see to the education of his children. The bonds of loyalty are normal and strong.

In some ways this is a more natural social order than bureaucracy. But political dominance and a correspondingly larger share of the plunder are the practical objectives to which the informal cliques address themselves. The clique groups aim to enlarge their "hunting territories" and thus their proceeds of public predation. Like intelligent predators they try not to exterminate their prey. The hunting territories comprise the old bureaucratic functions, preserved at first for show and now as a tradition. Tradition thus splits LDC into competitive functional territories, with the president sitting uneasily on top. Within the functional hunting territories, residual symbiosis remains. You still get service for a bribe which many businesses account for as unofficial "taxes," "sales promotional expenses," or "insurance."

Administratively, the civil service of LDC has become so top heavy that it has seized up, and administration has passed beyond bureaucracy. Although convention demands the bureaucratic facade of a government, all the crucial decisions are made outside the bureaucratic chain of the command. A pretense of functionalism remains, but there is so much duplication of functions that no power group needs to rely on the services of another. Some departments have their own communications networks, hospitals, weapons, vehicles, and so on. None of them works very well, but they permit each power group to avoid becoming the administrative hostage of any other.

Occasionally several government functions must get together in the interests of coordinated action, in which case the BSO exudes its old charm. Cooperation between departments usually degenerates into wrangling, however. Even when the cooperation is aimed at foreign aid grants, bureaucratic rivalry predominates. When one of their pet schemes seems destined to expire, foreign aid people dangle the dollar to induce the government to create a new agency reporting directly to the president. This new agency hopefully will not have to coordinate with the old bureaucracies. (This is how RAID got started.) But the old departments do not stand still when they are bureaucratically bypassed. They force various compromises so that they can tap into some of the foreign aid action. The result usually is more administrative confusion and a higher waste bill. The multiplier effects of roads that wash away or dams that do not irrigate are felt largely in Swiss bank accounts or in American and Japanese corporations manufacturing the construction equipment.

## THE PREBENDALIZED BUREAUCRACY

The bureaucratic practice of job ranking in preference to social rank probably arose from the medieval concept of prebendalism. As applied to government bureaucracy, an officeholder uses his official powers to reward himself in lieu of a salary. A medieval church abbot might retain a percentage of the church land rents; today a justice of the peace might retain a percentage of the fines he collects.

Prebendalism seems to have come out of the practice of "tax farming" that was common in many ancient civilizations. The tax farmer collected taxes in the form of goods from a district and turned over an agreed-on, fixed share to the state. He could keep what he could collect over what he guaranteed to pay the state; the predatory possibilities of such prebendalism were always clear. The salaried civil servant became a viable alternative to tax farming with the rise of the money economy and reliable tax collection systems. Civil service officials exchanged fixed salaries for the former practice of personal plunder of the public in rendering "civil service."

It was salary and, typically, career tenure which made possible the evolution of the concept of a civil service, along with the notion of honest if somewhat ponderous administration. With this type of civil service system, self-enrichment acquired through the official powers of office became known as corruption.

When government administration first changed over from prebendalism to civil service, illiteracy was its greatest ally. The fact that one had to read and write to become a government official limited the supply of civil servants. By the middle of the 19th century, the service was characterized by formal examinations for entry and tenure systems. Patronage declined, by public demand. By the standards of the day, salaries were often excellent; in Britain, they were elitist. The public came to assume honest administration, and public faith in government civil authority depended on systematic honesty.

Not only did illiteracy support honesty by limiting the potential supply of civil servants, but social pressure held down tendencies of overjobbing. A tiny number of well-paid British civil servants brought honest and reasonably efficient administration to half the world. True, they administered a smaller range of services than is required today, but the quality of administration was often incomparably better. Internal competition between departments was negligible. The social order had not become entirely bureaucratic, and loyalty and pride in good work were important. Job ranking prevailed, but there were far fewer levels. Civil servants thus had wide job latitude. Regulations tended to be general rather than agonizingly exact, because slow communications left little choice. The government decentralized administrative power out of necessity. Those on the working level had to decide if a decision was to be made.

Such a happy if temporary state of affairs would be impossible in LDC, which has a large, well-educated middle and upper class of youths with nowhere to go but into the government. In the industrializing West, industry expanded much faster than government, and consequently it absorbed the growing numbers of educated Western youth. Only by the 20th century would the effects of the Industrial Revolution be translated into effective political demand for expanded government services and pressure to "overjob" the civil services as a make-work device.

The Third World had a different experience. First, the transition from officials paid off in self-collected prebends to salaried bureaucrats would never be as complete as it was in the West. Some nations would approach the Western model, but others would not come close. An overriding reason was lack of useful employment opportunities for the educated. There was intense social pressure from the most powerful elements of society to make room in the civil service for their sons. China felt this pressure, and the rampant corruption that followed long before the West arrived in the Orient. Corruption of the prebendal sort led to the fall of the Manchu dynasty and later of the Nationalists.

In many Third World nations, the civil service (and the military, in some cases) became the road to riches. Wherever substantial elements of prebendalism remained, overjobbing reversed the trend toward the

Western model of civil service honesty. Instead of the lone official collecting recognized prebends (not always involving plunder), standing armies of parasitic bureaucrats evolved to live off the land.

Senior officials in the prebendalized bureaucracy could get rich through construction kickbacks, purchasing kickbacks, or payoffs from business firms wanting special treatment. Lesser officials helped themselves to the chickens of peasants or extracted payments from overloaded trucks. Everyone took bribes to bypass all the red tape set up first to legitimize overjobbing and second to encourage bribes to bypass the red tape. Some officials grew very very rich. Others enjoyed the sort of living to be expected of an important civil servant. Nearly all did better than their official salaries indicated.

As the process of overjobbing began, the hope of paying adequate salaries slipped away. Of course, good salaries in themselves do not guarantee honest administration, but without good salaries, the "discipline" of "wrongdoers" becomes next to impossible. Adequate salaries are a necessary if not sufficient condition of honest government. If you run a restaurant and pay your waiters nearly nothing, you can hardly complain about their accepting tips. Indeed, they will try to collect as many and as big tips as possible. And if you monopolize the restaurant business in a locality, your waiters soon go beyond "accepting tips"; they extort them. The help may also steal from you.

Attempting to expand the range of government services by a prebendalized government bureaucracy simply extends the hunting license. Set up an employment agency? Clients must soon buy their jobs from the government employment agency. Offer welfare services? Most benefits must be kicked back. Construct public housing? The civil servants wind up with the houses and then "rent" them out.

Public anger mounts accordingly. Along with being preyed upon, the public must listen to the rhetoric of being "selflessly served" by their "patriotic government officials."

## THE SPECIAL PROBLEM OF MAINTENANCE

The prebendalized bureaucracy cannot maintain anything well. New buildings fall into disrepair; new equipment breaks down; new construction falls apart or fails to work as designed. Most government employees are ever alert to areas to be skimmed internally; not everyone can tap directly into the public. Maintenance budgets, spare parts, and supplies earmarked for construction become favorite targets.

Third World nations almost never maintain something really crucial, such as the airplanes of a nationally owned airline, by themselves. Singapore, an island of honest administration in largely prebendal seas, accordingly does a booming business in aircraft maintenance and overhaul. The telephone system, water works, electrical distribution network, and such will normally exist on the edge of collapse if they are government owned. Nationally owned railways may all but cease to operate, and nationally owned ships may lie tied up most of the time in port. New equipment arrives, only to fall promptly into disrepair. Economists calculate the money required to put things right, while ignoring the institutional causes.

We can heap military equipment on such nations as a part of some broader political wisdom, but the complex equipment will never see effective use. If it breaks down, there it will stay until cannibalized. Maintenance advisors help, if they maintain it themselves in the name of training. Prebendalization of spare parts is to be expected. Equipment operators, condemned by civil service wage scales to peanuts but without prebendal opportunities, adopt practices quite similar to those of the British shop floor: They opt for on-the-job leisure. Operators, for example, often refuse preventive maintenance checks. Checking oil levels or filters in a bulldozer will not be part of the operator's job. He "drives" or "operates" only; maintenance people must do anything else. Such tactics frustrate American technical advisors, who must watch the new equipment furnished for the aid project break down ten times as often as necessary. But superintending this damage will only be half their problem. The other half comes from their own superiors, who explain (having consulted a cultural anthropologist) that the problem has to do with some arcane "status hierarchy of work in this particular culture." The American technical advisor is exhorted to explain to the local operators just how vital preventive maintenance is; they are not very sophisticated, but once they understand the importance of maintenance, they will do it. "But remember," the boss adds, "you are just an adviser. You can't give orders. We Americans can't afford to develop the image of coming over here and imposing our views on their culture."

Thus the adviser has been saddled with full responsibility and no vestige of authority.

He knows the cultural dodge for what it is. The operators, disgusted with pay a third of what private industry pays, have simply invented their own version of the British "work to rule." In terms as blunt as their culture permits, they let the advisor know they do not plan to change. By strict observance of the no-maintenance rule, operators cut their work day by two thirds. Thus they enjoy a *rate* of pay for time actually worked comparable to that paid in private industry.

The adviser writes a memo asking whether it might not be possible to allocate a bonus for the equipment operators, since the value of the equipment they are ruining is worth many times more than the bonus would cost. He receives a furious reply to the effect that the personnel and remuneration policies of the host government are no concern of his. He is instructed to confine his reports to statements on the technical progress he has made in reducing the equipment downtime. After a congressional watchdog group has discovered the shockingly low rates of equipment utilization, the adviser's real role as fall guy becomes apparent. His firm, which has the contract for advisory services, is sacked. A new lot of advisers then come in to perform the same role and risk the same fate.

Variations on this maintenance problem can be found in all less developed countries. More important than a catalog of such instances is understanding the processes at work, which arise far more from bureaucracy itself than from the wider culture.

## COMMUNISM AND PREBENDALISM

Prebendalized bureaucracies have been the ruination of foreign aid programs, American and others, throughout the Third World, although the problem varies with the country. Bureaucracy by itself causes enough problems. With prebendalism also, economic development and social justice become hopeless goals, and the objectives of communism are well served.

Communism benefits also because wholesale, systematic corruption always can be found in bureaucracy's terminal prebendal stage. Widespread corruption had crippled Russia, China, Cuba, and Vietnam long before communism moved in to exploit the resulting public outrage and frustration. A reaction to corrupt government, not an abstruse Marxist ideology, won the day for communism in these nations. It takes a pretty sorry mess before masses of people will support a "dictatorship of the proletariet." Our refusal to face the alienating propensities of prebendalized bureaucracy in Indochina were instrumental in getting the United States into the Vietnam War.

Communism contains the seeds of its own destruction because it has not solved the problem of bureaucracy, and it can never do this as long as it remains true to Marxist ideology. It is biologically impossible to put the world, or even one large society, into a single camp. We are a competititve species as well as a fraternal one, and the successful economic system must make room for both competition and comradeship. It must do this without autocracy or dictatorship in either territorial government or economic enterprise. Systems which fail to meet these critieria will ultimately succumb to the stresses generated by irreconcilable internal contradictions.

At first communist societies may seem viable because they may in fact be much better than the corruption they replace. Still, in my own opinion, free enterprise can adopt to fraternity much more readily than communism can adjust to internal competition. I say this because free enterprise has already demonstrated its fraternal viability, as will be shown in the next chapter.

## THE COMMON THEME OF THE BUREAUCRATIC BLUNDERLAND

Before leaving Part III, I want to review the common theme in the three widely diverse bureaucratic settings that have been discussed here. In all of them, we can observe too many cooks spoiling the broth. The "cooks" can work in any culture and be of any religious faith, degree of education, or ideology; regardless, if too many of them gain access to the kitchen, they will surely ruin the soup, and probably wreck the kitchen as well. While all bureaucracies have a potential capacity for incompetence, achieved incompetence will depend in large measure on the degree of overjobbing in bureaucratic operations.

In Britain, the pressure to overjob applies almost universally to blue-collar work. The result has been mounting physical waste in the industrial processes. In America, the tendency to overjob is more erratic, but when serious overjobbing arises in management and professional ranks, as in aerospace, catastrophic results can follow. In much of the Third World, the civil service or other government operations receive the most pressure to overjob, with typically disastrous consequences as widespread corruption becomes fertile soil for communist insurgents.

The social motive to overjob in all three of these examples is actual or threatened unemployment, reacting with the logic of bureaucracy's social order. All societies are subject to considerable pressure to find a place for everyone, and practical considerations often demand that these places be found in organizations. When a surplus of "place seekers" exists, organizations are forced, one way or another, to accommodate many of them. The bureaucratic organization must create fake jobs, make-work, call it what you will. By its own logic the bureaucracy can have no operational reserves of its own; everyone working for it must have a designated job, otherwise they have no "place." When things must be found for the surplus people to do, the useful content of all jobs tends to be corrupted. Useless procedures, "controls," and other forms of red tape will be developed. Layering will begin, and communications will become distorted. As alienation sets in, the pace of work will slow down and the average quality of workmanship will decline. The ratio of input to useful output will decline sharply as not only man-hours but physical resources are wasted. Bankruptcy will threaten the private enterprise, and prebendalism will threaten to engulf the public enterprise or civil service.

The danger of overjobbing reaches a particularly acute stage in the unindustrialized, overpopulated, less developed nations which are also short of arable land and lacking in natural resources. The way to avoid this danger is for society to adopt the fraternal social order in its organizations.

The challenge of economic development puts the system of natural social order to its greatest test. Japan's use of fraternity in industrial organization has met this development challenge, as will be shown in the next chapter.

# Part IV

## FRATERNITY IN ACTION

# 8

# Fraternity in Japan

## JAPAN'S DECISION TO MODERNIZE

A century ago the British Empire had reached its peak of industrial glory, and America clearly was becoming an economic giant. Germany, France, Italy, Russia, and Austria-Hungary rounded out the club of world economic powers. The least likely candidate for admittance in 1870 would probably have been Japan. Yet from virtually a zero industrial base, by 1905 Japan had become an important industrial power. In the intervening 35 years, it had taken on and decisively beaten China and Russia. Probably no nation has ever sprung more economic surprises on the world than has Japan in the past century.

For years, our attention was diverted by Japan's military surprises. But Japan could not have waged modern war without an effective industrial base. Indeed, the Japanese modernized their economy specifically to build up a strategic industry capable of autonomous defense. In response to fear of the "white peril" of the Western colonial powers, the nation moved from a feudal agricultural economy directly into modern industry and scientific technology in about 30 years. No other major nation in the world comes remotely close to this record.

The Japanese succeeded largely without foreign help of any kind, except for technical assistance which they paid for. No foreign aid, very few loans, and not much in the way of foreign capital investment helped Japan. Moreover, it had few raw materials to export and in fact had to import most of them, as it still does. To get foreign exchange Japan had to industrialize for export. Otherwise it was limited to silk and handicrafts for foreign exchange earnings. To add to Japan's problems, the Western nations imposed on it a number of unequal trade agreements which effectively took import duties from Japanese control.

159

Moreover, Japan had an anticommercial cultural heritage not unlike that of medieval Europe. Merchants were in the lowest class in a bureaucratic (functional) class system in which the warriors (Samurai) occupied the top slot. Then came farmers and artisans, in that order. An "untouchable" caste, the Eta, also existed, but they were few in number and socially insignificant.

Thus Japan did not have the "proper" cultural background for an enormous expansion of the economy. True, the motive was military rather than economic, but Japan could not just build shipyards and arsenals for a strategic industry, it had to develop a more or less balanced industrial economy. A balanced economy requires banks, insurance companies, steel mills, trading firms, transportation lines, textile mills, and on and on. To acquire these things entailed a vast commercial expansion that was foreign to Japanese cultural tradition. To add to the cultural confusion, it was not the merchant class that led the way but the warriors, who had previously hated commerce. The Samurai played the same role in Japan's industrial emergence that Calvinist merchants did in the West: agents of change.

In short, neither Japan's material resources nor its cultural heritage seemed to suggest its rapid economic rise. To this day Japan stands as the best example of the economic development the West has tried to encourage throughout the postwar years in the Third World. As a Third World development model, however, Japan was studiously ignored until very recently.[1] Japan had been crushed in World War II, and perhaps it was only natural to ignore the losers.

Before the war, Japan had a reputation for cheap, often shoddy goods. This provided another industrial surprise in World War II, when the Japanese produced generally superior weapons. Japanese battleships, aircraft carriers, and destroyers proved as good or better than ours, the Zero ranked as the best fighter plane in the world for about 12 to 18 months after it entered combat, and their optics were superior. True, Japan lacked good tanks, and their subs were neither very good nor well deployed. By and large it had few of the military niceties, such as a electronics, with which the American forces were endowed. But the surprise was stunning nonetheless, since it had been assumed that all of Japan's weapons would compare poorly with ours.

Another big economic surprise from Japan worries us now. It was Japan that forced President Nixon to declare his "new economic policy" and that was responsible for the subsequent devaluations. Yet no one witnessing the debris of Japan's industry in 1946 would have predicted Japan's economic power 25 years later, not even the Japanese. I first visited Japan in 1948 as a college student. Three years after the war,

---

[1] Gunnar Myrdal hardly mentioned Japan in his *Asian Drama*, for example.

there were vast areas of burned-out factories between Yokohama and Tokyo. I remember thinking that Japan had been knocked out of the industrial sweepstakes for at least 50 years. It did not seem possible it would ever compete with America in such fields as automobiles, electronics, or steel.

But fraternity is the most powerful social force in human enterprise. The fraternal social order behind Japan's spectacular break from feudal agriculture also powered its postwar recovery. The nation applied the social order of the tribal hunter to modern industry and advanced technology, with spectacular success.

## A FRATERNAL HISTORY OF JAPAN

Fraternity did not emerge merely from Japanese cultural values or Japanese religion. Rather, by accident of history and geography, the Japanese never quite abandoned the natural social order in economic affairs. The teamwork-releasing properties of fraternity proved almost as useful in Japanese agriculture as they had in hunting. At the community level, cooperation remained a social necessity for successful farming, since Japan's mountainous, mild, and wet climate made rice culture possible only with local-level cooperation in irrigation.

While Japan borrowed much from China culturally, it did not borrow China's bureaucratically coordinated hydraulic agriculture based on vast networks of canals. Japan tried this briefly but dropped the effort shortly after 500 A.D., for lack of purpose or need. As Karl Wittfogel explained in *Oriental Despotism,* Japan's water supply "neither necessitated nor favored substantial government directed works." Its terrain was compartmentalized by numerous mountain ranges, which "encouraged a fragmented rather than a coordinated pattern of irrigation farming and flood control." In Japan, Wittfogel notes,

> The rulers of the dominant political center effected a loose political unification at a rather early date, but they were not faced with hydraulic tasks that required . . . corvée teams. Nor were they conquered by the forces of an Orientally despotic state. They therefore failed to establish a comprehensive managerial and acquisitive bureaucracy capable of controlling [the rest of society] as did . . . the Chinese mainland.[2]

When an attempt to emulate China was made in 656 A.D. by digging a long canal, Wittfogel noted, it "struck the people as 'mad'; critics compared it with a useless colossal hill that was built at the same time."

Boye De Mente believes it was "the particular Japanese method of growing rice, based on a community-operated irrigation system with its requirement of harmony, mutual help, and self-sacrifice, plus untold

---

[2] Karl Wittfogel, *Oriental Despotism* (New Haven: Yale University Press, 1963), p. 197.

162

generations of life in feudalistic clans, that forged their basic character."[3]

Cooperation was studied in depth by John F. Embree, who lived several months in the Japanese village of Suye Mura during the 1930s. Embree designated the two outstanding features of *buraku* (hamlet) life to be cooperation and exchange. Cooperation he described as "the voluntary working together of a group of people. This implies that there is no 'boss'—no person who forces the people thus to work together. . . . The lack of bosses or chiefs in local social forms is very marked."[4]

Embree also noted that the basic cooperative work group, *kami*, had no designated leader. A *kami* usually comprised about five families, and groups of *kami* rotated "responsibility and work each year to a different group." Work on the irrigation canals, during the transplanting season, on road maintenance, and in bridge building depended upon cooperation without designated leadership. Embree described the construction of a small village bridge as follows:

> On the appointed day at about 7:00 A.M., one person from each house in the *buraku* turns up. If the bridge serves two *buraku*, members of each *buraku* work on a separate section of the bridge. Those who did not go to cut wood on some previous day will contribute straw for rope or matting for the bridge. Each person sets to work doing something. There is no boss, yet all gets done without confusion.[5]

House building, roof repairing, weddings, and funerals also elicited community cooperation, but everyone followed an exact exchange system. If one received help from others, one expected to repay it in kind. Perhaps the most difficult and crucial task Embree observed was the transplanting of rice from the seedbeds to the paddy fields. Every able-bodied man and woman would be in the fields transplanting. There were no bosses, even with work groups of up to 20 or so. Each year the sequence of transplanting rotated; the one at the head of the line one year would come last the next year.[6]

In the Japan of 40 years ago that Embree studied, the village headman was elected, and the position was regarded mostly as honorary. Virtually everyone belonged to associations of the type we call cooperatives for purposes of credit, irrigation, and purchasing discounts. The central government did not interfere in the associations or attempt to

---

[3] Boye De Mente, "Can We Learn from Japan?" in *Worldwide P & I Planning*, March/April 1970, p. 55.

[4] J. F. Embree, *Suye Mura . . . A Japanese Village* (Chicago: University of Chicago Press), p. 112.

[5] Ibid., p. 123.

[6] Ibid., p. 133.

dictate policy, but it did furnish an expert for agricultural extension services who had a farming background.

Since the end of World War II, agricultural productivity per man-hour has risen faster in Japan than anywhere else in Asia. Only two nations come close to matching the Japanese record, Taiwan and South Korea, both of which use almost exactly the same local-cooperative system as the Japanese. In fact, Japan exported this sytem to those countries after it occupied them near the turn of the century. While they did not love the Japanese as masters, they did retain Japan's local system of cooperation.

In the feudal era, especially during the Tokugawa period of 1603 to 1868, the Japanese occasionally used corvée labor for public works, although not on the scale of China. It was more like the old American road tax, which called for either labor or money. Except for taxes, the government historically left the farmers alone to manage their own affairs, and still does. Neither prewar theoretical absolutism nor the militaristic dictatorship which emerged in the early 1930s impinged much on the farmer or his way of life. Bureaucracy and its social order did not figure in the farmer's economic existence.

In this he differed little from his U.S. rural counterpart, although the practical requirement of close local cooperation is much higher for Japanese rice than, say, American wheat. Embree's description of cooperative Japanese house building resembles descriptions of an American barn raising, complete with drinking party. Actually the lot of the Japanese farmer in the Tokugawa era, socially, physically, and emotionally, probably was superior to that of an American sharecropper. He did not enjoy formal political rights in the Western fashion, but neither did he suffer arbitrary tryanny.

After the Meiji Restoration in 1868 and the introduction of Western technology, the Japanese population, still overwhelmingly rural, began to grow rapidly. Population pressure soon mounted on the available land, only about 15 percent of which is arable. As the population exceeded 30 million, underemployment mounted. Many were forced into the status of submarginal farmers, and some were forced off the land altogether. The losers furnished the labor supplies for industry. But when they entered industry, these dispossessed farmers usually found a social environment similar to the one they had left. Accordingly the alienation and anomie which so marked the Industrial Revolution in the West did much less harm to Japanese society. If anything, the Japanese factories became closer socially to the fraternal hunting bands than to farming, because there was competition between enterprises, something that had been muted in the rural setting. The concept of sharing, meanwhile, moved from the family to industry.

The Japanese admired Western technology and scientific achievement. Even before the Tokugawa Shogunate had been replaced by the Meiji Restoration, teams of Japanese (usually of the Samurai class) traveled the world to study the ways of the West at first hand. The previous 250 years (until Commodore Matthew Perry opened Japan to foreign trade in 1854) had been a period of self-imposed isolation, in which the only window on the West was a small Dutch enclave near Nagasaki. Japan had much catching up to do, and the teams went forth to learn.

## INDUSTRIAL BUSHIDO

While the Japanese accepted and copied Western technology, they found Western industrial relations to be so poisonous they decided they could not hope to succeed industrially if they copied that system. Indeed, they were horrified and repelled by it. They regarded it as barbarous that factory owners could treat workers callously and impersonally, as things rather than people. The Japanese regarded esprit de corps and teamwork as essential to collective success, in part from the Samurai code of Bushido. They could not imagine how Westerners expected worker cooperation under the commodity theory of labor, and the buyer-seller relationship seemed nonsensical in a cooperative enterprise. The nearest they came to it experimentally was with the use of labor contractors, a practice they found unsatisfactory and abandoned. That Westerners could discuss the sanctity of the individual and the layoff in the same breath seemed to most Japanese to be hypocritical poppycock.

The natural social order survived in Japanese agriculture by accident of geography. But the Japanese deliberately introduced fraternity into industry, partly out of reaction to the Western inhumanity they discovered. They adopted as a motto, "Eastern morality and Western science."

As the source of spiritual guidance for the Samurai warrior class, the code of Bushido influenced the Japanese culture as a whole. Westerners have often misinterpreted Bushido as a code which merely glorifies war, a misinterpretation that became inevitable during the 1930s when a militaristic government bent Bushido into a military code. But the code dates back into prehistory, and it survived many periods of sustained peace as well as endemic civil war.

Broadly, Bushido stresses self-sacrifice, reciprocal loyalty, frugality, valor, and honesty in private dealings. Thus it could compare to almost any fraternal oath sanctifying the existence of a bonded brethren. Its underlying concepts could serve as the basis for loyalty to any college fraternity, athletic team, Catholic religious order, or trade union, suitably adjusted for a particular purpose. Bushido's theme has a taproot which could go all the way back to the preagricultural hunting bands. Fraternally bonded hunters and similar groups have devised Bushido-type codes in cultures widely separated by time and distance, such as Sparta and the Iroquois Indians. This suggests something more than cultural learning alone; the Iroquois can hardly have been in touch with either the Spartans or the Samurai.

Japan disbanded the Samurai and other social classes once it decided to industrialize. But the code of Bushido became more than a code for the nation's military forces. It had penetrated the commercial world nearly 250 years earlier. Perhaps the most famous early example of the application of the fraternal code of the Samurai in the world of commerce is by the House of Mitsui, one of the largest trading firms in the world. Mitsui is the oldest Japanese *zaibatsu,* or industrial combine.

## THE HOUSE OF MITSUI

Mitsui traces its origins to the early days of the Tokugawa Shogunate and thus ranks among the oldest commercial enterprises in the world. The founder was an ex-Samurai, the son of Mitsui Tokayasu, a feudal lord who lost his fief in battle, retired to Ise province, and refused to participate further in the civil wars. This led in 1603 to Iyeyasu's first Tokugawa Shogunate. Upon succeeding his father, Mitsui Sokubei perceived that Tokugawa unity favored the peaceful arts more than warfare. With remarkable courage Sokubei abandoned his Samurai rank and class to undertake a commercial career as a brewer and seller of sake (rice wine) in Matsuzaka, not far from Osaka. Thus Mitsui voluntarily left the highest class to join the lowest class, the merchants (Chonin).

Sokubei's youngest son, Hachirobei, actually founded the House of Mitsui. Hachirobei became a money lender after study and apprenticeship in other family enterprises. An astute businessman, he accumulated capital for over 20 years and then, in 1673, moved to Kyoto and launched a new enterprise in commerce. Trading in dry goods, Hachirobei made several important innovations which paid off very well. Two of these were cash terms and a single price. Traditionally Japanese merchants carried long credit accounts, and prices reflected marketplace haggling as well as interest on credit and loss on bad debts. The Mitsui policy lowered the cash price considerably. Mitsui also sold a customer any size of material he desired instead of the "standard size only" policy generally in effect.

Mitsui also innovated in advertising. The firm often paid actors to "slip in a plug" for Mitsui during a performance, and it gave away paper umbrellas with Mitsui advertisements printed on them.

Mitsui's business grew rapidly as a result of these policies. Stimulated by the concessions to their convenience, customers flocked to the store. Warehouses were added until the Mitsui store became one of the sights of the city. Mitsui expanded its operations and opened outlets in Osaka and Edo (Tokyo). Business did so well that the Edo store employed over 1,000 before 1800.

Although commercial banking as such did not exist during the Tokugawa Shogunate, Mitsui and similar firms performed many banking functions. They accepted savings deposits, issued drafts, made commercial loans, and processed bills of exchange.

A "branch bank" was opened in Osaka, Japan's commercial center at the time, and Mitsui became a financial agent for the Shogunate in 1690. Hachirobei's commmercial inventiveness emerged when he convinced the shogun to adopt an exchange system in financial accounts. It had been the practice to transport government funds physically from Osaka's Treasury to Edo. Since Mitsui and other merchants purchased large quantities of goods in both places, the exchange system allowed bookkeeping entries to substitute for most of the physical transfer of funds, to everyone's advantage. Mitsui thereafter enjoyed great confidence from the Tokugawa. It became court banker (1707), and acted as central bankers not only for the shogun but for many feudal lords as well.

Ironically, some of the improvements and innovations made by the Mitsui organization helped smooth the way for the transition to a money economy. Money eroded the economic base of Tokugawa feudalism, as did the Mitsui innovation of double-entry accounting procedure.

After the Restoration Mitsui expanded rapidly, although many other wealthy commercial houses declined in importance or failed altogether. Mitsui performed a leading part in the organization of cotton, paper, and silk-reeling mills, with government assistance. Later, shipping, insurance, mining, and engineering works joined its traditional functions of banking, wholesaling, and retailing. Mitsui today ranks among the leading corporations of the world. It is even one of America's largest trading firms, unbeknownst to most Americans.

## The Code of Mitsui

The House of Mitsui was comprised of a main family and several collateral families, all of whom followed a code established by Mitsui Hachirobei as his "moral legacy" to the House he had labored to establish. The general rules of Hachirobei's code[7] read as follows:

> That which is set forth below is the testament of the founder of our family and therefore none of those who are to be born thereto should violate it.

---

[7] House of Mitsui, *A Record of Three Centuries* (Tokyo, 1937).

1. We are able to live in happiness today owing to our ancestors, and for this we should be thankful.
2. All laws and ordinances issued by the government should be faithfully followed by all, from the master to the lowest of employees. Gambling is absolutely taboo.
3. All members of the family should have a true spirit of cooperation. Those who stand above should be kind and charitable to those who are below, and those who are low should be respectful to those who are high.

   Members of the family may be on good terms now because they are brothers, but their children and grandchildren will be no longer so closely related and may not remain on as good terms. They should therefore be warned against change in their attitude of mind. They should be so taught as to observe the family rules with unchanging faith and fidelity and cooperate well with one another; otherwise, their house would never thrive or prosper. They should always be thoughtful and considerate of what others would have done by them. When one thinks of one's own interest only and judge others by one's own standpoint, there will be friction and discord, internally and among one's own folk.

   Self-indulgence and self-importance will always lead one's house to ruin. Be strict in self-discipline, be kind and helpful to those who are related with your family, and be industrious in your business.
4. Be always careful and cautious in your work or your business will fail. Good understanding and cooperation is necessary between those who stand high and those who work under them. No good house could be built unless there be a good master carpenter and good men working under him.
5. It is a matter of first importance how to select the men to work for you. You should not employ men whose idea of business is such that they, in pursuit of small gain, incur a big loss. Nor those who, in order to avoid a small loss, miss big gains.
6. Life in the countryside is simple and frugal but in urban places like Edo [Tokyo], Kyoto, and Osaka there is a tendency to luxury. Chonin are apt to become less attentive in business and more indulgent in luxury: this is the reason why their houses fall in the second or third generation. Of this point one should always be wary.

These rules were laid down for moral guidance, and their relationship to the moral code of the Samurai class to which Hachirobei's grandfather belonged is fairly obvious. A sort of commercial fraternity, initially on blood lines, was established which gradually replaced pure familial loyalty.

Special rules applied to the education of all Mitsui male children:

1. The boy children, when twelve years of age, should be put to work at the head office in Kyoto. They should be put on the same footing

and do the same kind of work as ordinary apprentices. When fifteen years old, they should be sent to the office in Edo and given training in actual business for a period of two or three years. Completing this term, they are to be brought back to Kyoto to learn how to lay in stocks and how to keep books. When twenty years old, they should again be sent to Edo to acquire proficiency in bookkeeping. Back again in Kyoto, they should divide their time between the head office and the shop in Osaka, acquainting themselves with the businesses of mercery, money exchange and drapery. When twenty-nine years old, they are to go to Edo to learn more of the drapery business and go about in Edo and places in the neighboring districts laying in drapery stocks.

2. Honorable orders may sometimes be received from the Shogunate and feudal lords, but honor and business should never be mixed. It would never do to make light of the business.

3. Members who go to Edo and Osaka for service should so conduct themselves as to become exemplars for others to emulate. When they work at branch establishments they are required to report fully to the head office on the business and internal conditions of those places. Orders or instructions from the headquarters in Kyoto can at times be inconformable with conditions on the spot. In such cases members of the family are to consult with senior clerks and take the best measures in their judgment.

4. It would not be well to expend much money on a big collection of costly curios. Wishes for stately mansions and costly household ornaments and articles can never be satisfied in full.

5. It would be well to follow the ways of Buddhism and Shinto or acquire the wisdom of Confucianism; but it would never do to become too much engrossed with any of them, because the family business would thereby be neglected. When any one should give himself up to Buddhism so that he became like a monk, or when any one should devote himself so much to Shinto worship that he became like a priest, his business would be certain to suffer, with the result of disobeying the true will of divinity of Buddha. It would also be wrong to make unjudicious donations of money to Buddhist temples or Shinto shrines. Divinity and Buddha are moved and grant protection only in response to the supplication of true hearts, their benevolence never being bought with money.

The last rule could be compared with the secularized Puritan ethic, which drew a distinct division between the business world and the affairs of the church. Other exhortations to eschew luxury and wealth also bear much similarity to the Calvinist-inspired instructions to the bourgeois. The notion of career-long rotational training also emerges, as does the avoidance of functional or job rank.

Faith in hard work, menial or otherwise, clearly emerges from the following rules for young members beginning their business training;

1. At the branch office they have to obey the clerks who are in charge of their training and make themselves useful in all possible ways. Their position is the same as that of apprentices.
2. They should never forget their own social position as traders. They should be polite in greeting all customers. Their faithfulness and attentiveness should go to the extent of putting customers' footwear in order when they stepped out of them to be shown in.
3. They should be permitted to wear only cotton clothes and their hair in such styles that they should in no way attract more attention than apprentices when customers come in.
4. During the daytime they are expected to do nothing but office work. Only at night are they free to attend to their own affairs, but never to stay up late.
5. Each meal must be taken in the culinary section with other apprentices, and their fare is to be as frugal.
6. There are many clerks and apprentices in the office and they are apt to talk well or ill of one another. But the young masters are never to lend an ear to whatever they might have to tell.
7. Besides business, they should apply themselves to the studies they have taken up and be properly drilled by masters so that they should not lose their accomplishments.

The particularities of time, place, and circumstance aside, the Mitsui code comes across today as remarkably sound. Cooperation and loyalty, the essence of teamwork, received heavy stress. The focus clearly centers on the whole enterprise, not the functional parts, but rotational training ensures familiarity with the parts. While Mitsui Hachirobei clearly set up a family enterprise, he also foresaw that kinship ties would fade with the passage of time. This prospect induced him to leave his moral legacy, to provide for the replacement of direct kinship ties with fraternal bonds attached to the enterprise itself. Hachirobei consciously chose as his model the Samurai code of Bushido.

The Mitsui code clearly stresses long-term success and survival, not profit maximization. The interests of the whole enterprise receive a sort of natural focus through symbiotic attention to the welfare of the customers. Mitsui was not alone in inculcating the Samurai ethic into commerce. A movement founded by Ishida Baigan (1685–1744) attempted to defend the commercial function against its lowly social status.[8] Baigan sought to improve the dignity of commerce by emulating the ideals of Bushido more closely. Traditionally, the element of symbiosis had been muted in commerce, while predation had been more blatant. "Our creed is greed" has been ascribed to merchants by customers in many a culture. Paradoxically, when Baigan sought to upgrade the service or symbiotic element of commerce, he turned to Bushido for

---

[8] R. N. Bellah, *Tokugawa Religion: The Values of Pre-Industrial Japan* (Glencoe, Ill.: Free Press, 1957), p. 160.

inspiration, supposedly the code of the master predator. But this is the point, of course. The truly fraternal code stresses the health of the enterprise, whether it is practicing predation, symbiosis, or both. The code of the "warrior" focuses not on the enemy, but on the "warriors," the fraternity. The team must achieve internal harmony to concentrate most effectively on external competition. Autocrats cannot durably impose such harmony. Fraternal codes, if part of the natural social order for human enterprise, do so much more effectively.

## Mitsui Policy in Industrial Practice

The code of Mistsui became, broadly speaking, the policy model for the other Japanese *zaibatsu* firms, initially Mitsubishi, Sumitomo, and Yasuda. Some Westerners have assumed that the Japanese willy-nilly applied clan feudalism to modern industry, but this is true only to the extent that feudalism partly subsumes fraternity. As the Mitsui story indicates, the Japanese had applied the fraternal social order successfully in commercial enterprise long before it decided to industrialize. They had tested it for a much longer period than most Western firms had existed. Though they copied the technology of the West, they did not substitute its alienating bureaucracy for fraternity.

Adam Smith had nothing to teach the Japanese on the division of labor. They had long since put into practice at the enterprise level Karl Marx's dictum on income sharing. The essence of Douglas McGregor's fraternal Theory Y model of organization had never been abandoned, even in agriculture. The only organizational models which the Japanese adapted from the West comprised the Prussian army, the British navy, and more or less the British civil service. Bitten by bureaucracy, the Japanese behave no differently from people in any other culture. In the functional separation of the military services, they created a sort of "bureaucratic rivalry" between the army and navy which played a crucial role in Japan's entry into World War II.

Westerners have regularly predicted the demise of industrial fraternity in Japan and its replacement with the bureaucratic social order. Because fraternal free enterprise capitalism has no Western intellectual model, in the minds of many Westerners such a creation cannot function. The Japanese are perfectly content with this Western view; they sometimes even seem to agree. If you are using a system with which you are creaming the competition and the competition claims your system doesn't work, why disturb their illusions? While they dream, you can use their markets. And if they want to attribute your commercial success to inscrutable cultural peculiarities, you have enough of them to distract the competition for decades. If they stumble onto the power of the natural social order in human enterprise, your anticipated dominance of the 21st century might be thwarted.

When, shortly after the war, it appeared that the Japanese might adopt American "management" techniques, it was due more to words than deeds. In fact, the postwar fraternal system was consolidated. Industry in Japan has never been more fraternal than at the present time, as borne out by surveys by both the *Oriental Economist* and the Ministry of International Trade and Industry (MITI).[9]

## THE NATURAL SOCIAL ORDER IN MODERN INDUSTRY

When the Japanese military decided to industrialize in the late 1800s and to achieve competitive equality with the West, Japan faced all the problems of a developing nation, and more. It was overpopulated, and the population growth rate was rocketing. Mounting underemployment brought intense social pressure to find "places" for the dispossessed Samurai and the farmers. Japan required many imports but had little of value to export; it had few industrial raw materials except for some coal of poor quality. Foreigners controlled custom duties and hence taxes, and the island empire was located well off the world trade routes. It lacked a tradition of science and scientific technology, and there was mass illiteracy and no public school system. Finally there came the self-imposed burden of creating a modern military machine from scratch, quickly.

Japan sought no foreign assistance; it even refused to borrow money, because it did not want to give the West a pretext for occupation should it default. Nor did Japan seek foreign investment capital, to avoid further intervention. The humiliating trade agreements Japan had been forced to sign made it very suspicious. In trade, Japan faced the problem that the various European empires had sewn up most of the potential markets in which it might compete. In all the Far East, only Siam (Thailand) remained an independent nation, and it also suffered from unequal trade agreements. China had been carved up economically among the Western powers. Other territories were occupied by France, Spain, Russia, Germany, Portugal, or Holland. By modern reckoning (which carefully avoids institutional analysis), Japan could not win.

Japan succeeded in the economic race because institutionally it entered jet against propeller-driven competition, and thus it could overcome its handicaps and its late entry quickly. But Japan's decision to compete militarily, wherein she enjoyed no compelling institutional

---

[9] De Mente, "Can We Learn from Japan?" p. 51.

advantage, led to her defeat in World War II. Japan's army matched the German in institutional effectiveness and its navy matched the American or British, but Japan enjoyed no overriding advantage, once deprived of the element of surprise and having suffered the attrition of sustained combat. The military social order draws on the natural social order, yet it also departs in significant ways. Because it had copied Western military institutions, Japan could only match or marginally excel them.

Japan also badly miscalculated its cultural "spiritual advantage" over the West in a military contest. After Pearl Harbor, Americans could marshal all the courage nature gives the outraged defender against blatant territorial intrusion. At Midway, badly outnumbered Americans fought effectively with generally inferior aircraft and less well-trained pilots. The Navy's last-ditch defense won a crushing victory which doomed both Japan's and the Axis powers' hopes of victory.

While broad cultural considerations enter into institutional effectiveness, it is the social order of the institution itself that is of overriding importance, because it will biologically release or inhibit effective teamwork. Similar social orders in different cultures tend to release the same kind of behavior, although the culture influences the value accorded the enterprise objectives, such as military victory, religious conversion, or commercial profit. In survival and territorial defense, however culturally defined, the influence of biology predominates, whatever the culture.

Japan's commercial ascendancy arose out of a culture steeped in a thousand years' tradition of strong anticommercial bias. This tradition has by no means completely died out, either in Japan or in the West, under the influence of Puritanism. An influential minority in both cultures still regards commercial enterprise with suspicion.

Probably no modern culture has a wholly consistent set of normative values. The broader culture should not blind us to the social order of the institution or enterprise itself, so that we assume it must reflect in microcosm the often inconsistent values of the culture. It might, but it might not. Japan's *zaibatsu* firms did so in some ways, but not in others. The Japanese were innovators in such things as the decentralized structure of the *zaibatsu*, which Americans later reinvented as the conglomerate.

The natural social order in Japan's fraternal free-enterprise *zaibatsu* corporations can best be discussed in terms of the fulfillment of the five social needs: identity, status, prestige, role, and reward.

### Identity

James Abegglen, the first American to describe the factory social order in Japan for a Western audience, compared a Japanese employee joining his firm to an American college student pledging a fraternity; both see the act as a lifetime commitment.[10] Just as joining an American college fraternity does not confine you to a functional identity within the fraternity, neither is the Japanese employee so confined. A Japanese firm accepts an employee after looking him over carefully, but it does not hire him to fill some vacant job. Typically even special talents are not considered, although class position and school will be of interest. The employee is hired more or less as a Marine is accepted into the corps, because it is thought he will "fit in." Typically, the employee joins a *zaibatsu* on a year's probation, after which he becomes a permanent employee and acquires career tenure.[11]

When you were a student you may have experienced a typical American adolescent identity crisis and joined a protest group, perhaps to do a bit of rioting. You are never more sour on the system than when you have no place in it. A Japanese who joins Mitsubishi Heavy Industries, for example, has no identity crisis; he now belongs to Mitsubishi. This association provides a clear and unambiguous identity for the rest of his career. He knows who and what he is.

His identity is not contingent on good times, either. Such decisions as whether to buy better equipment or alter the organization format do not endanger it; as long as Mitsubishi survives, so does he. He therefore develops an abiding interest in Mitsubishi's survival, almost automatically assuming that what's good for Mitsubishi is good for him. He would not consider career objectives that conflict with the goals of his company, neither would he be aware of putting personal goals aside to work for those of the company. He wanted to join the Mitsubishi team, and he selected as a personal goal the success of his team. He takes pride in the accomplishments of his enterprise, and his feelings of loyalty toward it seem to differ little from those he feels for his family or country.

The employee thus enjoys permanent and under normal circumstances irrevocable identity. He feels as loyal to Mitsubishi as a career Marine does to the Corps, an Etonian to his school, a Sigma Chi to his house, or a Jesuit to his order. All enjoy the uncomplicated and biologically natural experience of fraternal identity. They are free to leave, but without just cause and due process, they cannot be expelled. Such fraternal identity cannot be taken away arbitrarily or capriciously.

The Japanese *zaibatsu* employee, unlike his counterpart in the bureaucratic social order, cannot be relieved of his identity as an economy measure to protect the interests of others at his own financial and

---

[10] J. C. Abegglen, *The Japanese Factory: Aspects of Its Social Organization* (Glencoe, Ill.: Free Press, 1958).

[11] Japanese firms also hire temporary employees from the ranks of off-season farmers, retired people, students, or housewives. Temporary employees, who may comprise 10 to 15 percent of total employees, can be laid off.

social expense. He is safe from involuntary nomination, through unemployment, to be part of the body count in a war against inflation. Hard times will affect his income but not his enterprise identity, no more than the business cycle impinges on his family or national identity. A genetic imperative, not human manipulation, motivates his fully reciprocated sense of enterprise loyalty.

In the fraternal social order, the Japanese can obey human nature in their feelings of intense loyalty to their enterprise. Their social order releases the tendency to bond innately with the enterprise and with their economic brethren. As nature once selected out unbonded, contentious hunting bands from the savannas, the market now selects out the corporations of contending individualists. The functional bonding advocated by American management theories has allowed Japan to infiltrate markets the United States once dominated. Whereas Americans honor the star, the Japanese honor the team, and the market selects for effective teams, not prima donnas.

### Status and Prestige

The status system in a *zaibatsu* differs hardly at all from what the typical American experiences from childhood through college graduation. As you age you accumulate social rank at home, at school, at play, or in such formal groups as the Boy Scouts. If you grow up on a farm, your age might determine the nature of your chores, but your chores would not determine your relative social rank. At seven you might only feed the chickens or help weed the kitchen garden, but you would not be classed as the "chicken feeder" or "garden-weeder's helper." At 17 you might drive the tractor, but you would not draw your social rank from the title "tractor driver." If you prove inept at some chores you are assigned to others. Your talents influence what chores you draw, but this does not affect your relative social rank. Your prestige also relates to your talents but it does not disturb the social rank your age determines. Your prestige arises directly from performance of your chores, not from your talents.

The same relationships hold in school. Your class (age) determines your social rank, your grades (performance) your prestige. Only at the extremes of good or bad will your prestige change your social rank, when you skip or fail a grade. For members of groups such as the Boy Scouts, there is even a closer connection between status of social rank and performance prestige. Even here, however, your performance prestige will not focus on your "job," and your efforts to improve your social rank will not depend on any rating you receive as patrol leader, scribe, or whatever. Rather, you must pass special tests of competency which cover a wide range of functional areas which may or may not influence your job duties within your troop.

Your immediate superiors in the Scouting coordinating hierarchy pass judgment only on the beginner ranks, thereafter you must accumulate merit badges. To achieve the higher ranks, your performance will be judged by experts outside your own superiors; physicians, for example, may pass on your competency in first aid. Such outside experts normally have no personal axe to grind in passing or failing you, and if you fail, you can try again.

Your Scouting social rank merely modifies the age criteria, it does not eliminate it. As with your school class, personal performance can modify the age criteria, but not with respect to job performance in the enterprise. The jobs you draw, whether as patrol leader or class vice president, do not determine your social rank, and whether you learn much or little does not particularly affect your enterprise. If you have talents for your jobs you will likely perform them well, and your prestige will reflect your performance in these jobs. But prestige based on job performance and social rank based on age plus learning comprise two distinct hierarchies, and the coordinating instructions you receive as chicken-feeder, patrol leader, or class vice president comprise yet a third hierarchy. This is the natural way for humans, a legacy of our hominid past. So it is with Mitsubishi Heavy Industries.

Unlike the employee in most Western industries, the Japanese employee continues to play this status game. Social rank, prestige rank, and coordinating rank all remain more or less distinct. Age and education determine his social rank, and he achieves informal prestige and the esteem of his fellows, depending on his performance. His coordinating rank determines the assignments he draws, based upon his abilities. Simple trial and error, often in training, will usually determine who can do what acceptably well. Although there are exceptions, he normally rotates among a variety of assignments.

Over his career he will rise in status continuously until retirement, purely as a function of age. Those he enters the enterprise with will be those with whom he later retires. If he is especially bright and ambitious for personal recognition in the acquisition of social rank, he may find the system confining. He may, indeed, break away and start something of his own, another Matsushita or Sony Electric, a Toyota Motors, or even another Mitsui; all were creations of entrepreneurs in the best tradition of Western individualism. He can risk it on his own if he desires, but the ambitious employee is not likely to find a way to exercise his personal dominance instinct within the fraternal enterprise he has joined. The enterprise will not lend itself as a vehicle of personal ambition; to do so would adversely affect the enterprise status system and thus teamwork.

A very bright Japanese employee who performs consistently well for the enterprise, however, might be selected to join the ranks of upper management in his mid-forties. Normally he would retire at age 55, but in top management this limit no longer applies. He will rise to senior social rank about as rapidly as his counterpart in the West, but he will not do so as a boy wonder, unless he succeeds on his own.

Should he fail to win nomination to a top slot, he may be tapped for a presitgious upper-middle position. In this case, at age 55 he will move on to a senior level in another part of the enterprise, or he will retire. This system compares to our own military officer corps (with some significant differences, of course); the employee who joins Mitsubishi with a college degree might be said to do so as a second lieutenant. He can expect to retire at age 55 as a lieutenant colonel, but should he be tapped for service beyond age 55, at the upper-middle level, this rank could be comparable to full colonel. Beyond that would come the rank of general. To retire from the army as a lieutenant colonel signifies a normal career. If you retire as a full colonel you did well; if you retire as a general, you did very well.

The *zaibatsu* take care not to disturb teamwork when making these choices. Those selected move out as they move up, so no one is humiliated by seeing someone promoted over him. The Japanese have found that teamwork does not arise out of humiliation. They also almost never humiliate their employees by bringing in someone from outside the enterprise, although there are exceptions for retired civil servants in staff positions. As Ford's "coup" with Knudsen of General Motors, proved, "going outside" can prove disastrous. It never helps loyalty; to understand why, imagine an army which would recruit its leaders from its enemies.

A variation of the Boy Scout merit badge system is used by the *zaibatsu* to select upper-middle and top-management nominees. Because those in the immediate chain of command do not get involved in the promotion process, the employee has no need to fear his superiors politically. Perhaps the best way to convey how this selection system works is with Peter Drucker's description of the "godfather system," which follows.

> The Japanese take this system for granted. Indeed, few of them are even conscious of it. As far as I can figure out, it has no name—the term "godfather" is mine rather than theirs. But every young managerial employee knows who his godfather is, and so do his boss and the boss's boss.
>
> How is a godfather chosen for a young man? Is there a formal assignment or an informal understanding? No one seems to know. The one qualification that is usually mentioned is that the godfather should be a graduate of the same university from which the young man graduated— the "old school tie" binds even more tightly in Japan than it did in England. Yet everybody inside the company knows who the godfather of a given young man is and respects the relationship.
>
> The godfather is never a young man's direct superior, and, as a rule,

he is not anyone in a direct line of authority over the young man or his department. He is rarely a member of top management and rarely a man who will get into top management. Rather, he is picked from among those members of upper-middle management who will, when they reach 55, be transferred to the top management of a subsidiary or affiliate. In other words, godfathers are people who know, having been passed over at age 45 for the top management spots, that they are not going to "make it" in their own organizations. Therefore, they are not likely to build factions of their own or to play internal politics. At the same time, they are the most highly respected members of the upper-middle management group.

During the first ten years or so of a young man's career, the godfather is expected to be in close touch with his "godchild," even though in a large company he may have 100 such godchildren at any one time. He is expected to know the young man, see him fairly regularly, be available to him for advice and counsel, and, in general, look after him. He has some functions that reflect Japanese culture; for instance, he introduces the young men under his wings to the better bars on the Ginza and to the right bawdy houses. (Learning how to drink in public is one of the important accomplishments the young Japanese executive has to learn.)

If a young man wants to be transferred, the godfather knows where to go and how to do what officially cannot be done and, according to the Japanese, "is never done." Yet nobody will ever know about it. And if the young man is errant and needs to be disciplined, the godfather will deal with him in private. By the time a young man is 30 the godfather knows a great deal about him.

It is the godfather who sits down with top management and discusses the young people. The meeting may be completely "informal." Over the sake cup, the godfather may say quietly, "Nakamura is a good boy and is ready for a challenging assignment," or "Nakamura is a good chemist, but I don't think he'll ever know how to manage people," or "Nakamura means well and is reliable, but he is no genius and better not be put on anything but routine work." And when the time comes to make a personnel decision, whom to give what assignment, and where to move a man, the personnel people will quietly consult the godfather before they make a move.[12]

Like all systems of human judgment, this system produces misjudgments, but much potential bias has been kept out it. As Drucker points out, the godfather has no personal axe to grind. He cannot favor his particular school, since all his charges came from it. He is not swayed by the tensions between superiors and subordinates in the coordinating hierarchy. No doubt the chemistry of personal likes and dislikes plays a role in biasing godfather judgments, but the godchild's career will not be ruined by such misjudgment. The majority can safely expect to retire

---

[12] Peter F. Drucker, "What We Can Learn from Japanese Management," *Harvard Business Review*, March/April 1971, pp. 120–21.

at age 55. About as well as a human system can, the Japanese system removes status threats from the enterprise. Secure status eradicates the personal defensiveness which snarls Western corporations and bureaucracies.

The Japanese avoid making formal invidious comparisons between people who must work together as a team. They do not have merit ratings or efficiency reports. In every possible way they try to protect the dignity of every individual. This concern does not derive from false notions of individual equality; the Japanese, like all humans, vary in their particular abilities. The *zaibatsu* are like the family that attempts to integrate a handicapped child by concentrating on his strength rather than calling attention to his disabilities. The handicapped child suffers no penalty in family social rank, since he did not self-select his handicaps. Penalties could do nothing but harm; they have no chance of "improving" his performance. By protecting his dignity, the family encourages the less able child to do his best. The initial selection procedures of the *zaibatsu* do tend to keep the range of skill differences within manageable bounds; they do not mix morons with geniuses, but even the best have blind spots and areas of weakness.

Chances are that in his entire career in a *zaibatsu* the employee will never receive a "tongue lashing," be fired, or get passed over for promotion. If others stay on while he retires, he has not been passed over; rather, they were selected out for special treatment. Thus he will never have cause to become so concerned over his personal status that he forgets about his job. Because the enterprise guarantees his status needs, defensiveness is unnecessary.

The Japanese do have effective techniques for letting an individual know if he is getting out of line, but they do not involve direct criticism, which means loss of face. This enters the realm of cultural niceties. Variations on the natural social order inevitably reflect the broader culture, but we should not imagine that "saving face" is peculiar to the Orient. The Western enterprise which humiliates the individual loses him as a team player (and often altogether), as much as it would in Japan.

*Fortune* once quoted an American corporate psychologist as saying, "This status thing is our biggest bugaboo. We've got to get rid of it."[13] The Japanese recognize that status will not be "got rid of." To avoid the problems status can introduce, they take proper care of the individual's status needs. Status problems will hinder the enterprise to the extent its social order allows them to do so. You can no more rid individuals of a need for status than you can rid them of a need for food.

---

[13] R. C. Albrook, "Those Boxed-in, Left-out Vice Presidents," *Fortune*, May 1, 1969, p. 107.

## Role and Participation in Decisions

The Japanese enterprise, which attaches identity and status to the enterprise and not to the individual's role in it, depends on participatory decision making. Social rank is not equated with political power in the bureaucratic sense; the concept of the executive as a lonely decision maker of major enterprise policy and strategy is foreign to the *zaibatsu*. Despite Japan's historical theories of absolutist political power, they recognized that autocratic decisions are destructive for human enterprise and avoided them in the world of work. Before industrialization, when the Japanese faced the problem of social control of the underemployed, they had turned to a modified absolutist system. At that time Japan had to support over two million Samurai who were more or less exempted from work other than fighting, and strict hierarchies traditionally had governed their social relations. When industrialization required the coordination of work, they adopted participatory decision making as a means of determining the course of the enterprise.

At work the Japanese participate directly in decisions which affect their own jobs. A worker in Toyota's accounting department is not asked for ideas on styling, and one in production scheduling need not be concerned with theories for marketing strategy on the East Coast of the United States. The rule of reason applies. It is also enterprise policy to isolate questions of identity, status, and prestige from operating problems, so that individuals have little urge to participate in decisions unless they are well versed in the technical aspects of the problem. By freeing management from political and social questions, the Japanese enterprise achieves the Western goal of a management which can analyze problems rationally and more or less impersonally.

*Biological Roots of Decision Making.* American firms spend vast amounts of time and devote much philosophical energy to the decision-making process. The *zaibatsu* view the actual choice among alternatives as one part of a larger process which is concerned with (1) defining the problem properly, (2) evaluating the relevant alternatives, and (3) implementation of the decision. The actual choice tends to "fall out" by consensus. Once people agree on the problem, typically, one alternative will stand out from the others. Implementation follows directly.

If you are confident of the cooperation you can expect in getting a decision implemented, the American approach can "reach" a decision quickly by Japanese standards. However, often nothing much happens thereafter. In the fraternal enterprise, on the other hand, everyone with technical knowledge first agrees on the problem's definition. If the decision reached enjoys the support of the knowledgeable, they will work toward its successful implementation. This is the way of the wolf; the pack huddles and then collectively decides if it can successfully attack the prey. With human hunters, too, enthusiastic agreement, not blind obedience, had to motivate the attack on the giant mammoth or saber-toothed tiger. Today participatory decision making determines the battle tactics of the Israeli army. The Israeli G.I. can critique an officer's plans and suggest alternatives, all on a first-name basis. Indeed, the officer solicits the soldier's ideas, in open council. However, this is true only of the planning phases. Once combat gets under way, no one debates tactics, and the entire effort is devoted to winning.

In the *zaibatsu*, too, once the decision has been made, it will be acted on swiftly. Neither the Israeli solidier nor the Japanese employee brings a unique genetic advantage into play to achieve this. Rather, the fraternal system has damped out all the internal resistance which bureaucracy inevitably generates. Like the wolf pack which has somehow reached a fraternal "go" decision, they charge hard and enthusiastically. Ethologists do not know how the wolf pack reaches its collective decision either to charge the prey or leave it alone. But as Lionel Tiger and Robin Fox point out, something similar often seems to happen with athletic teams which have practiced together for a long time.[14] The "decision" to win seems to occur more or less collectively and spontaneously, without benefit of conscious intellectual thought. None of this argues in favor of mystical decision making, but it does suggest that biological influences are at work. We may not understand them, but that does not preclude our making use of them. The evidence suggests that for humans, bureaucracy destroys these processes.

***Bureaucratic and Fraternal Decision Making.*** No greater mistake could be made than to try to apply participatory decision making in a bureaucracy. The fraternal decision requires an environment that is free of functional status. American have a richly justified horror of bureaucratic committees, because members seem to go into the meetings prepared mainly to defend their own functional-political positions. They wrangle endlessly and decide nothing. Few ever make concessions in the larger interests of the enterprise which go against the interests of their function. Only when individuals have identities and status attached to the enterprise itself and not to their role can they focus on the best interests of the enterprise.

Nothing is less natural than to use role as the basis for identity and status. But even if the broader culture does this, as the Japanese once did (while ours never has), the enterprise need not make this mistake. One of the many paradoxes I have found is that the Japanese enterprise is more consistent with our broader culture, historically, than with their own in its rejection of social stratification according to function. Social

[14] Lionel Tiger and Robin Fox, *The Imperial Animal* (New York: Holt, Rinehart & Winston, 1971).

status in America arises mainly from money, whatever the source. Different occupations have different levels of prestige in America, of course, but the basis of prestige in American culture is vastly different from the stratified functional social structure of a bureaucracy. Physicians may have more social prestige than janitors, but the man who makes a mint providing janitorial services can outsnob the physician, even without classifying himself as a sanitation engineer. Job-title snobbery in America has very tenuous roots and has arisen mainly from bureaucracy itself, not the culture. For years many American corporations did not even use job titles. Workers were blue- or white-collar, but beyond that their jobs might have no formal designation at all.

The Japanese have a name for their participatory decisions technique: they call it *ringi,* or *ringi-sho.* Typically the proposal for a decision arises in the middle ranks; if this technostructure accepts it, top management's approval usually follows. A member of top management who has an idea finds someone lower down to originate it, and it then goes up in the typical way. The *zaibatsu* start with the premise that the real "power" *must* be in the middle, the technostructure.

John Kenneth Galbraith has pointed that out that de facto the same is true in the United States, but American industrial bureaucracies pretend otherwise.

Japan's fraternal decision-making process has been described by M. Y. Yoshino, who notes that although it is radically different from modern management concepts of decision making, it has made the administration of large business organizations possible in Japan. The word *"ringi"* has two parts—*rin,* meaning submitting a proposal to one's superior and receiving his approval, and *gi,* meaning deliberations and decisions. Yoshino describes the process as follows:

> When a decision to be made is of some importance, it is quite likely that a considerable number of prior consultations will take place with those who may be affected by it, as well as with those who are in a position to influence its outcome. In formal meetings and by informal means an exchange of views and some bargaining will take place. *It is only after a consensus is reached that the ringisho is prepared and circulated among various executives for their formal approval.* Even in these cases, however, it should be noted that the initiative of coordination and consultation often rests with lower levels of management.
>
> Furthermore, top management can only act on matters submitted by lower levels of management—it cannot itself initiate new ideas. In order for top management to initiate a new idea, it must choose a subordinate to prepare a proposal and circulate it through the formal channels. Thus, under the strict ringi system, the role of the president is, in effect, that of legitimizing decisions made by group consensus by affixing his seal of

182

approval. Under this system, top management is not expected to exert strong leadership. This is consistent with a tendency found in other large collectivies in Japan where the formal leader is considered only the ceremonial and symbolic figurehead, whereas actual control rests with his key subordinates.

Although lower echelons of management actively participate in decision-making, it is not quite accurate to describe the Japanese management process as decentralized, inasmuch as decentralization of decision-making authority, at least in the American context, presupposes a clear-cut identification of who is responsible for decision-making in the first place. As we have seen, this is not the case in the Japanese organization. Perhaps a more accurate description of the Japanese pattern would be that the decision-making authority is widely diffused, rather than decentralized, throughout the organization.[15]

The *ringi* system can be awkward at times; it typically works slowly in the preimplementation phase. But at least it does not confuse a process that is smooth on paper with human reality. A certain messiness is inherent in reaching and then effectively acting upon decisions which require the future cooperation of coordinated teams. Such techniques as decision trees and systems analysis can do no more than help; numerology will never substitute for cooperative teamwork.

The imposed decision, however honestly made, inevitably generates resistance and backlash. Dictums of blind obedience to "legitimate authority" can work only temporarily. If the lone decision maker occasionally accomplishes a brilliant Inchon landing he will more likely come up with a Waterloo. Inefficiency is compounded with risk when all power of choice is placed in the hands of a single individual in the large human enterprise. The effort to do so has ruined one power structure after another, throughout recorded human history. This is not the case in Japan, where Hirohito can trace his lineage back to Jimmu Tenno, the first legendary emperor, because the emperor has been symbolic head of state, never the chief executive. Centralized power at the top will topple the structure sooner or later by mislocating the social center of gravity.

Power diffusion is a central facet of the natural social order and thus of effective teamwork. The *ringi* process proves that power diffusion, or wide participation in decision making, can work effectively in profit-minded complex business corporations. And I use the word "proves" literally. Moreover, the system works the world around; Japan's *zaibatsu* merely represent the most comprehensive industrial example. Few friendship groups fail to rely on a participatory process when they engage in work, whatever its purpose.

[15] Reprinted from *Japan's Managerial System* by M. Y. Yoshino by permission of the M.I.T. Press, Cambridge, Massachusetts. © 1968 The M.I.T. Press. Emphasis is mine.

***Training through Job Rotation.*** In Mitsui's moral legacy, job rotation is an important element of the individual's role. While some employees do specialize, specialization is not the usual career expectation. Specialization improves expertise up to a point, of course, but beyond that point is the realm of "trained incompetence." This problem even affects medicine; the more the physician concentrates on particular organs, the less he can know about the patient as a whole person. In business and government, individuals who specialize within functions or techniques are less wise in applying their knowledge to the problems of the whole enterprise. Trained incompetence results from enforced seclusion from the problems of other functions.

If prolonged exposure to one function causes a bond to form between the individual and the function, he can lose all objectivity. In such a case, genius becomes a positive menace. Because bonding is subintellectual, a genius such as Field Marshal Haig is apt to invent brilliant rationalizations for silly tactics. A stupid man would never ignore entrenched machine guns against massed infantry; it takes a certain genius to circumvent such obvious disadvantages. The function-bonded genius can actually behave far more stupidly in many situations than a person of only average intelligence. Lack of objectivity can do vastly more damage than lack of IQ.

Expertise, however, does not require bonding. It only requires applied study, given some ability for the subject. It is possible to become expert on something without acquiring a social identity, complete with formal status based on a particular expertise. Indeed one can become an expert on many things in order to avoid trained incompetence in a specialty.

The fraternal *zaibatsu* firms rotate assignments frequently enough to avoid both functional bonding and trained incompetence. Employees often receive training in areas they probably will never use themselves, but this training gives them a better overview of the enterprise and improves their performance. *Zaibatsu* firms have become noted for brilliantly researched staff studies on pending decisions, but they do not rely on an expert, so identified.

Training can come on the job or in reserve, that is outside the worker's own unit. In reserve the Japanese employee might learn anything from computer programming to the tea ceremony. The use of reserves, at both white- and blue-collar levels, enables the Japanese to avoid overjobbing. By any gross manpower comparison, the Japanese overman as badly as the British do, but they do not create the sort of fake jobs which infest U.S. aerospace, the British shop floor, or the civil services of developing countries.

In the early days of industrialization, the Japanese had to man their enterprises with displaced illiterate farmers. The *zaibatsu* were under pressure to hire, more or less indiscriminately, both displaced farmers flooding into the urban areas and the disemployed Samurai. Thus, at blue- and white-collar levels alike, the Japanese overmanned, sometimes on a heroic scale. Overmanning depressed wages, but it avoided serious unemployment or the need for large state welfare programs. It also avoided most of the trauma, alienation, and social chaos which still afflicts the West. (Liberals often avoid the study of Japan because they find it awkward that private free enterprise and not Marxism pulled off this coup, without coercion.)

It could probably not be claimed that the the *zaibatsu* avoided over-jobbing altogether. But they did create marginal jobs, not out-and-out fake jobs. Further, the employee's identity and status do not arise from his job, and this has made all the difference between Japan and other developing nations. The entirely natural tendency to share the available work occurred fraternally in Japan and bureaucratically in LDC and Britain. Surplus labor thus became an asset in Japan, a liability elsewhere.

***The Reserve Concept.*** The use of internal reserves proved crucial to the *zaibatsu's* ability to turn surplus labor into an asset. An employee might spend up to 35 percent of his entire career in "reserve," training for a variety of skills. The reserve system makes it possible to achieve reserve strength, far greater internal mobility of labor, and much more flexible employees, in both skills and attitude. The pitfalls of dead-end jobs, work monotony, and on-the-job alienation are avoided. The training reserves were originally set up because the first workers were illiterate. Interestingly enough, where Japan fails to set up such reserves, Western-style job territorial disputes tend to break out. The Japanese bureaucratic employee behaves as defensively as anyone else.

The Japanese take the reserve concept for granted. They have not made operating doctrine of it as our own military does (two up, one back, and feed 'em a hot meal), but it works more or less the same. Worker reserves rotate, they engage in training, and they stay on the payroll like anyone else. The individual's formal social rank and identity divorced from his job eliminates the complication of deciding how much to pay people in reserve. The Japanese do not confuse the concepts of employment as a social relationship with labor utilization as an economic relationship.

The Westerner can easily miss the reserves unless he has been alerted to the system. For example, the following excerpt from Richard Halloran's generally fine book, *Japan, Image and Realities* makes no mention of it in describing employment practices.

> Japan has supposedly developed a labor shortage in the last few years. Industrial expansion has dried up the excess labor supply from rural areas and the young adults who are the result of the immediate postwar baby boom. Companies complain that they can't get enough people. The labor

shortage is an illusion, however, as it is predicated on the practice of employing ten men for three men's work. *The social ethic says that everybody will be given work and the income divided so that everybody has a minimum living wage at least.* The labor shortage could and may be solved by giving each employee more work to do and increasing his income. The amount of wasted labor in Japan would stagger even the best featherbedders in American Labor.[16]

I became aware of the reserves only when a former Japanese student of mine, defending high labor content in practical rather than social terms, seized on the military analogy almost in desperation. As a part of the overall fraternal social order, reserves clearly make sense. The *zaibatsu* avoid altogether the horrors of skill dilution which have recently crushed efficiency in the U.S. aerospace industry. Enormous sums spent to train people literally disappear in the American hire-fire cycle. Imagine the élan and ability of a combat army which hired and fired with the tide of battle so as not to "waste" manpower by keeping it "idle" in reserve.

### Reward

To its misunderstanding of the use of reserves, the West wed an entirely false notion that life tenure makes labor costs a fixed rather than variable expense. At first the *zaibatsu* could only pay "survival" wages, partly in kind, in order to finance a reserve training corps. But as productivity has grown (faster than anywhere else in the world), so have wages. With higher productivity, an increasing percentage of wages comes as a bonus which fluctuates essentially with cash flow or revenue. Thus a growing proportion of labor costs varies automatically with revenue.

In Japan the bonus usually comes twice a year, but wages are usually quoted without it. This gives an entirely misleading impression of how much a Japanese worker actually earns. For example, according to press reports, a blue-collar worker of the Akai firm with 15 years' service, married and with two children, received a year-end bonus in 1969 of nearly $6,000. His earlier bonus had come to about $2,000. His base salary came to about $4,000, and the value of his fringe benefits (medical care, housing subsidies, etc.) to perhaps $2,000 more. The total, $14,000, would hardly be considered sweated labor in any country, yet his "wage" might easily be reported at $4,000. Since the 1973 devaluations his actual income in U.S. dollars would be about $18,000. Akai, of course, is exceptional.[17]

---

[16] Richard Halloran, *Japan, Images and Realities* (New York: Alfred A. Knopf, 1969), pp. 152–53. Emphasis is mine.

[17] "Akai Announces Japan's Fattest Bonus," *Bangkok Post*, December 8, 1969.

## The Zaibatsu Answer to the Individual's Social Needs

The policies which the *zaibatsu* use to meet the individual's social needs can be summarized as follows:

1. Identity: The permanent employee has lifetime membership with the enterprise. (Should his particular "chapter" fail, his rights extend to other chapters in the "fraternity.")
2. Status: The employee has personal social rank unrelated to his role, which rises automatically as he gains in experience.
3. Role: The employee receives a wide variety of assignments and spends about 30 percent of his career training for them. He participates in decisions which affect his role.
4. Prestige: The employee's prestige varies with his personal performance in teamwork.
5. Reward: The employee's income varies (via a bonus) with enterprise performance. His share is determined by his social rank. Merit reward comes at the normal career end.

### THE FRATERNAL SOCIAL ORDER IN THE BROADER CULTURE

It would be misleading to assume that there are no frustrations in the *zaibatsu*. Mistakes are made and failures occur; foul-ups and boondoggles are not unknown. The *zaibatsu* are not perfect, but because they are fraternal they closely if imperfectly duplicate the natural social order for human enterprise. Perhaps they expect too much off-the-job togetherness; always being polite has its own stresses. Japan's sensational postwar economic expansion has created serious problems with physical ecology. But none of these problems has been compounded with the alienation and social demoralization of the West.

In any event, the Japanese have created enterprises which can cope. For example, they have reached a stage of affluence where resources can be comfortably diverted to ecological problems. But Japan had its priorities right; it saw first to sound social ecology before addressing the easier problem of physical ecology.

In discussing Japan's fraternal free-enterprise, profit-minded, and capitalistic *zaibatsu* corporations I have avoided the culturally particular as much as possible. The niceties of the tea ceremony and negotiating procedures in business deals were simply ignored, so my account would not serve as a guide for those who want to do business in Japan. My reason for ignoring cultural aspects was to avoid confusing the culturally particular with the fraternally general. Fraternity can apply anywhere, not necessarily in the specific Japanese form.

I have stressed that a fraternal social order can operate in any culture because of its compatibility with the human biosocial needs. The particular mechanics of the application, however, cannot escape the influence of the broader culture. An attempt to create a fraternal social order exactly like the Japanese one in any other culture would probably incur great difficulties. While the broad social policies of the natural social order are applicable in all cultures, there is a good deal of room for cultural variance in the details of each application.

There is one aspect of Japanese culture which could make the Japanese more susceptible to deeper fraternal bonding than might hold true in the West. Appendix A discusses the concept of social imprinting, which occurs roughly in the second six months of life. The infant becomes socially imprinted, for better or worse, mainly by how often and how closely he is held. Holding facilitates an infant's future social bonding properties. The Japanese, like most Orientals, believe in holding the infant, if only in a back pack, as much as possible before he can walk. Possibly the well-imprinted Japanese would bond more deeply in later life with his enterprise than the typical Western male might. Even so, this would not change the teamwork-releasing properties of fraternity. It might mean, however, that a Western fraternity could take fewer liberties with the individual and still retain loyalty.

As a final note, I might mention a potential cultural problem which the very closeness of Japanese fraternity could present in an era of multinational corporations. America's more heterogeneous culture probably provides the potential for a more genuine international fraternity than would Japan's. Other things equal, this could give an international Ford a genuine advantage over an international Toyota.

# 9

# Variations on the Theme

## THE MILITARY

As the oldest direct descendant of the hunting bands, the military establishment retains many fraternal characteristics. The infantry squad of nine or ten men is the hunting band reincarnated, and the squad, not the soldier, forms the basic fighting unit of any army. When General S. L. A. Marshall studied the reactions of the World War II combat soldier under fire,[1] he suggested the following situation: Assume 100 soldiers are deployed by putting one man in each foxhole. Every soldier thus fights as an individual. Then assume an attack on the 100 defenders by a squad of 10. Each defender will feel himself outnumbered by ten to one! The defenders, unable to draw on each other for moral support, are likely to break and run.

This example illustrates our ability to face danger collectively more effectively than we do as autonomous individuals. Under the stress of danger we probably react little differently than did our ancestor *Australopithecus*. The human male prefers to face danger in primary groups of 7 to 11. No experience (including sex) more exhilarates the human male than successfully overcoming danger or meeting some other suitable challenge within a fraternally bonded band.

The Iroquois, Samurai, Borneo headhunters, and Norsemen, among others, engaged in perpetual low-grade warfare. They fought more for sport than for conquest. As Lionel Tiger and Robin Fox have pointed out, war is a specific male problem, not a general human one.[2] Agricul-

---

[1] Samuel L. Marshall, *Men Against Fire: The Problem of Battle Command in Future War* (New York: Peter Smith, 1948).

[2] Lionel Tiger and Robin Fox, *The Imperial Animal* (New York: Holt, Rinehart & Winston, 1971).

ture downgraded hunting as an economic requirement, but the hunter's urge to seek danger in fraternal association remained. Robert Ardrey developed this thesis in some depth in *African Genesis*.[3] Behaviorists, especially those of a pacifistic bent, fear that admitting to a biological risk-taking urge somehow justifies war. Actually the evidence is pretty clear that overcoming *any* sort of challenge, particularly an economic one, satisfies the risk-taking urge. We *do not* have a gene which commands men to behave violently and destructively, as Eric Fromm points out.[4] Rather men have a generalized urge to overcome challenge in fraternal association. Indeed, they prefer to do so in the broader survival interests of their economic community rather than in destructive violence. Nevertheless, violence can satisfy the male urge for risk taking if other outlets do not exist. Early agriculture did not fill this need.

## The Fighting Farmer

Farmers make better fighters and soldiers than hunters or merchants do. The challenge of farming does not compare to the challenge of fighting. Farming has problems which must be met, but the subsistence farmer often can only *react* to nature, watching helplessly as flood or drought threatens life. Thus the farmer has a bottled-up challenge to overcome. He can fight back to the visitations of a foreign foe, or even *initiate* the visitation. War can satisfy male urges that farming cannot.

Teen-agers of any background make the best soldiers. Several innate urges peak during adolescence: the risk-taking urge, the urge to conform to the norms of one's fellows, and a willingness to sacrifice life on behalf of bonded brethren. When a rural background lacking in satisfactory outlet for fraternal challenge is added to these urges, you have the makings of a real warrior. A teen-age farmer will outfight a city boy on the attack every time, other things equal. Defense is a different matter, since both benefit from nature's injection of courage into all territorial defenders. What hampers the city boy in aggressive war is that he is more likely to have been presented with satisfactory fraternal surrogates to hunting. An atmosphere of commercial competition also somewhat dissipates the urge to violence, physical danger, and destructiveness. The city boy's early fraternal experiences and his acceptance of a commercially competitive way of life make him a doubtful conqueror. Because he has no bottled-up biological motivation, he does not qualify as a natural warrior.

---

[3] Robert Ardrey, *African Genesis* (New York: Atheneum, 1961).

[4] Erich Fromm, "Man Would as Soon Flee as Fight," *Psychology Today*, August 1973, p. 35.

Many warlike peoples, upon achieving commercial success, have abandoned their warlike ways. Scandinavia and Switzerland are European examples. Britain's record as conqueror sagged decidedly after the onset of the Industrial Revolution. The "playing fields of Eton" may have served Wellington well, but he was lucky to be fighting a defensive battle at Waterloo. For as Eton and industry grew, imperial aggression slowed, ceased, then rapidly contracted. Agriculture, not industry and commerce, frustrates the imperial animal enough to motivate military conquest. Had the United States remained an agricultural nation, we might well have gone on an imperial rampage, redefining our Manifest Destiny to apply not only coast to coast but pole to pole. Merely gathering in nature's bounty is not enough for the human male. He began to foresake that life 20 million years ago, and returned to it only 10,000 years ago—"man's great leap backward," to quote Tiger and Fox.[5] Japan's commercial triumphs may well defuse any future Japanese aggression, since there no longer is a large pool of subsistence farm youth. It is no wonder that the Samurai kept the merchants at the bottom of the social heap, since the commercial life threatened the motivation of the warrior much more than farming did.

The military life is far from a satisfactory hunting alternative. Even among such warriors as the Iroquois and Samurai (and at roughly the same time), signs appeared that the disadvantages outweighed the advantages. The Iroquois Confederation (reputedly a model for the U.S. Constitution) was formed under the urgings of Hiawatha, who hoped to keep internal peace, within perhaps 100 years of the time Tokugawa Iyeyasu brought endemic civil war to an end in Japan.

## Autocratic Leadership and Underemployment

The modern military establishment has even less to recommend it as a fraternal outlet. For the one thing the destructive power of nuclear weapons makes the risk of war a risk of extinction. Aside for this unacceptable danger, there are other problems. Since the Industrial Revolution, war between modern nations has become episodic, and the military life, like industry, suffers from gross underemployment. Idleness always endangers the human animal's psychological balance. When years and even decades pass by between wars, the military life degenerates into largely empty ceremony and contrived activity requiring exaggerated social deference (ESD).

Prolonged underemployment or idleness always necessitates stern dominance orders to maintain social control. Yet education makes such control seem tyrannical and pointless. Garrison spit and polish does

---

[5] Tiger and Fox, *The Imperial Animal.*

little or nothing to improve combat effectiveness. The more educated the rank and file, the more they see this. The soldier can only spend so much time training and so much time in housekeeping chores; after that, he must invent things to do. Educated soldiers resent busy work even if it prevents trouble, because they not only need to keep busy, they want to do so usefully. Nothing will be more resented than imposed "displacement activity."

The Israeli army has avoided the problem of peacetime garrison idleness by allowing most Israeli soldiers to live useful civilian lives between wars. Israel's small size makes civilian reserve deployment practical, since most Israeli soldiers can arrive at their unit within hours of a mobilization order. Thus, in combat, the Israeli army can behave "naturally" because garrison "discipline" has been dispensed with.

ESD may control the idle, but it also interfers with effective combat operations. Most modern armies impose ESD in peacetime but abandon it in combat. The natural warrior state almost never gives evidence of autocratic leadership, belief in "blind obedience," or ESD. The Iroquois, rated as among the most effective fighting Indians in North America, hardly used leaders, let alone ESD, in their raids. Consensus of objectives and tactics before the raid, together with practiced teamwork, made the strong leader redundant at the unit level. Man for man, most Indians outfought the Army; they were simply overwhelmed by both numbers and technology.

Of course it is necessary to create a coordinating hierarchy to oversee a complex operation. Discipline must prevail, but even so, a doctrine of blind obedience will interfere with efficiency. General Robert Nivelle's grisly offensive in the spring of 1917 which led to the revolt of the French Army is testimony to the dangers of the autocratic commander. Nivelle started out with a good enough plan, but he so publicized it that the Germans learned of it and made appropriate defensive adjustments. Thereafter, as Nivelle's own staff clearly saw, his plan was simply a program for the slaughter of the French Army. Nivelle followed through on the original program and ruthlessly suppressed staff criticism, even after all his preconditions for success had vanished.

Such military catastrophes throughout history fail to support the contention that military leadership must be autocratic. Only if the war is being fought with the objective of thinning out the male population can a case be made for the military autocrat. It is no argument to observe that the autocrat in command of a particular catastrophe was a "poor commander" or "bad strategist" or whatever. The problem with autocracy is that to succeed it depends on godlike men, which nature has not seen fit to evolve. Nor is the alternative anarchy, as the Israeli army has proven. Between autocracy and anarchy stands fraternity, nature's own solution.

Generally speaking, naval (and more recently air) operations have experienced fewer problems with autocratic leadership and underemployment. Overmanning on naval vessels does raise problems of idleness, since manning must reflect the rare chance of combat and possible subsequent damage, not the normal needs of the ship's operations. The average naval vessel has perhaps three or four times as many people as it needs when it is not fighting or in maneuvers. The old idea of the captain as absolute autocrat has eroded considerably, and for good reason. When captains shanghaied their crew, they needed a cat-o'-nine-tails to keep them in line.

## Natural Social Elements in Military Society

Despite underemployment and autocracy, the military still retains many technical elements of the natural social order. Social rank and job function remain separate. The chain of command differs from the hierarchy of social rank. Informal prestige also has independent status; the individual can receive recognition for individual valor or outstanding service independently of his rank or job. The medal is a visible reward for bravery.

Individual identity, status, prestige, and reward all occur more or less in the natural way in the military. The same cannot be said of role. Typically the individual soldier must perform make-work without much opportunity to participate in deciding what he does or how he does it. The opportunity to participate rises with rank, but the weak link in the military social order remains with role. This weakness arises from the underlying problems of peacetime underemployment and substitute make-work that is autocratically coordinated.

Nevertheless, the military discovered the division of labor long before Adam Smith. Most organizational techniques used by industry to coordinate division of labor effectively were borrowed from the military, which innovated the chain of command, line and staff, the project organization (task force), market research (intelligence), and even operations research. The corps-unit form of organization adopted by the military is discussed in Appendix B.

## PATERNALISM IN THE FAMILY ENTERPRISE

Fraternity in economic affairs is most clearly illustrated by the family-initiated enterprises. The family enterprise founded by Mitsui Hachirobei was later promoted into a fraternal conglomerate, an entirely natural development. An extended family forms a better foundation for a family business than a nuclear family, because it will have a better chance of going fraternal. An enterprise based on the nuclear family alone is apt to become paternalistic, and at best paternalism will be mildly autocratic; at worst, viciously so. An authority contest between an aging paternal autocrat and an aspiring son can endanger the enterprise, so that the family risks losing control even if the enterprise survives. Autocratic authority can be addicting, but it serves the individual's own interests poorly, however much it is savored.

In an enterprise based on an extended family, including brothers and cousins, it is possible to avoid paternalistic autocracy. When the founder passes from the scene the succeeding head will more likely reign than rule, and the top job will not be open to political contention. The descendants will think in terms of perpetuating the enterprise rather than contending for personal control. Operating control will find its natural place near the middle of the enterprise. Dominance struggles will always endanger the enterprise, however, unless fraternal policies are made official. The enterprise which does not apply fraternal policy to all permanent employees may backslide into paternalism or get waylaid by bureaucracy. To distinguish between kin and other employees in terms of policy sets up pointless internal stresses.

America rose to industrial greatness with the family enterprise. Those industries that allowed themselves to be subverted by bureaucracy early, such as railroads and steel, earned a reputation for indifferent management. Others, such as duPont, ESSO, General Motors, Sears, Weyerhaeuser, IBM (which, like Japanese firms, even had company songs) and others held off bureaucracy for a long time.

My first job upon getting out of college in the early 1950s was in the corporate headquarters office of the Weyerhaeuser Company at Tacoma, Washington. Never have I witnessed such loyalty to a company by its rank-and-file employees. No one ever criticized the company as such. One might not like certain individuals, but the company was above direct criticism, by general consent. The pay was not very high, but the bonuses usually were quite generous. Tales of the Great Depression when Mr. Weyerhaeuser (I forgot which one) reputedly dipped into his personal fortune to meet the payroll were common.

I was the greenest of new employees, but only four levels existed between me and the president. I felt no sense whatever of being stifled by bureaucracy, although I harbored no illusions of social equality. If my social rank was low, I was new and young. In so flat an organization, one's social rank really did depend on seniority. One could almost take life tenure for granted, assuming reasonable diligence. Job titles and job descriptions had just come into use, but nobody paid much attention to them. Pay was an individual thing, only loosely related to one's job. Yet I knew of no one with a reputation as a "goof off." There were few petty rules, yet hardly anyone tried to take advantage. This was what American capitalism was all about—at least I thought so, as a white-collar overhead employee. Had the Korean War not intervened, I might be there yet.

The atmosphere at Weyerhaeuser could be described as paternalistic, but this would be misleading. The firm actually was comprised of quite a few separate corporations, most of them headed by family members. Yet the average employee felt bonded to Weyerhaeuser, to the whole fraternity, or so it seemed to me. The employee's attachment transcended loyalty to any particular family member; the Weyerhaeuser name itself evoked pride. Transfers of employees between enterprises were common, but the identity of Weyerhaeuser prevailed. The practical difference between Weyerhaeuser's white-collar employees in the early 1950s and today's *zaibatsu* would have been small. Weyerhaeuser made good profits in a highly competitive industry. I do not know what has happened since, but hopefully Weyerhaeuser still enjoys comparative freedom from bureaucracy.

## THE BELL TELEPHONE "FRATERNITY"

One American enterprise which approaches fraternity despite enormous size and some bureaucratic elements is the Bell System. No comparable-size enterprise anywhere operates more efficiently. Certainly no other telephone company which I have had to endure throughout the world comes remotely close to Bell's good service and low prices. True, in recent years, service has started to decline in some places. Perhaps the bureaucratic malignancy has started to spread, which would be a great pity.

I know of Bell mainly as a West Coast customer; I cannot comment on its internal operations. But it is a healthy sign that not one person in a hundred could name Bell's chief executive, even though nearly everyone buys its service. Fraternal leadership tends to be muted and low profile. The reputation centers on the enterprise itself, not its leader.

Another evidence of fraternity is Bell's reputation for promoting strictly from within and never firing anybody. A professor from Harvard Business School has advocated going outside for "new blood," suggesting that "It would shake the industry to its boots." Unfortunately, it would. Many share the professor's naiveté on the relationship between loyalty and teamwork, thus betraying a thinly veiled view of the manager as godlike and the employee as clodlike.

## THE MAFIA

The natural social order in human enterprise by no means guarantees its pursuit of the paths of righteousness. The Mafia is reported to gross something like $40 billion annually from its nefarious operations.[6] If so, it takes in more revenue than any other enterprise in the country, outside of government. Perhaps no group illustrates better the economic staying power of fraternity.

The Mafia is a true tribe comprising many bands of predators. Frequent territorial disputes between bands often lead to bloodshed. Disloyalty merits the death sentence. Loyalty, the rock of any fraternity, governs internal relationships, in prison or out; members are even said to take a loyalty oath in blood.[7]

The Mafia takes good care of its members' social needs. They enjoy permanent identity. Status depends entirely on social rank, which is patterned after military rank. There is role or job flexibility, and job title does not determine social rank. Prestige, in the best fraternal fashion, depends on accomplishments. Reward varies with the proceeds of the gang to which one belongs.

Of course, its underworld status and the character of its operations lays a stress on the Mafia which a normal fraternity would not have to endure. Voluntary departure can be risky. The Mafia's reputed restriction of the full rights of fraternity to those of Italian and preferably Sicilian descent could ultimately undermine it. Unbonded hoods would never have the same fraternal commitment to the enterprise. The male offspring of the regular fraternal members may become corrupted with the broader society's ideals of virtue and honesty. They may pair bond with non-Italians and thus father progeny to uncertain membership eligibility, or attempt to channel the fraternity into the avenues of legitimate business. Time can introduce all sorts of problems which will lay stress on a policy requiring pure Italian descent for fraternal membership.

A departure from this policy would introduce other stresses, at least temporarily. Given the importance to the Mafia of Harlem and other black ghettos, for example, are blacks to be admitted into full membership? If blacks are kept out of the inner circle, they might form rival groups. They could organize along the same fraternal lines, using their basic Mafia training, and then eject the Mafia as a territorial intruder. On the other hand, if blacks do join the inner circle, a difficult and perhaps uneasy period of suspicious adjustment would follow. Defections by either side would probably increase, making the whole enterprise more vulnerable.

This same suspiciousness could arise with any other non-Italian element of course, not just blacks. Such problems are crucial because of the illegal nature of the operation. In principle any fraternity founded

---

[6] Peter Maas, *The Valachi Papers* (New York: G. P. Putnam's Sons, 1968).

[7] See *Time*, August 22, 1969.

on narrow ethnic grounds would suffer from similar traumas in broadening the membership base, but a legal enterprise will not be nearly so jeopardized by possible transitional disaffections.

The legal enterprise also can usually count on its symbiotic purpose to unite factions, whereas the Mafia has largely predatory aims. Any endeavor which puts the sole emphasis on predation will defeat itself; it will either exterminate or hopelessly alienate its prey, unless a mutually useful exchange occurs. The Mafia enjoys an element of symbiotic appeal because it thrives on the fact that prohibitive consumer "blue laws" demand almost total community support if they are to be successful. Majority rule never works; any time a sizable minority wants to consume something—the services of prostitutes, gambling, drugs, etc.—it will usually find a way, and the Mafia fulfills this "need." The more heterogeneous the society or community, the less will the simple fact of illegality matter, because some groups will always feel others simply seek to impose their own standards. Thus the blue laws put the Mafia in business and keep it there, with the help of the police. Unpopular blue laws almost guarantee the corruption and ultimate prebendalization of the police, who sooner or later take payoffs to look the other way.

## THE KIBBUTZIM

The Israeli kibbutzim began as a more or less Marxist experiment on the local level. The kibbutz experiment predates Israel's modern-day existence as a nation; indeed kibbutzim were an important element in the achievement of independence. Although some of the early kibbutzim looked to the Soviet Union for spiritual guidance, they have grown disillusioned with Russian communism and now stand mainly on their own merits and traditions. Marxian premises still influence kibbutznik thinking, but the dogma has been softened.

The typical kibbutz began as an agricultural commune. The founders were usually idealistic young people who wanted to abandon the "decadence" of bourgeois urban life but who tended toward doctrinaire social arrangements. The typical kibbutz nevertheless organized an economy in line with fraternal elements in Marxist ideology. An important difference between the kibbutzim and Russian communism, however, is that collective ownership stops at the kibbutz boundary. Members own their particular enterprise collectively, but no others. The kibbutzim began as farms but have since branched out into various types of light industry and some services. As an economic enterprise the typical kibbutz relies heavily on the natural social order to meet individual social needs, avoiding the bureaucracy of a Russian collective farm almost completely.

## Exceptions to Fraternity

But while achieving substantial economic fraternity, the kibbutzim saddled themselves with a number of unnatural and superfluous policies. Child rearing was all but taken out of the hands of mothers. This disrupts parental bonding, which is as much to the disadvantage of mothers as it is to children. Peer group bonding can make up much of the deficit for the children, but to this day, according to M. E. Spiro, intergenerational friendships rarely go deep, nor does parent-offspring attachment.[8] Disruption of normal kin bonding does not seem to prevent adults from normal bonding to the enterprise, but the tenuous kinship bonds probably breed tensions which otherwise would not appear in later life. Unlike the Japanese, for example, members of a kibbutz often exhibit much verbal aggression toward one another.

Perhaps they lack sufficient social imprinting as infants during the crucial period. The kibbutz might assign only one full-time nurse to three infants. Though the parents visit their offspring, this is not enough to allow them to form normally deep parent-child attachments. Segregated quite rigorously by peer group, the children bond to each other but then rarely pair bond as adults, almost as if they were siblings. This works in its fashion, but the kibbutz is too big to take over all the nurturing duties of the family.

Another mistake in the early days (which has now been largely corrected) was to confuse the advantages of belongingness with togetherness. No adequate allowance was made for individual privacy, which ultimately proved frustrating. When practical concessions were made to reality, an idealistic commitment to "group dynamics" (togetherness) was quietly moderated. (Here I refer to life off the job, not to teamwork on the job.) Possibly a relationship exists between early social imprinting, bonding, and a capacity for togetherness.

The early kibbutzim tried to leap from the pair bond directly to the economic community, bypassing both the nuclear and the extended family. The kibbutzim were saved from breaking up because of this unnatural attenuation of family life by common causes such as Arab hostilities, other threats, and their defense role. The large economic community cannot do family nurturing duty effectively, and nothing has yet replaced family nurture for infants. The family is a sort of missing social link in the kibbutz system.

Another factor affecting the early kibbutzim was that agricultural work lacks something of the competitive thrust for the enterprise as a whole of either hunting or commerce. The early kibbutzim disowned the notion of competition, but however hard we try, we cannot disown

---

[8] M. E. Spiro, *Children of the Kibbutz* (Cambridge, Mass.: Harvard University Press, 1958).

our biological heritage. Informal competition for internal kibbutz prestige thus can be fierce. Moreover a somewhat xenophobic outlook on the rest of the world soon emerged. Such aggressive resentment has been softened in recent years, in part with the rise of kibbutz industries, but it found expression in a challenge to outside forces. In all of Israel's wars, the soldiers furnished by the kibbutzim have been among the best.

### Meeting Indivividual Needs in a Kibbutz

In other respects, the kibbutz meets all the individual's social needs in a successful economic enterprise. The kibbutznik does indeed enjoy permanent and everlasting identity with the enterprise. If anything, status may be a bit too equal. It seems to rise informally with seniority, but this translates only tenuously into greater privilege, such as preference for senior members if the kibbutz improves housing quality.

Generally the individual performs the work for which he is best qualified and which he desires to do. Unpopular jobs rotate. So do managerial jobs, but mainly among those who have demonstrated a capacity for them. Political control remains with the membership as a whole; only it can eject a member for conduct threatening to the enterprise, for example. In the natural fraternal sense, management exerts technical authority nonpolitically. This applies even to deployment; work rosters are made up by committees whose members rotate. Nearly everyone will occasionally draw an assignment which entails some management authority and responsibility. Such tasks warrant no special privilege and are, therefore, not particularly popular. Managerial chores often require work in addition to normal duties, which hardly improves their desirability.

Generally the least desirable work in the kibbutz appears to be "family" related. Food preparation, laundry, clothes making, and child nurturing have been largely taken over by the kibbutz. Judging from Spiro's account of the problems this caused in Kibbutz Kiryat Yedidim,[9] a net loss was incurred from taking family work out of its natural clan setting. The bulk of these chores still fell to women, because women were not always physically strong enough for heavy field work. Thus early attempts to ignore sex differences in work assignments did not work out; biology usually prevails over ideology when the two conflict. The ideological denial of family life may explain why men generally find kibbutz life more satisfying than women do. Because women cannot perform their natural role in the natural way, some women experience a lack of fulfillment.

---

[9] Ibid.

There is no formal job ranking; the kibbutz spiked this bureaucratic malady early. While people have strong work preferences based on their abilities, no pecking order exists. The coordination of work depends on the muted leadership of classic fraternity, as Spiro describes it:

> The position of foreman, like the other managerial positions in the Kibbutz, is elective; but the manner of election depends upon the nature of the branch. In those branches in which the workers are permanent, the foreman is elected by his fellow workers in the branch. Where the workers of a branch are temporary, however (because of the distasteful nature of the work, so that its membership rotates) the foreman is elected by the town meeting. The foreman is an administrative, rather than a policy-determining, official. He makes the daily decisions concerning the number of workers, in addition to his permanent crew, he requires: where and how they are to be allocated; what machinery he will require. Since almost all permanent workers in a branch are experts in their work, the foreman is merely a temporary primus inter pares; temporary, because this responsibility rotates among the members of the branch. Policy decisions concerning the branch are made, therefore, by the entire branch, and not by the foreman alone.[10]

The kibbutzim began with the premise that political and management authority should be divorced and that no special social majesty should attach to the management function. This does not deny importance to the management function, nor does the policy assume that everyone has the competence to manage. The kibbutzim early discovered that management skills, as all other skills, are distributed along a bell curve. Not everyone has the competence to lead, but some management skills do not require "leadership" talent. Money management, for example, or a flair for scheduling work efficiently does not necessarily tax charismatic abilities.

Thus the kibbutzim recognized that if management tasks are invested with exalted social status, the talented and untalented alike will strive to get them. Technical management tasks will be avoided whenever possible if they have no special status. And stripped of political power, the management job will not appeal to those with a surplus dominance drive. Status and dominance drives exist as ends in themselves, independently of each other and of any incidental talents required for politically powerful positions of high status.

According to the legends of bureaucracy and conventional management wisdom, a kibbutz cannot function. For one thing, no one would be motivated to work; everyone would lie down on the job. Stripped of euphemisms, conventional management theory insists that people

---

[10] Ibid., p. 82

work for only two reasons, fear and greed. If this were really so we would probably have remained small-brained primates.

Spiro believes the most interesting and the most crucial aspect of the kibbutz economic system is economic motivation. His description of personal motivation on the kibbutz is worth quoting at length.

> . . . In the absence of private property, and of money, it is obvious that the profit motive does not operate in this society. Moreover, this is not a stratified society in which persons in authority compel their subordinates to carry out their responsibilities. Kiryat Yedidim has no supreme political authority—other than the group itself—and its economic executives and managers serve, as had already been noted, at the pleasure of the people. Nevertheless, despite the absence of those economic motives that have become conventional in other western societies, the chaverim successfully operate an economy of no small proportions.
>
> It should be noted in the first place that the absence of the profit motive does not imply that other conventional motives are absent from kibbutz economic behavior. The chaver has at least four personal motives for not shirking his economic responsibilities and for working hard and efficiently. As is the case in capitalist society, the harder he works, the greater the economic returns he receives. It is true that the returns from his labor do not accrue to him directly, so that he does not see the immediate effects of his productivity. Nevertheless, his own standard of living is dependent upon that of the group which, in turn, depends upon the productive capacity of its members. Everyone is aware of the fact that if he were to "take it easy," and, that if others were to do the same, then he, along with the rest, would suffer. Hence, one important source of work motivation in Kiryat Yedidim is the motive of personal economic improvement.
>
> It should be remembered, moreover, that most chaverim have deliberately chosen to live a rural life and to work in an agricultural economy. Furthermore, the chaver, in most cases, works in a branch which interests him the most. Consequently, the average person enjoys his work, deriving pleasure from its actual performance, as well as from its end product. What Veblen termed, "the instinct of workmanship," or what is called "mode pleasure"—in contrast to "end pleasure"—are as applicable to the average chaver as they are to anyone else. In short, a second personal motive for economic behavior consists in the fact that the average chaver derives intrinsic satisfactions from his work.
>
> Competitive pride is a third source of economic motivation. The average chaver is a permanent member of a particular economic branch—the orchard, the wheat fields, the dairy, etc.—and his immediate attachment and identification is with his branch, taking pride in its success, and becoming depressed by its failures. And though he wishes to see the entire kibbutz prosper, he derives great satisfaction from knowing that his branch contributed its share—or more—to this prosperity. Hence, he is motivated to work hard in order for his branch to receive a favorable rating in this informal competition. To note but one example: normally

the most productive branch in the kibbutz is field crops, and the workers in this branch generally show a perceptible superiority over those in other branches. The year in which the author's research was conducted, however, was a drought year, and the yield from the grain harvests was low. Thanks to artificial irrigation, however, the vegetable gardens had a highly successful year. The pride of the garden workers in this fact was apparent to all.

A final personal motive for efficient and productive economic behavior is prestige. It will be remembered that labor is one of the paramount values in the culture of the Kiryat Yedidim, and that hard, efficient labor is a necessary, if not sufficient, determinant of prestige. In the absence of the profit motive, the respect of one's fellows has become an important motive in this society. Few are willing to jeopardize this respect by shirking on the job, and since most work is performed in cooperative work groups, shirking would be spotted immediately. Given the importance of labor in the kibbutz hierarchy of values, public opinion—or daat hakahal, as it is known—is a highly important factor in work motivation.[11]

Despite the stresses from unnatural family life, the kibbutzim have survived to quite literally make the desert bloom. Kibbutzim clearly can no longer be classed as experimental. The Weberian contention that only bureaucracy can effectively coordinate large-scale enterprise is proven false by the kibbutzim and *zaibatsu*. Together they demonstrate the effectiveness of the natural social order along a wide spectrum of human economic enterprise.

The initial kibbutzniks had to make a complete and abrupt cultural shift from the ethos of private accumulation to fraternal sharing. Moreover, as Jews, they had to learn a new line of work after centuries of competitive commercial endeavor. Generally the Jews had no tradition of agricultural activity. (The Japanese made about as abrupt a shift in the reverse direction, from agriculture to industry.) The founders of the kibbutzim, moreover, had spent almost all their formative years learning a culture diametrically opposed to the kibbutz life style. Their successful transition suggests that early cultural learning to the contrary poses no insuperable obstacle to the fraternal social order in economic enterprise.

The kibbutzim also have demonstrated that ideological commitment to biologically unsound social arrangements will either fail or cause problems. Ignoring sex differences in work assignments failed, and the refusal to form family living groups causes continuing problems, particularly to women. We cannot change behavioral predispositions by learning or ideological propaganda.

I do not argue that everyone should live a fraternal economic exist-

---

[11] Ibid., pp. 83–84.

ence but that the overwhelming majority would find fraternity preferable to the bureaucratic social order. Those who fear the tyranny of the group over the individual have much more to fear from the bureaucracy than from fraternity. The individual has no safeguards in the BSO, whereas he has many in the natural social order. Nor do I argue the relative merits of the "lone wolf" existence and a collective endeavor in any social order. Each individual can answer this question for himself, as he does in Japan and Israel and, for that matter, in Britain or America. In any event, collective endeavor is here to stay. The issue boils down to what kind of social order best achieves humane efficiency in collective endeavors, fraternal or bureaucratic? I argue that fraternity wins hands down.

No two cultures hold theological views on the spiritual importance of the individual versus the group at greater variance than do the Jews and the Japanese. However, each in its own way has found the natural social order to be humane, effective, and profitable in its collective economic affairs.

# Part V

## LIFE WITHOUT BUREAUCRACY: FRATERNAL FREE ENTERPRISE

# 10

# The Fraternal Enterprise

## WHO STANDS TO LOSE?

The policies of the fraternal enterprise provide essential social nutrition for employees, who respond with more self-discipline and cooperation and generally superior teamwork compared to how they respond to the bureaucratic social order. Both employer and employee benefit in the fraternal enterprise, because they cease being artificial adversaries and become natural partners. The adversary relationship between capital and labor is imposed gratuitiously. Were it otherwise, sole proprietors would be at continual odds with themselves over the clash in interests between the capital they invest in their businesses and the labor they put into them.

Many managers, particularly at the top, intuitively know that partnership is the basis for teamwork, without which efficiency falters. Yet few managers understand the social foundation which must be built before such teamwork can be achieved. They do know in some general way that employees should be treated as people, and they may treat those with whom they deal personally with courtesy and respect. But at a hierarchical distance, corporate policy and not the personality of the top man governs. The results often are at odds with those the president personally seeks.

When corporate policy assures a foundation for fraternity, genuine esprit de corps emerges and teamwork comes easily. Top management does not have to tread lightly in matters of human relations. Its problems in this respect are solved by its respect for the fraternal social order.

The accomplishment of any social change has at least two dimensions. First, the goal must be desirable and must seem to be desirable to those it affects. Second, almost no change can be made without some difficulty to someone, no matter how beneficent the change. If robust good health were to become the norm, for example, the medical and dental professions would be in trouble.

Those who would stand to lose most by widespread adoption of the fraternal form of enterprise are the trade union hierarchies. As now organized, trade unions, have a vested interest in perpetuating the adversary relationship between capital and labor. They acquired this interest innocently, to be sure, for capital initially created the rift, and the trade unions responded. If this rift were closed, the resulting partnership between capital and labor would undercut the trade union movement by removing the "enemy." As police "need" criminals, physicians "need" the sick, and civil rights crusaders "need" bigots, so trade union officials "need" corporations, public or privately owned, they can identify as "grasping, selfish, and profit-mad" and managements they can charge with seeking to "victimize helpless workers."

Any proposal to fuse the identity of the employer and the employee in the enterprise would threaten the existence of the trade union movement. Unions depend on a brotherhood of the trade, not of the enterprise. This originally made sense for independent artisans, as it now makes sense for physicians or attorneys. But even as an Army physician has little need for the AMA, so would an employee of a fraternal business enterprise have little need for the AFL–CIO.

Should any serious attempt be made at corporate conversion to fraternal social policies, trade union officials predictably would try to block or at least slow down the transition. Much would depend on the strategy and tactics employed to deal with the unions. Elbowing them aside would probably incur the most resistance. An effort to negotiate a transition in the usual way would probably fail, however, and might be worse than merely ignoring the unions. Trade union officials are no more likely to negotiate themselves out of existence than anyone else; they, too, will fight to preserve their identity and status, even though the justification for their existence may have disappeared.

In the long run, however, resistance by trade unions will succeed or fail depending on the outlook of the membership, not the elected officials. If rank-and-file union members see fraternal enterprise as a better bet for themselves, they will turn their backs on the union. The crucial question then becomes how rank-and-file employees will regard fraternal enterprise. If they do not see it as of positive benefit to themselves, the advantages of a fraternal enterprise will remain academic. Therefore, the first viewpoint to be considered is that of the employee, union or nonunion.

## ADVANTAGES TO THE EMPLOYEE

The fraternal social order has four major advantages to employees, including management employees. First, employment security would vastly improve and become something of a vested right of tenure, and pay would reflect the indivdual's personal rank and the relative success of the enterprise. Second, good times or bad, the employee could look for steady promotion as he rises in rank, which is personal and unconnected, at least directly, to job assignment. Third, the employee would avoid the monotony of dead-end jobs and be allowed to broaden his skills by rotating between operational and reserve training assignments. Fourth, the employee would not be alienated from his enterprise but would enjoy the more natural feeling of loyalty to it and to his fellows, in exchange for the fraternal protection it accords him. He would not fear arbitrary abuse, even unintentionally administered. In short, he would enjoy human dignity in cooperative enterprise as his own "identity crisis" and struggle for status ceased. The employee's loyalty would center on the enterprise, not on its leader. He would experience fraternity, not paternalism.

### Tenure and Pay

Widespread tenure requires an end to the fixed rate of pay as it now applies, whether stated in hourly, weekly, monthly, or annual rates. We have stressed that an employee's income should rise or fall with enterprise revenue. Many different approaches could be used to accomplish this; a base rate of pay combined with a large but fluctuating bonus is one possiblity. Two conditions must be observed, whatever the scheme. First, a large percentage of the expected annual average wage must be free to fluctuate with revenue. Second, the formula used for calculating the relationships between enterprise revenue and employee wages must be crystal clear, subject to outside audit, and legally binding. It cannot be subject to manipulation by top management. This caveat would not prevent the formula from allowing a provision for retained earnings in very good years, so that something could be put aside for use during bad years. Provision should also be made for periodic review of the formula.

The Japanese approach such matters with much informality, largely because they lack a tradition of exploited labor in the Western sense. Moreover, the essence of the Japanese system is very old, and custom there has almost the force of law. U.S. industrial history, which traditionally treats capital and labor as adversaries, is quite different. Here there can be no murkiness in the formula itself and, equally important, no room for ambiguous definition of accounting terms. In my view, for example, the best definition of revenue or sales would be cash actually received, not sales contracted for.

To firm up the partnership of capital and labor, I believe the ideal scheme would divide between profits and wages all revenue remaining after all other expenses had been met. Other expenses would include such corporate costs as taxes and, interest on loans as well as costs of producing and distributing the product, such as utilities, raw materials, depreciation on plant and equipment, supplies, fuel, and freight. The logical division between profits and wages would depend on the nature of the business; capital would get a heavier cut in capital-intensive industries and a smaller one in more labor-intensive areas. On the average, I suspect the normal range would be 80 to 90 percent wages, 10 to 20 percent profits. The idea of what is fair in a given case would probably be influenced by an analysis of the average split that had actually prevailed over some reasonable past period.

*Pay the Point.* The split between profit and wages aside, the problem also concerns the relative distribution of wages among the employees. In this regard, rank could be expressed as "pay points." Suppose, for example, that six levels of rank were decided upon and that the highest rank counted as six points, the lowest rank as one point. The total number of rank points for all employees would be added together and then divided into revenue available for wages. The result of this calculation would determine the pay value of a rank point for the pay period in question. The individual's pay would accordingly be determined by multiplying the value of a rank point by the number of points he held.

A point system might work in practice as follows: Assume a company of 1,250 people who between them have 6,500 rank points. Then assume that in some year the company sells $210 million worth of its product. If the cost of raw materials, energy, utilities, interest, and so on (in other words, everything but profit and payroll expense) was $130 million, $80 million would remain to be divided between the stockholders and employees. If we assume an 80/20 split ($64 million to the employees, $16 million to the stockholders) then the value of a pay point would be $64 million divided by 6,500 total points, or $9,846.15, including fringe benefits and before taxes. In this case the lowest paid person would gross $9,846.15 and the highest paid, six times that amount, or $59,076.90 per year. Of these sums a percentage, say 10 percent, might be withheld for retirement trust funds and medical insurance. Another percentage, say 10 percent, might be withheld for income maintenance insurance whenever the value of a pay point dropped below some predetermined level, say $6,000.00. Then the gross pay for tax purposes would be $7,876.92 per pay point, making $47,261.52 the highest pretax income.

Suppose the following year a recession caused sales to decline by about 25 percent, to $158 million. We can assume the cost of all outside purchases would drop proportionately, so that this cost would amount to about $100 million, leaving $58 million to divide between employees and stockholders. Employees then collectively would earn $46.4 million; stockholders, $11.6 million. Given this sharp a downturn, assume the company fails to replace all who quit or retire. If total turnover were 5 percent and only 1 percent new hires occurred, the number of employees would drop by 4 percent, to 1,200. Assume also that this same drop occurred in the total number of rank or pay points. Pay points might now number 6,240 in total, so that the value of the pay point during a recession becomes $7,435.90 gross. Given deductions for retirement and income maintenance insurance, the value of a pay point for tax purposes becomes $5,948.72. Since $6,000 is the floor for income maintenance, less than 10 percent would be deducted for income maintenance insurance. About 9 percent sales decline could still occur, therefore, without dropping below the income floor by suspending payments into income maintenance reserves. Sales would have to drop by almost 40 percent, in other words, before cutting into the trust reserves for income maintenance.

The accumulation of pay points or a downturn in sales would not influence chances for promotion. The value of a point would fluctuate, but not the seniority and other criteria by which points are accumulated.

Manpower employed temporarily would not come under this pay scheme. Temporary employees or, more precisely, contract workers would be classed as an outside expense. This practice has already become widespread with the use of the services of such firms as Manpower, Inc., Kelly Girls, and Office Overload by businesses and the personal services contracts often used by the federal government.

As outsiders, temporary employees would have fixed wages (or fees), typically for a fixed (or approximately fixed) period of time. These fees, which might be calculated on an hourly, weekly, or other basis, would have a prior claim to the regular payroll. Generally, temporary help should probably not average more than about 10 to 15 percent of total headcount, except perhaps in purely seasonal industries. Their term of contract might be by the day, week, or month, but probably would be less than a year under normal circumstances. A minority, but still a significant number, of people in the labor force prefer temporary to permanent employment, including housewives, seasonal farmers, school teachers, students on vacation and semiretired people. In this somewhat limited area we can think of a free market as setting "prices" for "jobs" for those for whom the traditional ground rules of Economic Man make at least a modicum of sense.

### Promotion Criteria

No hard-and-fast criteria which universally apply to promotion in rank can be identified. While each corporation should establish its own criteria, certain guidelines can be laid down. Whatever else governs promotion, seniority would have to play a significant role. Seniority equates precisely with experience, and promotion is in rank, not in job. Pushing people up and into jobs purely by seniority can produce some grim results, as the British experience attests. The same does not apply to the use of seniority for promotion in personal rank.

Man's need to progress steadily upward in formal status as he grows older counts as one of his most basic social-psychological needs. Almost every culture pays at least informal deference to age, and many make the requirement for such respect highly explicit. If only one criteria for promotion could be used, seniority would have to take precedence over merit, because the former is highly objective and not subject to human misjudgment. We cannot say the same for merit; the merits of U. S. Grant as a general are still subject to debate, for example. Moreover, merit is highly fragmentary. George S. Patton was an able field general but a disaster as a diplomat. Business history is full of examples of brilliant founding fathers going on to failure; Henry Ford's enterprise was saved only by the timely intervention of Henry Ford II in 1946.

Nevertheless, merit can be introduced as a promotional criteria if a reasonably objective standard can be defined and applied outside the chain of command. Educational attainments would qualify, for example; in practice, education is used to determine the employee's entrance level. Only rarely do the less well educated object to this, given equal experience. Special skills in which tests of proficiency can be passed, also serve as a test of merit; this is the basis for the traditional apprentice-journeyman-master levels in the craft trades. The foreign service gives extra pay credit for foreign languages learned—the more proficiently learned, the more credit given. Those who fail to achieve language proficiency rarely regard it as unfair that the better linguists get more pay, even in precisely the same job. The key to successful merit-based promotion (always in addition to, not instead of seniority) is criteria that seem fair to those who fail to qualify for their "merit badge." Above all, the chance for favoritism must be minimized, as must the incentive to achieve promotion via the political route, or by "apple-polishing."

The criterion of job performance could be applied, provided the judgment is that of peers, not superiors. Peers have more detailed performance knowledge in the first place, and they feel less resentment at the application of such subjective judgments by those of their own rank. However, an end to bureaucracy would mean the substitution of a more open team approach for the notion of tightly defined job responsibilities. The open team allows for much greater freedom in fitting individual talents to tasks. Thus in the fraternal social order differences in individual performance levels would typically be smaller, because the tendency would be for people to do what they do best.

Peer group rating might be the U.S. counterpart of the Japanese "godfather" system, which would probably not be workable in the United States. Such rating might accomplish the same ends, keeping politicking and favoritism to a minimum and helping select candidates for top management.

In the example above, a reasonable approach to the six-level tier of personal rank for pay purposes would go as follows: Seniority alone might carry a person to grade 3, superior education to grade 4, added skill proficiency to grade 5, and a top peer group rating to grade 6. Budgets could be established to set maximum and minimum percentage limits for each grade or rank. For example, grades 1 and 2 together might comprise 35 percent of employees, grades 3 and 4, 25 percent each, with 10 percent in grade 5 and 5 percent in grade 6. Generally speaking, the larger the enterprise the more grade levels would be permissible, but no more than ten grade levels should be used, to avoid exaggerated social distance. Three levels would probably be the least required, depending on size. Intermediate steps between levels could also be used.

### The Rotating Reserves

When business conditions are poor and production is curtailed, the question arises of how to keep people usefully occupied. In the fraternal enterprise of the example above, it is conceivable that by eliminating make-work and unnecessary tasks it had created a reserve of 20 percent on the average, or 250 people out of 1,250. In the slump, the headcount fell by 4 percent, or 50 people, purely by attrition. We can assume reserve manning still might rise to about 450 people. Those assigned to reserve status would normally be those whose turn was nearest for normal rotation. Reserve status would not influence rank and hence pay.

I have suggested that training is the ideal reserve duty. Other reserve duty could involve marginal work or catching up on delayable maintenance and other things put off in busier times. More people might be deployed to sales and promotional work, and vacations could be incorporated into reserve time. But training would be the standard goal of reserve duty, and it would continue at reduced levels even in the busiest of times.

In-house reserve training programs, through which everyone rotates periodically, would counter many problems which now face the employee. Reserve duty would do much to eliminate the frustration and alienated monotony of narrow dead-end jobs, which increasingly affect white-collar as well as blue-collar employees. Professional employees who use reserve duty to keep in touch with new techniques in their fields would suffer much less narrowing of interest and on-the-job obsolescence. Periodic training would allow all employees to learn more about the work of the enterprise as a whole and to put their own specialties, if they develop them, into better perspective. Much better communication could be opened up between professions and specialties, since all would focus on the goals of enterprise.[1]

The absence of make-work at all levels would also be a boon to employee morale. A reserve training program would make it easier for people at all levels to identify needless tasks and get rid of them. The level of workmanship could rise as people took pride in the workmanship of their enterprise. The reserves would be the obvious place to become more proficient in a variety of skills upon which merit promotion would depend. The reserve concept makes it easy to award these "merit badges" outside the operating chain of command.

Another form of reserve manpower might use retired personnel for temporary work in peak periods. The earlier the normal retirement age, the more feasible such retired standby reserves would be. Both parties would benefit from this voluntary arrangement. Such temporary workers would not participate in the pay pool, but they would have a prior claim to it. The fraternal enterprise's retired employees would have had a wide range of training in the special needs of the enterprise, because of their operational experience and rotational reserve training.

Conceivably, much of the training and proficiency testing of the reserve program could be the province of the trade unions. Corporations already concede this principle with engineers, for example, whose certification comes not from corporations but from colleges or state licensing boards. Training and testing would provide a useful, indeed vital, economic role for the unions that is broadly within their existing functional identity but has no pernicious side effects. Management favoritism and victimization would be outflanked, since seniority and peer group evaluation would comprise the other promotional criteria.

*Entry-level Training.* It can be said that the earlier the age of recruitment, the more thoroughly and naturally will an individual iden-

---

[1] One reason why the Marine Corps provides America's most effective tactical air support in combat is that a Marine pilot must take infantry training. Thus he can provide his "specialized service" with a more realistic understanding of his client's needs.

tify with and form bonds to his enterprise. The earlier the age of entry into an enterprise, however, the more important it is for initial assignments (or a probationary period) to stress training instead of immediate work.

Evidence suggests that somewhere between 16 and 18 is the ideal age of entry into any proposed lifetime career. Attachments and other emotional bonds formed during late adolescence tend to be life's most durable and lasting. The biological explanation probably reflects the fact that in most primitive hunting bands, young men leave the band of their youth (break away from the family, in other words) to marry and become hunters in a different band of the same tribe. They loosen one set of attachments and acquire another. Nature seems to have programmed the male human animal to desire this in late adolescence. Corporations would do well, by both themselves and teen-agers, to recognize this biological tendency.

A probationary period which requires serious effort seems to improve the bond between the individual and his band once he passes this period. Usually the end of the probationary program is marked by ceremony and formal rites of passage. At no other time in his life will a male be so receptive to trials, rites, and ceremonies which can cement the bond between himself and his enterprise. Nearly every fraternal organization in every culture has such a program. Late adolescence does not just happen to be an impressionable (bondable) age; rather, it served the evolutionary purpose of bonding the young hunter to his new band. Taking advantage of the bonding power of adolescence could also help ensure the survival of private free enterprise.

With a 17-year-old entry policy, business recruits would enter as trainees in every sense of the word. They would not be hired for specific jobs or necessarily even for specific skills. Normally the probationary period would last between six months to a year, during which they might be put through rather strenuous challenges before becoming full-fledged members of the fraternal enterprise.

Should such a program become widespread it would greatly benefit teen-agers, particularly those not especially adept at pursuing academic higher education. They would be faced with a much more realistic challenge at the very time of life they are genetically urged to break loose of parental care and begin to make their contribution to their own and society's economic survival. Indeed, an argument could be made that very large fraternal corporations should take in all new entrants at about age 17, even those who would benefit from higher education. Such corporations might form their own "service academies" for the higher education of young recruits. General Motors in effect has its own engineering college, as did Boeing at one time, and many firms already have extensive training programs.

The charge that such an educational focus risks adverse inbreeding is largely a red herring. Massive infusions of "outside blood" at all levels into our major corporations and the civil service have gone hand in hand with the increasing bureaucratic ossification of these institutions. The other side of the inbreeding myth is equally unfounded, namely the idea that job hopping is some kind of passport to greater individual fulfillment. Granted that some individuals do indeed benefit from job changes, the fact remains that far more frequently they pay a stiff social-psychological price. According to research, the job jumper's health suffers from the stress of continual multiple disruptions.[2] A change can mean changes in job, company, career, location, and friends, all at once. Most people who change jobs probably do so out of the frustrations of bureaucracy. They seek greater fulfillment mainly in the negative sense of fleeing from an adverse situation. They rarely climb some nicely graduated career ladder of "more responsibility" and "greater challenge" in a series of carefully calculated moves leading to "fulfillment." This pattern is much more likely for those who, at an early age, joined corporations which have retained the policy of promoting largely from within.

### Life On the Job

The work itself in a fraternal enterprise would be built around the open team approach. There would still be many tasks that are best done by individuals, of course, but teamwork would be the norm. Drudgery and boredom would not disappear, since they can creep into the most fascinating task, but there would be far less monotony.

Challenge would be greater because most trained workers would boss themselves. There would still be the management function of coordination and technical direction, but the work teams would sort out the details themselves within the established guidelines. Consequently management input could be less, which has usually proven to be the case whenever the open team approach to task performance has been tried. Morale, teamwork, and self-discipline typically soar in these experiments in the United States, but the experiments still flounder during layoff periods. Lack of flexible pay formulas and employed manpower reserves prevent many of these experiments from surviving the inevitable fluctuations in demand.

Job enrichment in the fraternal firm would have two sides—on the job itself and in training. On-the-job task assignments would typically be loosely defined and flexible, thus improving the chance that individual skills will be matched to the task at hand. Much would depend

---

[2] From the research of Dr. Thomas H. Holmes cited in Alvin Toffler, *Future Shock* (New York: Bantam Books, Inc., 1971), pp. 328–30.

on the nature of the work. Factory or office; capital or labor intensive; assembly line, continuous process, or job shop—each is subject to inherent frustrations which would remain whatever the social order in the enterprise.

The fraternal enterprise is not, of course, some utopia or nirvana. Personality conflicts would still persist. Hard times would continue to alternate with good times, and belt tightening would periodically be necessary. Unpleasant tasks would still have to be done, and mistakes would continue to occur. But with a fraternal social order, employers and employees might well dispense with most of the woes gratuitiously foisted upon them by bureaucracy (as described in Part II).

## ADVANTAGES TO THE STOCKHOLDER

Many stockholders have little interest in the companies they have invested in, aside from the hope of buying low and selling high. Others are happy to remain ignorant of corporate operations, provided the dividends continue. And some investors, those who sell short, actually look hopefully for corporate hard times. While some stockholders do take a deep interest in corporate operations, because they have seats on the board or are company officials or employees, stockholders as a whole have no particular reason to care what kind of social order prevails so long as it does not threaten their equity or profits.

Generally stockholders are accustomed to the notion that the price of stocks can fall as well as rise and that losses can occur as well as profits. If fraternal corporations replaced their bureaucratic counterparts, nothing much would change from the average stockholders' point of view. There would be bull and bear markets, as profits and dividends continued to reflect interaction between demand and the efficiency with which the company meets it.

Nevertheless, several developments would be to the advantage of a fraternal enterprise stockholder. First, a much improved level of efficiency could prevail, and dividends would probably rise. This would reflect not only improved profits but also reduced corporate need to retain earnings, either for expansion or working capital. Bank loans would be easier to obtain for these purposes, since principal and interest repayments would come ahead of wages (and profits). Since employees and stockholders would be partners in splitting the sales dollar, employees would no longer have a prior claim to wages over profits. Thus losses would be much less likely, and some return on investment would be almost certain, even in the worst of times.

As the debt/equity ratio increased through greater bank borrowing, so would the average return on investment. This, and not greater book value from retained earnings, would cause any rise in the stock's market price. Only in the early transition period would the stock of the fraternal corporation be likely to experience a big jump in price. The first companies to move to fraternity, especially corporations with depressed values, might enjoy a spectacular improvement in stock price levels, but thereafter fluctuations would be much less volatile than has been true in the past two decades. Speculative fortunes would be unlikely, even with a crystal ball, except in new industries and businesses. The value of fraternal blue chip stocks would tend to be stabilized.

## The Position of the Owner-Operator

The stockholders who would risk the most in a switch to fraternal ground rules would be owner-operators or, in larger corporations, very large stockholders who also act as presidents. Henry Ford II would be an example, as would Alfred Sloan during his reign as president and later chairman of General Motors. Sloan created a semifraternal management structure which heavily stressed semiautonomous operating divisions. Crucial policy decisions were made by groups, not individuals. Sloan's reforms came in the early 1920s as part of an attempt to avoid bankruptcy, after GM had suffered a loss of almost $38 million in 1921. No loss has since been incurred; even in the bust year of 1932 GM stayed in the black (if just barely), and it made a hefty $83 million in 1933.[3]

Sloan's blueprint has been widely copied most notably by Ford Motor Company, at the insistence of Henry Ford II. Other companies, such as Du Pont, Sears, and Esso, also created management structures similar to Sloan's in a more or less conscious effort to ward off bureaucracy. When General Robert Wood decentralized Sears into a flat organization with 400 store managers reporting directly to him, he warned that "If we devise too elaborate a system of checks and balances, it will only be a matter of time before the self-reliance and initiative of our managers will be destroyed and our organization will be gradually converted into a huge bureaucracy."[4] Of course some administrative work was handled with staff assistance, but Wood gave all Sears store managers direct access to the top. He also showed his antibureaucratic bias in other ways, including this statement:

> The greatest danger of any executive—the danger is greater the more active, able and aggressive an executive is—is to surround himself with a staff and to build up a duplicate organization. Personally, I try to avoid this by having only an office assistant and a personal secretary.[5]

---

[3] Alfred P. Sloan, *My Years with General Motors* (New York: McFadden-Bartell, 1965).

[4] Reprinted from *Strategy and Structure* by A. D. Chandler by permission of The M.I.T. Press, Cambridge, Massachusetts. © 1962 The M.I.T. Press, p. 315.

[5] Ibid.

The point is that in America's most profitable enterprises, the top men have eschewed autocracy. They backed off because bureaucracy did not pay; their resistance was pragmatic, not theoretical. None of them completely rid their corporations of the bureaucratic social order, especially at the worker level, where the myth of Economic Man remained in force. Despite the pragmatically correct insights of such leaders, a broad drift toward bureaucracy has been evident since the late 1950s. This tendency is associated with a general decline in performance standards, checked occasionally by improved technology.

Today's owner-operator has much to gain from the application of fraternity to his enterprise. To gain this advantage, he must recognize that his ownership of physical assets does not equate with ownership of the people he employs. He will get more out of his employees in a fraternal system than through autocracy, however well intended or paternalistic. True enough, owner-operators have wide legal latitude to treat their employees autocratically, but the exercise of this right can lead to shaky performance and even disaster.

Only the owner-operator with some inner need to play the tyrant would have much to lose with the fraternal social order in his enterprise, and the loss would be psychic, not financial. Weighed against this "loss" would be the psychic advantage of knowing that he will leave an enterprise that is much more likely to survive and prosper.

## ADVANTAGES TO MANAGEMENT

Management would also benefit by the change to a fraternal enterprise system. What managers would lose in "majesty" they could gain in the much more important psychic reward of camaraderie. It is common for managers to complain of their loneliness at the top and the difficulty of real fellowship or fraternity with subordinates. This is both true and unnecessary, merely another of bureaucracy's aberrations.

When decisions are reached fraternally, the decision makers can afford to concentrate on the proper definition of problems before rushing to a judgment. Moreover, once the decision is reached, the process of implementation goes much faster and more efficiently, for two reasons. First, the decision will have more positive support and less covert resistance. Second, more people who must do the work will understand the reasons behind it and have a better idea of what must be done.

One of the main advantages to management would be the duffision of political authority, which would ensure corporate rather than personal acceptance of the responsibility for results. When things go wrong, top managers would not have to indulge in public hypocrisy, accepting rhetorical responsibility for failure but shifting actual blame and its consequences downward.

Things can go wrong in any situation, of course, but in a fraternal social order the relevant question would be "Where did *we* go wrong?" not "*Who* is to blame?" Top-ranked people would no longer have to pretend to godlike powers of omniscience. With no need to waste time in a scapegoat search and with a minimum of personal ego involvement in decisions gone wrong, corrective action can take place much faster and more effectively. I suspect, in fact, that more money can be saved by faster corrective action on poor decisions than could be saved by better decisions. The future will remain just as obscure to the fraternal corporation as it is to its bureaucratic counterpart, pending invention of a reliable crystal ball.

Planning could at least come down to earth, however, because planners would no longer work under the distortions of reflexive optimism. Without fear of retribution, they could work on the premise that business fluctuates down as well as up. Particularly in growth and cyclical industries, this would free them to study dispassionately the implications of hard times as well as good.

A little discussed problem is the firm's inability to reduce prices to stimulate sluggish demand. To illustrate, let's take the best case, and suppose that a firm sells a "price elastic" product wherein a reduced price stimulates enough new sales to increase total revenue. Rigid wage rates make the firm's unit costs inelastic. If the profit margin is narrow a unit price cut results in a loss on each unit sold; the higher the sales, the greater the losses. So, instead of cutting prices to pump up sluggish demand, the firm cuts production, lays off labor, and possibly even *raises* its price. This straightforward relationship between "sticky prices" and rigid wage rates causes stagflation or simultaneous inflation and unemployment. Nothing mysterious is going on.

Management in a fraternal corporation would thus be able to use price reductions much more flexibly than at present. They could reduce prices as a stimulant to sluggish demand, because without rigid wage rates they would not be forced to regard their price structure as sacred. Should a price reduction fail to stimulate demand as much as hoped, no disaster need follow, because wages would be tied to sales.

Losers could be dropped from the product line more expeditiously, with no fear of mass layoffs resulting. By the same token, U.S. firms would be less inclined to let previous investments (as in open hearth steel making) delay conversion to better technology (as with basic oxygen), thus allowing foreign competition to get the technological jump on them. Nor would the threat of strikes from mass technological unemployment distort the decision.

Overriding all would be the end to the guerrilla war between management and labor. Euphemisms such as "dynamic tension" between management and labor do not change the fact that nearly everyone in our economy suffers as a result of such tension. The place for competition is between corporations, not within them. In the fraternal enterprise, it would be possible to avoid the immense management effort now devoted to periodic wage and work rule negotiations, grievance problems, and other so-called "labor problems" which are essentially the political consequences of bureaucracy rather than the result of some immutable economic law.

Finally, the corporation could greatly reduce the enervating and costly power struggles which routinely erupt in the executive suit. This form of "labor trouble" (which is what it is) has probably become most acute in the past decade. The introduction of differing views would inevitably cause some conflict, but a much healthier institutional framework would exist for resolving differences in point of view.

The truly vicious element which infests the typical bureaucracy is the contest for purely personal power (or its illusion). Charismatic influence might remain, but it would not be reinforce with wasteful, counterproductive, and institutionalized autocratic powers of office. People would continue to contend for presitge, but this contest would have few of the invidious consequences of contending for power. Unfortunately, most men of great talent, energy, and drive (and even many without these attributes) succumb to the almost instinctive rationalization that whatever furthers their ambitions for power also best serves the enterprise. Thus they will shamelessly use whatever resources of the enterprise they control to serve their personal ambition. Bureaucracy in this respect regresses human behavior by perhaps 20 millions of years as men literally go "ape" in trying to reach the top.

# 11

# The Fraternal Free
# Enterprise Economy

Government spending as the solution to all problems has fallen into disfavor. Americans have grown weary and suspicious of it; even liberals have become jaded. For 40 years, ever since the Great Depression, we have put up with enormous waste in government spending in defense and others areas in vain efforts to "create more jobs" and thus achieve full employment. The spending solution has not only failed to create full employment, it has also fueled inflation. The result is stagflation, or co-existing unemployment and inflation.

In this chapter I will argue that we can cure stagflation by eliminating jobs and spending less, paradoxical as this may seem. We need only replace the social order of bureaucracy with that of fraternity.

The chapter will examine broadly the improvements that might reasonably be expected in a fraternal free enterprise economy. Among these are full employment in good times and bad, stable prices, lower taxes, less government, and generally, a much improved social climate. Moreover, the free market would be freed to do its job of resource allocation through the expression of consumer choice.

## FULL EMPLOYMENT

If, through fraternal free enterprise, our economy rid itself of all its useless jobs (something like 15 to 20 million, I suspect) and deployed a like number of people into corporate training reserves, we could save probably $250 billion. Fluctuations in the business cycle thereafter would translate into fluctuations in the ratio of reserve to operational manning. If, in addition, the economy also allowed wage rates to fluctuate with sales revenue, business firms could forego the layoff as a means of cutting costs. Labor costs would become a variable expense, and employment levels could remain relatively stable throughout the business cycle.

Once these simple but crucial changes in ground rules were made, a host of seemingly intractable economic and social problems could be dealt with. Any problem to which the fact or threat of unemployment contributes would be reduced; the welfare mess, racial tensions, crime and juvenile delinquency, and a great deal of personal tragedy could reasonably be expected to be ameliorated. Pressure for government spending at all levels to create jobs or make-work would decline. Some of the largest consequent savings would be in defense procurement, but substantial savings could also be made in public works and other programs supposedly devoted to the development of human resources. Spending pressure would also be lessened in areas such as police and welfare.

We need only substitute stable employment levels and fluctuating wages for rigid wage rates and fluctuating employment levels. Hard times would continue to alternate with good times, but the burden of a slump would be more evenly distributed, and the pernicious side effects of economic downturns could largely be avoided.

By no means would fraternity deny the employee the bracing effects of competition. Competitive efficiency would indeed determine wages much more directly than it now does. While bankruptcy might be less likely, it would remain the ultimate penalty for inefficiency. The bind would be felt, however, long before the point of bankruptcy is reached. There would be no more situations such as Douglas Aircraft's in 1967 or the Penn Central's in 1970, when reasonably good profits abruptly disappeared, to be replaced by the specter of bankruptcy. Douglas was saved by merger, and Penn Central went into receivership. The majority of the employees responsible for Penn Central's difficulties, through restrictive work practices on the lower levels and an ossified bureaucracy on the upper levels, did not suffer much. The stockholders, however, took a 95 percent drop in the price of their stock.

All the employees in any fraternal enterprise would suffer roughly proportional financial consequences for inefficiency, but mass unemployment would not normally be a threat, even in quite severe contractions. In hard times, unemployment would probably center on people not in the permanent labor force—those who prefer temporary work. Many of these employees would not be entirely dependent on such work.

The absorption of maturing youth into the economy could proceed without undue interference from the business cycle's normal fluctuations. Unusual conditions, such as an earlier baby boom which comes of age in the midst of a recession, might cause strain, but otherwise all youths who wanted to enter the corporate world could do so. Any trauma for the individual about his employment future would be largely due to his youth. The corporate-bound young person need not worry about having chosen the wrong line of work, because he would not lock himself in at an early age to any particular speciality. He could instead anticipate a career-long process of learning in various jobs and training in reserve. His identity would attach mainly to his enterprise, not to any particular task he might perform.

As industries changed in relative importance, fraternal corporations, particularly conglomerates, would place more new recruits in the dynamic sectors and fewer in the declining ones. In extreme circumstances such as a plant closure, the surplus personnel could be transferred, either temporarily into reserve or directly into other operations. Such transfers would eliminate much of the so-called frictional umemployment—people temporarily out of work "between jobs"—which is usually estimated at from a third to a half of total unemployment. Some frictional unemployment is admittedly benign; for example, a person who quits one job with the promise of another two months later could use the two months to repair his house, go fishing, or do whatever he pleased. But even temporary unemployment can be traumatic if it triggers a host of disruptions in the life of an individual and his family.

There would be an end to the fear of mid-career and "past forty" involuntary unemployment, either temporary or long term. The lives of people at all levels are increasingly being devastated by this problem. Higher education has long ceased to be a secure defense. Indeed, the better educated, upper levels of white-collar workers have probably reached an all-time low in employment security. Blue-collar union workers protected by job seniority have the advantage in this regard.

The most economic damage done by fear of unemployment, however, is due to the reaction of the employed, not the unemployed. For every person who actually loses his job, ten others will be fearful. The defensive measures the fearful take are not designed to benefit the enterprise, and fear of rejection can destroy loyalty. Teamwork will inevitably suffer under conditions of doubtful employment security.

## STABLE PRICES

An economy made up mainly of fraternal enterprises would promote price stability in several ways. All three types of inflation discussed in Chapter 4—cost push, wage ratchet, and fiscal—could be better controlled in such an economy.

### Cost-Push Inflation

Employment security and an end to make-work would reduce waste, and thus the cost-push inflation imposed by the hire-fire cycle would decline markedly. There is no way to measure how much avoidable waste occurs in our economy. It obviously varies by industry, corporation, and the state of the technical art of production. Extrapolating from the situations in which I could closely observe the waste firsthand and in some detail, I suspect that the raw materials, parts, supplies, fuel, and energy that are avoidably wasted (including outright sabotage) could average 20 percent. Waste is probably highest in aerospace, where the waste in failed projects approaches 100 percent, and lowest in farming. I do not include here what the consumer "wastes," of course, nor do I include the damage caused by such visitations of nature as floods or hurricanes. My standard includes an allowance for reasonable rates of scrap, wasted motion, accidents, and experimental failures. The zero defects objective sounds nice, but it is unobtainable as a literal standard.

Under the influence of Keynesianism, we tended to take a bland view of waste. If steel yields were lower than possible, this waste employed more people in coal mines, iron mines, oil drilling, and so on. If alienated auto workers tended to waste steel, steelmakers benefited. The Defense Department has financed a parade of overengineered flops and goldplated weapons to promote jobs, both in the Department and among defense contractors. As A. E. Fitzgerald discovered, the one who tries to fight this waste directly wages a losing battle. According to Watergate hearings testimony, even the White House, under a supposedly cost-conscious Republican administration, decided to let Fitzgerald "bleed" as he fought to preserve his Air Force job against illegal dismissal.[1]

The growing scarcity of raw materials would not seem to encourage further such profligacy. However, we cannot count on necessity to induce a greater concern for resource conservation as long as the motive to waste remains rooted in job protection. British experience attests to this, as noted in Chapter 5. Britain has to import nearly all its raw materials, and throughout the postwar era, it has had the greatest necessity to conserve scarce raw materials. Still the British waste more productive resources than even the Americans do, because defensiveness is so firmly entrenched.

The fraternal enterprise would have the deepest of motives to conserve productive resources. Every sales dollar which had to be paid for raw materials would be one less dollar in the wage and profit kitty. Every employee of a fraternal enterprise would thus acquire personal incentive to conserve resources, with no fear of unemployment. The institutional cause of cost-push inflation would ultimately vanish in a fraternal free enterprise system.

---

[1] The testimony of Fitzgerald on the actual cost of the C-5A which led to his dismissal from the Air Force is discussed in Chapter 6. Fitzgerald was ordered reinstated by the Civil Service Commission as an aftermath of the Watergate testimony.

## Wage-Ratchet Inflation

The fraternal free enterprise system would also mark the demise of wage-ratchet inflation and give enormous scope to the possibility of price reductions. Because all labor costs would be variable, if a lower price failed to stimulate demand it would be no disaster for the firm. This would give every business much greater latitude in the use of price reductions to stimulate demand in a recession, a prospect which has become increasingly rare.

Average wages would tend to be closely related to average productivity, without the benefit of government guidelines. Average real income would continue to rise as technology improved, but with much greater latitude to adjust wages to short-term changes in demand. In turn, price adjustment would be easier. Thus the free market could resume its traditional role of efficient resource allocation without government interference. Supply and demand would come into better balance much more quickly for a wide range of goods and services.

The free market would indirectly continue to determine the operational demand for labor and its wages. But under fraternity it would be a question of rotating between operations and reserves, not employment and unemployment, while the wages of everyone in the enterprise would rise and fall with the market. Wages would not fall by arbitrary management action, nor for that matter, would they rise in that way. Granted that promotion in rank would be independent of the market, the wage each rank got would be determined by competitive efficiency in the marketplace.

## Fiscal Inflation

Another source of inflation which fraternity would decrease is that caused by deficit government spending, or fiscal inflation. To some extent pressure for deficit spending would be lessened as cost-push and wage-ratchet inflation decreased. For example, unit costs of defense procurement would no longer take off like missiles. Contractors who were not threatened by wage ratchets, labor turnover and skill dilution, and a built-in tendency toward make-work could learn to live with their cost estimates. The Department of Defense would not have to face the dilemma that if it paid a contractor only the agreed-on price it would bankrupt its source of supply. If a contractor underestimated costs, wages would suffer for all its employees. This prospect would have a sobering influence both on contractor cost estimates and cost performance.

Probably no private sector of the U.S. economy suffers more from overmanning than aerospace overhead and engineering groups. Since they could not be laid off in the fraternal setting, they would have to be redeployed, partly into reserve and partly to other activities. If such operations were demanned, engineering costs could come way down. This could put the industry in a good position to bring the United States back into commercial shipbuilding, while retaining its aerospace technical lead.

Overmanning in the public sector also contributes to the fiscal inflation caused by budget deficits. Relative to the services they perform, both the civilian and military forces are overstaffed and overranked. With nearly 850,000 men, for example, the Army proposes a mere 13 combat divisions of about 165,000 total troops (roughly 13,000 men per division), surely one of the worst "teeth-to-tail" ratios in the world. The military as a whole has more colonels and generals for 2.5 million regular forces than it had for 14 million during World War II. In 1972 there were 5,172,027 people on the federal payroll at a cost to the taxpayer of about $57 billion, a significant chunk of the federal budget. The right kinds of reforms in the civil and military services would lower costs while improving quality. Fraternal reforms, of course, would preclude mass firings, in recognition of the facts that the hire-fire cycle has created much of the problem and any genuine reforms require the cooperation of the people who must carry them out.

Overall, the fraternal economy would look forward to much better price stability. Ending make-work and operational overmanning and substituting reserves in training would halt most cost-push inflation. Linking wages and profits to revenue would damp down wage-ratchet inflation and introduce more latitude for price reductions. Combined with fraternal reform of government, these developments could eliminate nearly all peacetime budget deficits and the resulting fiscal inflation, while reducing the scope and size of government.

The remaining source of price inflation would concern supply and demand, mainly in relation to basic raw materials. When oil runs short, for example, the price will rise unless technology provides cheaper substitutes. Even here, to the extent cost-push waste is reduced, pressure will be taken off scarce raw materials.

## SOCIAL WELFARE

The fraternal economy would also make it possible to cope more effectively with a wide range of social problems. Obviously, a full-employment economy would end the social trauma and backlash reactions of unemployment. This in turn would reduce the pressure on many other social problems, such as race relations, debilitating welfare handouts, and crime.

### Race Relations

No claim is made for a sudden brotherhood of man with the adoption of a fraternal free enterprise system. As used here, fraternity is specific to the enterprise, not universal to the species. Universal brotherhood is biologically not feasible; there never has been (and indeed never will be) a universal brotherhood of man in the usual meaning of the term. Intraspecies rivalry is part of our biological heritage; the problem is to find workable ground rules to regulate the rivalry.

The fraternal economy could reduce racial tensions by eliminating some of their major sources. The last-hired, first-fired problem which has harassed many blacks since World War II certainly could become a thing of the past. As a result, a whole host of "equal opportunity" red tape in the form of well-intentioned but largely futile government regulations would cease to have much relevance, except perhaps at the entry level.

With full employment and a social ranking system which made rank independent of function (job title) and which was heavily weighted by seniority, any racial competition for jobs would soon vanish for lack of purpose. Fraternity stresses formal equality of function and ties social rank directly to the individual, not indirectly to him through his job. His identity thus hinges on his enterprise, and his rank defines his social place in it. Substantial upward social mobility for everyone is built into the system. The individual's enterprise identity would tend to assert primacy over his other identities, such as job, race, religion, or ethnic background.[2]

If the fraternal enterprise recruited entrants at age 17 or 18, all entrants would bond to the enterprise and to each other, regardless of race. Racial minorities would especially benefit from such a practice, since under present conditions many of them enter the work force permanently at about that age. Indeed, the case can be made that the enterprise and society both would benefit by recruiting even those with the potential for higher education at age 17. James Coleman, chairman of the Panel on Youth of the President's Science Advisory Committee, believes we keep people in the essentially artificial school environment too long, thus tending to delay maturity. Coleman's panel suggested getting the young out of school earlier into "other organizations" and alternating work with study. The fraternal corporation would be the ideal vehicle for such a program, which would be much more relevant for such career courses as business administration, economics, or engineering. Meanwhile, those not suited to higher education need not suffer in their career prospects or waste time in activities for which they

---

[2] Those who systematically marshal maximum consciousness around these identities might not agree that their displacement to secondary status would be a good thing—at least not for their own careers.

lack talent. Those interested in a purely academic education would probably not embark on a corporate career in the first place.

With such a recruiting pattern racial animosities within the corporation could be reduced to a long-run minimum, but personal prejudices would probably persist. The problem might never disappear, but the most damaging results of racial animosity might well be avoided. The experience of the multinational corporations in this respect is encouraging. People of diverse races, cultures, and creeds work together in reasonable harmony, bound by a common tie of economic interest. Overt signs of racial or ethnic prejudice tend to become subcultural taboos in such enterprises. I have witnessed the most outrageous bigots at all levels conform to this taboo.

Covert prejudice could persist, and it is possible some minorities would be silently discriminated against in the assignment of top positions. In the fraternal enterprise, however, top management would have lost its false majesty and its sense of being at the top of a competitive pecking order. Without arbitrary political power, and with the intensity of the struggle to reach the top lessened, the motive to discriminate would be decidedly repressed.

## The Welfare State

A full-employment economy would deal a severe blow to the welfare state by removing most of the reason for its existence. It would not be possible for the welfare state to disappear overnight, but fraternal free enterprise would bleed off its recruits. Full employment and recruitment at age 17 would disrupt the self-perpetuation of the hand-out existence.

The equating of social welfare with economic handouts is one of the great blunders of 20th-century liberalism. Most liberals now acknowledge the mistake, recognizing that for social welfare people must have a useful role which allows them to contribute to the community. Makework is no answer, obviously. Full employment, with the free market merely determining labor force utilization, is a much sounder solution.

Under fraternal free enterprise, I conjecture, federal, state, and local government could get out of the welfare business in 15 or 20 years. Much would depend on the speed of the transition away from bureaucracy and to fraternity, of course. The federal government could ultimately forego old-age social security payments as well, except possibly on some residual level. Corporations could certainly look after their own retirement costs. An ideal target period would be the 1990s, when the ranks of the "depression babies" will begin to retire somewhat before the "war babies" would do so after the turn of the century.

Conservatives may not understand how right they were when they claimed free enterprise could solve the welfare problem better than the government could. But the solution can be approached in the wrong way. This approach was verbalized by a former General Motors vice president, John Z. DeLorean, who suggested that "Every business-man must get outside the corporate walls and join the battle to rid this country of poverty, prejudice, and unequal opportunity."[3] The only way businessmen can do any good on these issues is inside the corporate walls, for this is the scene of the decisive battle. It can never be won outside the corporation until it has been won inside.

### Crime and Delinquency

The potential of young people for crime or delinquency is exacer-bated by well-intended child labor laws and the tradition of long-term schooling. These laws and traditions fight biology. When the juices of the hunter start flowing at age 16 or so, particularly in boys, they need to be able to get away from home, to start pulling their weight, to take risks, and to form bonded peer groups.

Society erects many obstacles in the traditional setting for most young people who seek to gratify these urges. Substitute activities such as team sports, college fraternities, and similar groups outside the arena of economic survival are not adequate to overcome these obstacles. For many youths a life of crime, far from being a social maladjustment can be objectively viewed as a more healthy psychological response. By this I mean that crime can be a more biologically natural response to the hunters' urges than many of the substitutes that have been proposed. Crime is certainly more dangerous and damaging, for everyone in-volved, however, and it would be illogical to expect the victims of crime to look kindly upon the "naturalness" argument.

The point is that biological urges can be successfully suppressed only at inordinately high costs, direct and indirect. Teen-age urges should be catered to in as natural a way as possible, in order to channel them in socially useful directions. Since we cannot literally return to the hunting life on a large scale, as has been suggested by Paul Shepard, we need to satisfy the essential urges which hunting entails.[4] In the fraternal enterprise, providing a certain sense of economic adventure and risk within closely bonded teams working to support themselves and the enterprise which accords them a social identity, a definite status, and permanent sense of belonging will satisfy these urges. The specific activity involved becomes almost irrelevant.

Criminal activity also satisfies these urges. The Mafia owes much of its resiliency to its borrowing from the social order of hunters. When

---

[3] *Seattle Post-Intelligencer,* August 24, 1973.

[4] Paul Shepard, *The Tender Carnivore & The Sacred Game* (New York: Charles Scrib-ner's Sons, 1973).

the Mafia departs from this tradition, as in its periodic efforts to create an "El Supremo," a vicious and usually lethal power struggle typically follows.

There are other inducements to crime besides youthful frustration. Sumptuary blue laws are often disobeyed on a wide scale because people resent being told by an impersonal government what they cannot consume. Such laws may even lend the allure of forbidden fruit to the proscribed items. In bureaucracy, blue laws also serve a vital make-work function for law enforcement agencies and customs officials. They can induce secondary crime because they result in increasingly higher consumer prices, until consumers turn to crime to be able to pay the price demanded. As consumer costs rise, so do potential profits, and high profits attract a sophisticated and well-organized criminal element which is prepared to make appropriate police payoffs. Organized crime and the police form a truly symbiotic relationship, both heavily dependent on each other and both nourished by the make-work-creating and market-expanding potential of the blue laws.

The recent "hippy" movement and the accompanying drug subculture were not simple phenomena. In part they can be analyzed as the concurrence of (1) blue laws, (2) the fruition of the postwar baby boom as it reached late adolescence (3) the rapid postwar spread of bureaucracy in business, which increased alienating social distance, and (4) lack of useful "places" in industry for young people and the concurrent growth of college enrollments, leading nowhere for many. Initially, the Vietnam War was not much more than a catalytic agent. All these factors were more or less worldwide; the Vietnam War was not. The war played no role in the 1968 French student revolt, for example.

In the fraternal economy, nearly all vocational and most higher education occurs within the enterprise. Since it is the enterprise which will ultimately use the educational product, there is no good reason for the taxpayer to subsidize the process. Private schools would remain, because not everybody would want to enter business, but the student subculture which dominates the ethos of the 18- to 25-year age group would tend to be dissolved. In addition to the enforced delay in maturation, there is an often unrealistic and sometimes irresponsible character to the adult student subculture. By the very wildness and excess of its protests, the group was itself responsible for delaying America's recognition of its policy mistakes in getting entangled in Vietnam. Japan, where the fraternal enterprise flourishes, is not immune to this problem. Masses of youths are encouraged to go to college, thus delaying their entrance into a life of responsibility and leaving them beset by doubt and frustration.

Higher education should not be divorced from reality and responsibility at this critical emotional juncture of a young person's life. The problem of extended education is less severe when the training offered is for a known and reasonably certain career. In the fraternal economy, the public school system could concentrate on basic skills, leaving vocational and some professional education to the corporate users, who would alternate work and education over the whole career of the individual. Private colleges and universities, would be for those interested in largely academic education and professions not primarily related to business and industry.

## PUBLIC POLICY

No new law would be required for an enterprise to implement a fraternal social order. Should the goal of a fraternal free enterprise economy come to enjoy wide public support, however, enabling legislation of the right sort could certainly speed the transition. This would be particularly true for corporations whose employees are represented by many different and often competitive unions. Other changes would relate to antitrust and tax laws.

### Labor Law

In general the law should encourage, but not compel, corporate fraternity. The emphasis should be on positive inducements related to the social and economic advantages of fraternal free enterprise. In labor law, the inducement could be that corporate fraternity would probably achieve, even exceed, the goals labor law has fought to achieve, not altogether successfully. A fair inducement, therefore, might be a law exempting the corporate fraternal enterprise from such laws as the Taft-Hartley Act or the jurisdiction of such agencies as the Equal Employment Opportunity Commission.

In lieu of present laws, certain standards which would amount to a sort of employee bill of rights would have to be met by the enterprise. These rights would stress such issues as tenure, rank independent of job, criteria for promotion in rank, rotational training, and the agreed split between wages and profits after other expenses were paid. Thus its own legal binding "bylaws" stipulating certain standards would replace labor law for the fraternal corporation. These bylaws would virtually eliminate the exercise of arbitrary political authority by management over pay, rank, promotion, and tenure of the individual, who would become a member of his enterprise, not just an employee.

### Antitrust Law

Fraternal free enterprise would make it possible to rid antitrust law of its excessively vague strictures, provided a postive goal were adopted. Recall that the ideal fraternity is a confederated conglomerate in a widely diversified range of businesses. Congress might, for example, "enfranchise" $X$ number of fraternal conglomerates, no one of which could control more than $Y$ percent of any particular industry. Perhaps every conglomerate would have to choose between certain industries; it might choose between being in industry A or industry B but could not be in both. The purpose would be to ensure that the conglomerates would be each others' suppliers and customers, to some extent. Certain areas of the economy might well be reserved for small independent enterprises.

Such guidelines would be much more useful and straightforward than the existing metaphysical prohibitions. These are build around the amorphous notion that mergers or combinations "which *might tend* to result in restraint of trade" violate the antitrust laws. (Emphasis mine.) Almost any merger *might,* and almost none (short of outright monopoly) *would* restrain trade. This is hardly good law.

### Tax Law

Tax law holds the most effective promise for fraternal inducement. In recognition that the fraternal corporation would relieve the taxpayer of many present burdens, corporations that adopt fraternity should be relieved of certain taxes. Employer contributions to unemployment compensation would not be necessary, since employers would cease causing unemployment. More importantly, the corporate income tax, now roughly a $37 billion per year corporate cost, could be phased out. The loss of this tax revenue would be offset by twice as much or more in reduced federal expenses, to say nothing of state and local expenses. Several other advantages would accrue. Corporate losses would no longer be underwritten by offsetting past losses against current taxes, and thus the capital-raising potential for new enterprises which do not have this tax shield would be improved.

Profits, however, would not escape tax. Because most new capital expansion would come from bank loans, most profits would be paid out as dividends. As such, they would be taxed as income to the recipients. Wages arising in the fraternal enterprise should also be taxed at a lower rate to encourage the transition.

### UNION OPPOSITION

The fraternal economy promises nothing but bad news for trade union officials, at least in their present roles. The modern trade union needs a rapacious management against which it can defend its members. Without an "evil" opposition, unions would have little reason to exist.

Unions, however, cover only about a quarter of the work force. Their own questionable activities have dissolved the idealized aura they once enjoyed. Much of the union membership is less than wholly ideologically dedicated to the cause. They view unions pragmatically, as a force they need to stave off capricious management action, not as an abstract good to be defended and maintained.

More fundamentally, of course, it is difficult to live and work in a state of divided loyalty. The enterprise is the natural focus of employee loyalty, if its own policies would only permit it to serve this function. Modern unions thrive only because personnel policies typically frustrate this loyalty and so antagonize workers that they seek out unions.

While union officials can no doubt delay a genuine transition to fraternal free enterprise, they could not stop it. Still, fraternity does not preclude a union role. We have already mentioned the form it might take—a supervisory role over reserve training and perhaps control over "skill ratings" used for promotion. This would point unions back to their original role in apprenticeship training, but on a much enlarged and more comprehensive basis. Higher union officials might also be brought directly into the fraternal enterprise, at suitably high rank, of course. One nice thing about fraternity is that it needs no victims or bodies. No class needs to be wiped out or even suffer expropriation of assets. Many of us, exbureaucrats ourselves, know that bureaucracy, not bureaucrats, is the villain.

# APPENDIXES

# Appendix A:

# The Biology of Fraternity

The argument that our evolution as hunters predisposes us to the fraternal social order has a solid biological basis. The purpose of this appendix is to explore this basis in more detail, but in nontechnical terms.

Social scientists differ in the extent to which they believe environment or heredity determines human behavior. Most, however, accept the premise that behavior reflects an interaction between the two factors.

Learning plays a recognized role in behavior, but even it is not free of genetic influence. Inner drives command us to learn to walk at about age one and to talk at about age two. If only learning and the environment were at work, an adult could be expected to learn a second language much more easily than a child learns his first language. The reverse is true. Our "behavioral biogram," to use the term of Lionel Tiger and Robin Fox,[1] tells us to learn a language early in life, and we do so with comparative ease. Thereafter the task becomes increasingly difficult. Thus language, like much of human behavior, reflects various kinds of interaction between heredity and environment. This discussion will stress the biological influences, not to dismiss learning and environment but rather to highlight some of the biological influences which interact with environment to produce behavior.

A number of biological processes influence human behavior and help to explain it. The most important processes in understanding the systems of human enterprise we have explored are (1) neoteny, (2) im-

---

[1] Lionel Tiger and Robin Fox, *The Imperial Animal* (New York: Holt, Rinehart & Winston, 1971).

printing, (3) bonding, (4) territoriality, (5) releasers, (6) genetic inequality, and (7) the genetic pool. This appendix will also discuss the biological foundations of the five human social needs identified in preceding chapters as the basis for any enterprise system.


## NEOTENY

Desmond Morris defines neoteny as "a process by which certain juvenile or infantile characteristics are retained and prolonged into adult life."[2] Perhaps the most obvious biological evidence is the absence of body fur in the human being. Many primate infants enter the world naked, but only man, the "naked ape," retains infantile nakedness as an adult. This has helped man to survive, because it allowed the loss of body heat for the hominid hunter stalking his prey across the torrid tropical savanna, and it reduced drag, allowing man to swim better and fish more easily.

By prolonging childhood, neoteny also played a crucial role in the development of man's big brain. The chimp, one of our nearest intellectual rivals, arrives in the world with his brain at 70 percent of its final size. Within six months the chimp's brain has grown as large as it will. Humans have only 23 percent of their final brain size at birth, and it does not reach 100 percent until about age 23. The human brain continues to grow nearly ten years *after* man can reproduce, compared to the chimp's brain, which ceases growth six years *before* it can reproduce. The gap between sexual and intellectual maturity marks the time during which adolescent boys innately court great risks. Innate risk taking gave courage to the inexperienced hunter. When intellectual maturity was wed to hunting experience, the result was a wiser, more cautious "professional."

Because of the human's lengthy maturation period, dictated by the need for the brain to develop to its final size within the limits of primate anatomy, all birth for humanity is "premature." Utterly helpless as an infant, man must endure an extended period of nurture within a "social womb" if he is to mature properly.

The length of the helpless period during which physical dependency is gradually shed, produces another neotenous adult characteristic. As man grows more physically self-reliant, he gains in status of the kind we call social rank. His need to improve his social rank continues as he grows into adulthood.

The human's 20-odd year period of development can be separated into six phases: (1) infancy, (2) early childhood, (3) late childhood, (4)

---

[2] From *The Naked Ape* by Desmond Morris. Copyright 1970 McGraw-Hill Book Company. Used with permission of McGraw-Hill Book Company.

early adolescence, (5) late adolescence, and (6) entry into adult life. Physical changes in these periods more or less coincide with status changes. As dependency fades, there is a corresponding increase in social rank and privilege.

Within about 18 months after birth the infant literally takes his first steps toward physical self-reliance by learning to walk. By age three or so he has learned to speak his first words, and by age six he is both reasonably agile and fluent and can begin to take on minor responsibilities. He sleeps less, can feed himself reasonably well, and can see to other physical needs without aid. Indeed he fights off assistance, because of an inner drive for physical self-reliance. After age six his growth slows down but he continues to improve his motor and verbal skills and begins to imitate adult ways. His physical growth spurts again at puberty, tapers off after about 17, and ceases at about age 23. In late adolescence he acquires his adult form.

The neotenous character of social seniority rank can be illustrated by the fact that the six childhood stages of seniority are recapitulated in adult organizations time and again. Seniority (greater maturity) is typically a major criterion for "promotion" in rank, whatever the member's ability. And consider the example of a family with two children of the same social rank who have distinctly different levels of some factor such as intellectual ability. No normal parents would humiliate the less able child by withholding social rank and privilege; indeed, they would attempt to minimize the importance of the intellectural difference in every possible way. They also might encourage the less able child to seek some area in which he can excel, such as mechanical, artistic, or athletic skills.

## IMPRINTING AND BONDING

Imprinting is a type of learning which occurs quickly, needs little reinforcement, and can endure for life. Bonding refers to strong attachments that are deeply felt and, normally, mutually reciprocated. Loyalty and love are associated with bonding, which often occurs through the process of imprinting.

An example of imprinting is the attachment to a mother figure made by newly hatched birds. The British zoologist Desmond Morris describes bird imprinting as follows:

> Many young birds, when they hatch from the egg, must immediately form an attachment to their mother and learn to recognize her. They can then follow her around and keep close to her for safety. If newly hatched chicks or ducklings did not do this, they might easily become lost and perish. They are too active and mobile for the mother to be able to keep them

together and protect them without the assistance of imprinting. The process can take place in literally a matter of minutes. The first large moving object that the chicks or ducklings see, automatically becomes "mother." Under normal conditions, of course, it really is their mother, but in experimental situations it can be almost anything. If the first large moving object that incubator chicks see happens to be an orange balloon, pulled along on a piece of string, then they will follow that. The balloon quickly becomes "mother." So powerful is this imprinting process, that if, after some days, the chicks are then given a choice between their adopted orange balloon and their real mother (who has previously been out of sight), they will prefer the balloon. No more striking proof of the imprinting phenomenon can be provided than the sight of a batch of experimental chicks eagerly pattering along in the wake of an orange balloon and completely ignoring their genuine mother near by.[3]

Human imprinting and the resultant bond formations occur at different periods in life, depending on the bond being formed. The human infant bonds first with a parent, normally the mother, but he must develop in his "social womb" before his senses enable him to experience imprinting and parental bonding. Indeed, parents must form this bond with the infant first, or they may not care for the child properly.

Most mammals share certain endearing characteristics as infants which lead us to call all puppies, kittens, and babies "cute." "Cuteness" tends to release in the observer feelings of tenderness, compassion, and a desire to fondle, smile and coo. The human infant's positive reaction to the tenderness, the smiling, and the cooing plays a vital role in his imprinting, to form his side of the child-parent bond. The most sensitive period comes after the infant gains some initial motor control and his sight improves enough to enable him to recognize people. This imprinting period occurs from the sixth month until the child starts to walk, perhaps at 12 to 15 months.

The imprinting we receive as infants, roughly in our second six months of life, largely determines our other bonding properties for the rest of our lives. Properly imprinted, we will develop a healthy social behavior. Improperly imprinted, we can develop all sorts of psychological maladies which inhibit proper social development. We can form shallow relationships, be more selfish, show less concern for others, and have difficulty forming other bonds.

Imprinting tends to develop from simple situations involving the senses. In much of the Orient, usually where the extended family retains nurturing responsibility, remarkably good deportment can be observed in very young children By American standards, this good-mannered obedience is regarded almost with a sense of awe. In rural

---

[3] From *The Human Zoo* by Desmond Morris. Copyright 1971 McGraw-Hill Book Company and Corgi Books. Used with permission of McGraw-Hill Book Company.

Thailand, this is the result of a simple procedure: Someone always has hold of the infant, whether the mother, the father, an older child, a grandparent, or an aunt or uncle. The very young infant practically never need feel neglected. On the rare occasions his elders put him down, they rush to pick him up the minute he starts crying. The Thais believe that if a helpless, lone infant receives a serious fright or shock, his "spirit" will depart from him, a disaster in their belief. This primitive "superstition" may indeed contain a germ of biological truth. The behavior of the infant whose spirit had been frightened away would compare to the behavior ethologists attribute to poor social imprinting.

Nature never designed the small nuclear family to carry the full burden of nurture. Constant holding of an infant for many months places too much of a demand on any mother; the task has to be shared out, or the child will receive inadequate social imprinting. The extended family serves this need.

To satisfy the need to be close to a protector, the infant monkey can hang on to its mother's fur coat. The human infant retains much of this prehensile reflex, but his mother has lost her fur. Thus the human infant must be held, preferably by the mother but otherwise by any familiar person. As the Austrian ethologist Hans Hass has noted, "The mother is the natural partner, but another person is equally capable of giving the child what it needs as this juncture."[4] More or less continuous physical contact with familiar people during this crucial period of social imprinting opens, in Morris's terms, a large emotional bank account for the child. By sharing the burden of nurture during the critical period of social imprinting, the extended family opens this account. The infant is thus helped to identify himself with other people, and his ability to function well socially and develop healthy, durable bonds is enhanced.

Cribs and play pens which protect the infant but nevertheless isolate him do not further social imprinting, nor do such tranquilizers as propped bottles or pacifiers. Some ethologists suggest that the greater independence of mind that characterizes modern Western children is due to lack of imprinting. "A moderate attenuation of basic trust may thus help one cope with the problems of contemporary life," to quote Hass.[5] This implies that a slightly paranoid view of other people may be helpful because one cannot, in fact, trust one's fellow man. To me this argument seems circular: Improperly imprinted, we do not trust, so we cannot be trusted. This would argue for more improper imprinting to instill more distrust as a defense against untrustworthiness.

Following the parental bond is the fraternal bond, for which the sensitive imprinting period is about age 16 to 18. Fraternal bonding

---

[4] Hans Hass, *The Human Animal: The Mystery of Man's Behavior* (New York: G. P. Putnam's Sons, 1970), p. 164.

[5] Ibid., p. 165.

applies mainly to the male, the hunter. Little evidence from any culture indicates a strong female equivalent outside the family.

Because the need to provide care in prolonged childhood made bisexual hunting impractical, the hominids developed a division of labor based on sex. The men hunted, the women maintained the camp, cared for the children, and gathered what they could find. Different bonding properties developed—fraternal for men and family for women. Anatomical differences between the sexes, other than those of the reproductive organs, also developed. Today few women can execute a satisfactory overhand throw, nor can other primates. Only a male human can manage this maneuver, which was clearly useful in throwing rocks at intruders or prey.

Other sorts of bonding arose to accommodate the male's fraternal bond. Bonding with particular mates and children, in addition to the hominid's bond with his hunting fraternity, encouraged sharing with those with whom he had established a permanent bond. Thus the pair bond unites man and woman in a nuclear family. While away on the hunt the man could count on his mate's loyalty. The woman's kinship bond with the greater or extended family helped ensure mutual loyalty. While the husband hunted, the wife had social companionship of both sexes and all age groups within the family bond. Her family "rank" rose as she grew older, bonding her more closely to the kinship group. The female thus felt no more urge to compete in the hunter's world than the hunter did in hers. These relationships are discussed further in the section on the genetic pool.

## The Hunter's Fraternal Bond and Muted Leadership

Fraternal bonding among hunters greatly changed the nature of leadership. Morris notes that before man evolved into cooperative hunters, he probably lived in social groups similar to those seen today in other species of apes and monkeys. In typical cases, Morris says, "each group is dominated by a single male. He is the boss, the overlord, and every member of the group has to appease him or suffer the consequences. . . . The whole life of a member of such a group revolves around the dominant animal."[6] Morris goes on to say that, with the growth of the cooperative spirit which was necessary for successful group hunting,

> . . . the application of the dominant individual's authority had to be severely limited if he was to retain the active, as opposed to passive, loyalty of the other group members. They had to want to help him instead of simply fear him. He had to become more "one of them." The old style

---

[6] Morris, *The Naked Ape,* p. 34.

monkey tyrant had to go, and in his place arose a more tolerant, more cooperative naked ape leader. . . . The total dominance of the Number 1 member of the group having been replaced by a qualified dominance, he could no longer command unquestioning allegiance."[7]

Mutual trust and loyalty, comradeship, and shared dangers and rewards buttress the fraternal bond. That teamwork, voluntary and cooperative, arises in such an atmosphere is hardly surprising, since the most effective performance is achieved when everyone agrees on the objective. Consequently the most effective teamwork requires participatory decision making. As the hominid hunter evolved, a desire to participate in the decisions he had to carry out was encoded in his behavioral genes.

The desire to share the products of these decisions, including praise or blame, also developed. A genetic reluctance to accept personal blame for collective failure helped channel man's dominance instinct away from autocracy. The quality of decisions was improved by the participation of those who had to implement them. Better decisions speeded the implementing process by which teamwork controlled for natural selection.

Another bond, which probably involves less imprinting and more conventional learning, binds man to his community or tribe. This bond is seen today as patriotism, nationalism, ethnocentrism, or class and race consciousness. It enabled the hominid genetic pool, or intermarriage population, to expand beyond the local hunting band itself but to retain its exclusiveness. The logistics of a hunting economy put a rather severe limit on the size of a hunting band and its dependents. A tribal bond facilitated intermarriage between adjacent communities, promoted peace with tribal neighbors, and encouraged mutual assistance and collective defense from the incursions of rival tribes. Thus the fraternal social order comprised a fraternity or a confederation of politically independent chapters. The genetic pool is discussed in a later section.

## TERRITORIALITY

Territoriality, or the defense of a male animal's territory, exists in many species, as Robert Ardrey notes in, *The Territorial Imperative.*[8] A British birdwatcher, H. E. Howard, first observed territorially among birds in 1920.[9] It helps to "space out" or limit growth of a species and operates mainly within a species. Several species can occupy a given

---

[7] Ibid.

[8] Robert Ardrey, *The Territorial Imperative* (New York: Atheneum Publishers, and London: Collins, 1967).

[9] Ibid.

territory peacefully, because they rely on different resources under normal circumstances.

Territoriality works on an individual basis for some species, and for others it works collectively. A common pattern among birds and fish is for the males to stake out the territory and the females to compete for the males that have the best territory. Bird song does not hail the joys of spring but warns competitors to keep out. Normally the defense has the advantage in a natural setting. The deeper the incursion, the more the territorial defender gains in courage and the more the intruder loses his.

Territorial defense often is equated with status defense. With no territory, some birds have no status. For humans, many things can take on the coloring of territorialty; usually both social status and economics enter the picture. Workers attempt to stake out craft territories and to defend them from the incursions of other craftsmen. Professional people, scholars and government agencies behave in similar fashion. When territoriality attaches to occupations and jobs, this helps space them out. Moreover, the erection of entry barriers defends an occupational territory from the overcrowding which occurs when additional members diminish the occupation's status by reducing average economic returns.

## RELEASERS

Ethologists refer to releasers as innate release mechanisms or IRMs. The releaser governs which of our instincts command our attention at any one time. We can behave in many ways, but not all at once. Order must prevail in the parliament of our instincts. We can be conditioned to respond to certain artificial releasers, as Ivan Pavlov's experiments demonstrated, but these are not IRMs. Dogs, for instance, will not salivate to the sound of a bell in nature but they can be so conditioned in laboratory experiments.

Other laboratory experiments have proven that genetic conditioning elicits may behavioral responses, as with the orange balloon "releasing" the mother-imprinting response in birds or ducklings. In mother turkeys the sound of cheeping chicks releases a brood-tending instinct. If a concealed loudspeaker emits the cheeping sound from within a stuffed polecat (a natural turkey enemy), the mother turkey hen takes the polecat under her wing. If the hen is deprived of her hearing she may eat her own young because the appropriate signal failed to reach her and thus release her brood-tending instinct.

Hass has prescribed criteria for releasers, noting that they should be

> . . . as simple, unmistakable, and infrequent as possible. The simpler they are, the simpler need be the receiving apparatus and the less the effort

involved. The more unmistakable they are, the fewer failures of communication; and the more infrequent they are, the smaller the risk that other animals will use the same signal and so give rise to dangerous misunderstandings.[10]

The literature of ethology contains hundreds of such examples.

It has been noted above that the appearance of profiles tends to release tenderness and affection in humans. Konrad Lorenz, a founder of modern ethology, lists seven features of profiles: large head; high dome; large eyes in the midportion of the head; short, stubby legs; softness; chubby cheeks; and ungainly movements.[11] Comparative profile forms which trigger our brood-care instinct are illustrated in Figure 7. That men and dogs react in the same way to the same visual stimulus or releaser clearly suggests long lineage. A normal dog has innate inhibitions against aggressing human infants and puppies alike, because he reacts to the cuteness signal in the same way.

It is not necessary to detail here all the various releasers to which

**Figure 7**
COMPARATIVE PROFILES OF
INFANT AND ADULT FORMS

Source: Conrad Lorenz, *On Aggression* (London: University Paperback, 1969).

---

[10] Hass, *The Human Animal*, p. 164.

[11] Conrad Lorenz, *On Aggression* (London: University Paperbacks, 1969).

man responds. Our main concern is with the way the social order will either release or inhibit cooperative behavior in human enterprise. The hominid could not intellectually exhort his teammates on behalf of teamwork, and coercion and fear would work only poorly, if at all. To succeed as a hunter, he had to have a genetic program for teamwork.

Moreover, the perfection of the social order which released cooperative teamwork necessarily preceded the substantial evolutionary enlargement of the human brain. Nature must design both a social order and an anatomy which can make use of a greater brain before substantial improvement in mental powers will be developed. Other primates, as Morris points out, have the requisite anatomy, but more intellectual capacity, even enough to permit language, would conflict with the primate social order based on autocratic dominance. Wolves do have an appropriate social order based on teamwork, but their fourfooted anatomy prevents them from making much use of a bigger brain.

## GENETIC INEQUALITIES

Winston Churchill, whose varied talents and accomplishments won him many admirers, was at one time or another a generalissimo, First Lord of the Admiralty, cavalry officer, newspaperman, painter, bricklayer, novelist, historian, connoisseur, adventurer, and prime minister.

Yet if all humanity had all Churchill's talents but no others, the range of talent found in the human genetic pool would contract to a small percentage of its actual size. Churchill also had disabilities; he made many serious mistakes and proved hopelessly incompetent as Chancellor of the Exchequer. Many a man performs brilliantly in one role but behaves poorly in another.

Were all men really equal, mankind would be highly vulnerable—a disease which killed one man could kill all men, for example. Nature therefore broadly distributed weaknesses as well as strengths among the individuals who comprise the genetic pool, and inequality among individuals plays an important role in survival. Like territoriality, inequality helps space us out. Hopeless confusion would result if we all sought to learn and achieve the same things we all did equally well.

Talent is often mutually exclusive, however. Weight can be an advantage to a boxer but a liability to a jockey. A vivid imagination can prove a serious disability for some kinds of work in which the unimaginative excel, and the reverse also holds. Research has indicated that the imaginative genius does well on menial, undemanding physical tasks because his flights of fantasy prevent boredom but do not interfere with the work. The same person might botch a clerical task which requires close attention to detail. Those lacking much imagination, however, might find the challenge of accuracy absorbing their attention.

The wider the genetic inequalities among individuals in a group, the greater the need for participatory decision making. Within the narrowly prescribed range of abilities in a monkey tribe, the dictator makes sense. The monkey tyrant makes his best decisions alone, without advice from his inferiors. Not so with the emerging hominid, and even less so for modern man. We must bring many individual into the decision process. Large numbers of people raise difficulties, but this does not alter the principle.

Wide-ranging consultation protects man from the inevitable blind spots and disabilities of the lone tyrant, however gifted. We resist autocracy by genetic command. No matter how noble the intention of an imposed decision, we resist it, do not cooperate, procrastinate, conspire against it, resort to sabotage. Even duly constituted, entirely legitimate authority will not endure if it seeks to impose decisions against the desires of a substantial minority.

## THE GENETIC POOL

The tribe formed the primitive genetic pool. Perhaps 99 percent of the pair bonds formed within the tribe. For reasons I will explain later the typical hunting tribe numbered about 500 people scattered around the tribal territory in perhaps eight hunting bands of about 60 people each, including dependents. The tribal confederation of perhaps 12 or 13 tribes scattered over an area approximately the size of Crete or Cyprus followed the development of the human's big brain.

### The Basic Unit of Society

The individual is often regarded as the basic social unit. Obviously without individuals no society could exist, but neither could individuals exist without society. Moreover, the individual nurtured without social contact and hence proper imprinting never becomes a truly human being. Such individuals can form no society if they are later thrown together. This dependence of the individual on early social imprinting for normal social development holds for all primates. It has been proven experimentally among monkeys many times. It cannot logically be argued that the individual is society's basic social unit if he cannot be created without social intercourse and cannot function without social imprinting. It can be concluded, however, that the individual represents the anatomical unit of the species, and the tribe comprises the basic social unit.

The tribe is comprised of a number of separate social components, none of which functions as the "basic" component. Rather each plays a special role in the system. In discussing an aircraft, we would not call the wings, engine, tail, or fuselage the basic component. All must be present in the proper relationship for the aircraft to fly. We could claim, however, that the engines of an aircraft, more than anything else, dictate the nature of the wings and other components. So it is with the tribe. The fraternally bonded hunting band dictated much of the design of the other social components of the tribe and of the social order which systematically bound the tribes together.

## The Pair-Bonded Nuclear Family

The two anatomical units of the tribe, man and woman, must meet and mate to keep things going. The pair bond, together with the offspring formed and partly sustained by it, has the primary role of reproduction. In the primitive hunting band the role of sex assumed importance as the method of ensuring proper bonding and helping to sustain it. The quick and relatively casual copulation of other primates gave way to a more intense human experience. Instead of the periodic sexual urge tied to rut or estrus that is found in other mammals, human sex became a year-round activity. The vagaries of the hunt thus were not in conflict with a periodic sexual urge. In any event, the desire to eat takes precedence over sex. Sex, in whatever random order, could be fitted in between hunting expeditions, and prolonged denial could be compensated for later with commensurate indulgence.

The hunter also looked forward to a return to his children. Bonded to them and to his mate, he not only was willing to share with them but experienced a compulsion to do so. Their helplessness and cuteness helped release his protective and sharing instincts. He did not feel obliged to just any woman or child, however, but only to those bonded to him. This was the basis of the nuclear family.

## The Extended Family or Clan

That the nuclear family does not well serve the nurturing and imprinting needs of the helpless infant has been established. Social imprinting demands a totality of attention which one or two people cannot provide alone. Thus the role of nature's nurturing unit, can be ascribed to the extended family, comprised of many generations and relationships. It also helped hold the natural reproduction unit or nuclear family together. Not only did the female need help with nurture, she also needed social companionship and group status.

Females, biologically more driven to talk than men, could provide more continuous language modeling for the developing infant (whereas much chatter during the hunt could give the game away). Chatter with a largely unresponding infant or conversation with very young children could not satisfy the female's urge to talk, however. She also needed adult social companionship while the men hunted. The members of the extended family filled this need for one another.

Today the withering of the extended family puts a stress on the pair-bonded nuclear family nature never designed it to withstand. Both parties to modern marriage expect from it a fulfillment it cannot, in isolation, deliver for most people most of the time. Not only does divorce increase under these circumstances, but the death of either husband or wife in the nuclear family leaves the survivor emotionally stranded. In the extended family, he or she would remain part of a socially cohesive unit united with kinship ties.

## The Hunting Band as the Economic Community

In the natural social order, several extended families, probably about five of them, banded together to form the economic community which shared the returns of the hunt. This community numbered about 60 people divided roughly into equal numbers of males and females, adults and children. Thus the economic community had available to it, on the average, about 15 able-bodied hunters, but perhaps only 7 to 11 would participate in any one hunt. If all were away together, it would leave the base camp vulnerable to danger. The reserves, therefore, played a vital role in hominid evolution.

Besides base camp defense, the reserves had other uses. When injuries occurred on the hunt, replacements were vital. Those in reserve could at the same time practice individual skills and teach the maturing boys their tactics. Overall, reserves facilitated two vital ingredients of a successful hunting economy: risk taking and operational flexibility.

The hunting band could adjust its size in accordance with the dictates of the hunt, perhaps within the range of 5 to 11. Team hunting could not have made necessary adjustments if it had not had rotating reserves. The failure of many of today's economic enterprises to provide for employee rotating reserves creates pressures to legislate the size of work gangs or crews. Failure to conform rigidly to exact gang size, no matter what the real needs, may lead to strike action.

## The Tribe

The economic community which the hunting band and its rotating reserve corps supported comprised an independent chapter of the larger tribe of fraternal hunters. Perhaps eight such chapters might comprise a minimum tribe, which would be viable as a self-sustaining genetic pool of about 500 individuals. Such a size was effective because less than 1 percent of the marriages would have to be between tribes to prevent inbreeding, and a genetic pool of 500 encourages rapid diffusion of selectively advantageous genetic mutation.

Tribal confederations also arose, especially during the transition to agriculture. The confederation may have been the beginning of human politics. But the tribe itself functioned as the genetic pool; it did not comprise either a political or an economic operating unit.

## HUMAN SOCIAL NEEDS

When certain social needs are met, they release cooperative teamwork, self-motivation, and self-discipline in the individuals engaged in group activity. Identity, status, role, prestige, and reward comprise the major needs. The nature of the social order is defined by the way it caters to these needs. If the social order accords the individual a permanent identity, a rising status, a challenging role with variation and participation, equal opportunity to compete for prestige that is objectively measured, and an equitable share of the proceeds of group endeavor, he will cooperate willingly as a team player.

When the social order meets human needs in such a manner, the individual enjoys natural liberty, equality, and fraternity. Note, however, that by liberty we do not mean freedom from responsibility to others, by equality we do not refer to genetic equality, and by fraternity we do not imply a brotherhood of man. The individual will enjoy freedom from autocracy and arbitrary authority. He will have equal opportunity to achieve prestige under competitive conditions that are not marred by human misjudgment. And he will enjoy brotherhood within his economic enterprise, which engages most of his attention.

### Male Identity

Man achieves identity mainly according to the bonds he forms. When he has difficulty forming permanent bonds, he experiences an "identity crisis." The fraternal bond to his fellow hunters established the identity of the adult male in the hunting society. In the human male, the urge for fraternal association in adventuresome activity has become a drive at least equal in importance to sex in determining masculine psychology. Because Sigmund Freud largely overlooked fraternal bonding and its role in male identity, he overstated the importance of sex as a subconscious motivator.

The crucial time for fraternal bond formation occurs during adolescence, when the human male becomes subject to another imprinting process. The male friendships he forms between, roughly, 16 and 23 will be the most durable of his entire life. Those he forms before and after will not have the same depth of imprinting. Economics, not sex or even politics, lies behind the evolution of the fraternal bond.

Rites of passage play an important role in the formation of this bond. Before the bond becomes formal, the individual has to prove himself worthy. Typically the novice hunter had to endure an extended period on his own. He had to perform feats of skill and perhaps endure calculated torture to test his courage. Such tests have appeared in surviving primitive tribes in such diverse locations as Asia, Africa, and America.

The growing boy knows that his failure to succeed in this trial essentially denies him a male role for the rest of his life. Instinct, however, equips him at this very stage of life with an urge to court great risks, the ability to accept considerable pain, and an overwhelming compulsion to "prove himself." In the hunting economy, conditioning channeled instinct into the pathways of the hunt. Later the urge to take risks became expressed in 400 hp. cars, drug experimentation, and student riots.

Lionel Tiger has argued that the urge for males to band together "can only be elicited (or released) and manifested by real social contact with other other males."[12] Tiger provides numerous illustrations of male bonding which do not appear to include rites of passage, at least no formal or obvious ones. But rites of passage probably increase the impact of imprinting the fraternal bond. At the critical adolescence imprinting stage, they may forge such strong loyalties that the individual thereafter is immune to temptation to break them.

Conjecturing why it took so long for man to undertake much social innovation after he had acquired his big brain, with its capacity for abstract reasoning and imagination, Robert Ardrey suggested: "The humiliating truth must be considered: the arrival of that giant organ to which we attribute human ascendancy had no more effect on our way of life than a fair raise of pay at the office."[13] He believes the reason is that the stern demands of cooperative hunting kept the individual in a "repressed" state. Possibly, but an equally good case can be made that the intensity of the fraternal bond and the loyalties it sparked left individuals without motivation to innovate in ways that might undermine their bond. Far from feeling repressed, the individual likely enjoyed life. He had no motive to apply his newfound imagination to change. A permanent bond and the crystal-clear identity which it conveyed, along with other elements of the social order, fulfilled the individual. We still tend to resist change in situations we find satisfying.

The permanence of the fraternal bond, by crystalizing individual identity, frees the individual from the self-absorption and introspection of an identity crisis. Thus released, he is also free to contribute as a team

---

[12] Lionel Tiger, *Men in Groups* (New York: Vintage, 1970), p. 426.

[13] Robert Ardrey, *The Social Contract* (New York: Atheneum Publishers and London: Collins, © 1970) p. 351.

player. Once formed, the bond normally becomes permanent. Only treason would be acceptable as a reason to eject a fraternal member.

In addition to the fraternal bond, the male hominid also experienced kinship bonds: the pair bond with his mate, a parental bond with his children, and a bond with the tribe as a whole. These bonds completed his identity, with the exception of skill development. In the natural course of events, given his bonds, he would develop these skills to further the good of the bonded groups that accorded him his identity.

If a hunting community grew too large for the available game, it might well split into two sections. One would move off and occupy adjacent territory, but because of common language and kinship ties, the branch-off group would remain within the tribe. According to Lewis Morgan, one of the first to study the social structure of American Indian tribes, such splits occurred routinely and amicably among the American Indians.[14] The splitting, often on the basis of extended family, would cause no disruption of identity for the individual.

### Female Identity

While we have focused on the fraternal bond in male identification, the female bond with the extended family group should not be over-looked. Morgan notes that prior to the rise of civilization in Europe and its imposition on North America, hunting tribes often had a female, not male, lineage. Female lineage tended to bond the female more closely than the male to the extended family clan. The male, indeed, often entered the extended family from the outside, perhaps from another hunting community within the tribe, perhaps from another extended family within the community. Stern taboos prevented marriage within the extended family of the American Indian. Further, the hominid would not necessarily associate the act of copulation with childbirth nine months later. Paternity might not only be in doubt, its very fact might go unrecognized. Maternity was the only certain criterion of descent.

Morgan describes the female lineage of American Indian tribes this way:

> Kindred were linked together chiefly through the bond of their mater-nity. In the ancient gens [extended families] descent was limited to the female line. It embraced all such persons as traced their descent from a supposed common female ancestor, through females, the evidence of the fact being the possession of a common [family] name. It would include this ancestor and her children, the children of her daughters, and the children of her female descendents, through females, in perpetuity, while

---

[14] Lewis H. Morgan, *Houses and House Life of American Aborigines* (Chicago: University of Chicago Press, 1965; originally published 1881).

the children of her sons and the children of her male descendents, through males, would belong to other [families], namely those of their respective mothers. Such was the [extended family] in its archaic form, when the paternity of children was not certainly ascertainable . . .[15]

For females, the ordeal of childbirth, even without a formal rite of passage, served as rough equivalent to the physical ordeal of the young boy entering the hunting band. In both cases casualties could occur. Young girls would sometimes die in childbirth, young boys would sometimes fail to return from their ordeal in the wilderness. The female bond to the extended family and her own identity would be enhanced by childbirth, like the fraternal bond of the hunter.

Female lineage and her strong extended family bonding also allowed the male to be more mobile. On marriage he left one family to enter another, but he still looked to the fraternal bond for his primary male identity. His sons would look to the band of hunters, not exclusively to their fathers, for male modeling.

### The Myth of the Autonomous Individual

The big brain which improved human hunting proficiency also gave birth to an amazing range of abilities having nothing to do with the hunt. The idea that one's true identity can be found mainly in skill development has given rise to the myth of the autonomous individual who fears submergence in the group as a threat to individual identity. Partly this confusion arises from failure to distinguish between bonded and nonbonded groups. Bonded groups in their natural state do not tyrannize the individual, but nonbonded groups certainly can and do.

Genetically, the key to self-fulfillment lies in our bonded identities; skill development remains a genetic side issue. This is attested to by famous and talented individuals who have difficulty trying to find themselves. Those who must ask "Who am I?" lack the proper bonds. Searching within themselves may enrich the psychiatric profession, but it will not help them reach a satisfactory answer; they search in the wrong place. The autonomous individual exists in no branch of the primates, if by that we mean an individual who can satisfy his identity needs in isolation or without social belongingness.

Man does not require the "togetherness" of most other primates. If he is well bonded, his identity will be sufficiently clear to allow him to withstand periods of isolation without undue pyschological damage. One of the better examples in recent times was the behavior of Japanese soldiers who held out in isolated areas for decades after the end of World War II. Some endured almost complete isolation, but so

---

[15] Morgan, *Houses and House Life of American Aborigines,* pp. 4–5.

bonded were they with their comrades and their country that they survived in reasonably good mental health. Without any bonds, the individual has no identity and could only exist as a vegetable, if at all.

The prestige an individual enjoys within his group, bonded or not, does affect his identity and self-esteem. But in the unbonded group the individual tends to strive for stardom. Failing, he feels defeated, often bitter; succeeding, he can become unbalanced from an overnourished ego. He may suffer the disappointment of setting a goal, achieving it, and then discovering his success is largely illusionary. The premature deaths of some entertainment stars as a result of suicide, drug overdoses, alcoholism and so on hardly attest to the success of self-fulfillment from fame based on talent.

In the bonded group, the success of a group reflects on all the individuals in it. Individuals may be singled out for some special contribution to the overall success, but instead of a single star, the glory is distributed, to nourish all egos and contribute to all individuals' identity. Group success avoids ego overnourishment beyond the individual's capacity to live up to his reputation.

Achievement and prestige do not substitute for identity bonds, however. Our emotions do not prepare us to cope with the role of superstar because genetic inequality makes us fallible. If we attempt to develop our talents at the expense of our bonds, we risk obscuring our identity in a search for self-discovery.

There are two major sources of the modern American identity crisis. For women, the rapid erosion of the extended family creates difficulties which many cannot resolve within the limitations of the nuclear family. For men, the rise of impersonal bureaucracy has effectively preempted fraternal bonding opportunities in two ways. First, male *banding* in bureaucracy does not of itself achieve fraternal *bonding* because by its very nature bureaucracy discourages effective fraternal bonding. Second, large-scale enterprise has greatly reduced the opportunities for male self-employment in the cooperative semifraternal communities of traditional small-town America.

## Status, or Social Rank

It has been noted that as the child matures and becomes more self-sufficient, he gains in privilege. The six phases the child passes through in reaching adulthood accord him growing social rank, or status, and man retains his need for advancing status or social rank into his adult life. In the natural social order of the tribe, seniority was equated with social rank. The individual rose in social rank as he aged and gained in experience and, presumably, wisdom.

Social rank based almost entirely on seniority did for the early hunters in part what the dominance order did for other primates. Social rank specified who came first and who last. Age-status, however, did not have much to do with specifying who did what. Position was not normally influenced by rank, not even the position of chief, if indeed there was a designated chief. Many, perhaps most, hunting bands had no chief at all. Morgan called a group of several extended families whose male adult members formed a hunting band a phratry (the word has a common root with fraternity, and both imply brotherhood). In discussing the Iroquois, Morgan noted that "There was no chief of the phratry as such, and no religious functionaries belonging to it as distinguished from the gens and tribe." Morgan also noted that "The phratry was without governmental functions . . . these being confined to the gens, tribe, and confederacy."[16]

By the time Morgan wrote, of course, hunting had ceased to be the primary economic activity for the Iroquois. Even by the time of European settlement the Iroquois had made a partial transition to agriculture, and the phratries had become primarily military in purpose. Each phratry, Morgan noted, had a distinct military organization, a peculiar costume and banner, and a head war chief, and tribes went to battle by phratry.

A council of elders held the political power and named the chief of the hunting band. The post might well rotate. No special status or prestige attached to being chief. Morgan describes how the Iroquois lived under such a system:

> All the members of an Iroquois gens were personally free, and they were
> bound to defend each other's freedom; they were equal in privileges and
> in personal rights, the sachem and chiefs claiming no superiority; and
> they were a brotherhood bound together by ties of kin. Liberty, equality,
> and fraternity, though never articulated were cardinal principles.[17]

Morgan goes on to suggest that this may explain "that sense of independence and personal dignity universally an attribute of Indian character." (Until, I might add, that bureaucracy known as the Bureau of Indian Affairs entered the picture.)

According to initial reports, a recently discovered Tasaday tribe in the Philippines includes six families with 13 children and has no leader. A truly Stone Age group, the Tasaday know nothing of cultivation, or war. They apparently need no leader to trap monkeys, fish, and dig for roots; decisions are reached in open council.[18]

Some observers who compare contemporary human hierarchies

---

[16] Ibid., p. 14.

[17] Ibid., p. 8.

[18] John Nance, "Lost Tribes of the 20th Century," *Seattle Times,* July 19, 1971.

with the dominance orders they find in baboon troops or hen flocks draw a wrong conclusion, that a pecking order prevails in human affairs as naturally as in the hen house. Others have noted that the behavior of animals in a zoo gives grossly misleading clues about animal behavior in its natural state, and bureaucracy surely is a "human zoo."

The primate pecking order could not serve in the hunt, because pecking orders do not enlist voluntary cooperation. Therefore the team design evolved. (See accompanying diagram.) By substituting the horizontal team structure for the vertical totem pole of dominance, the individual hunters could concentrate on teamwork rather than dominance struggles. Teamwork becomes possible when social rank is taken out of open competition and based instead on seniority. Within families today social rank typically reflects seniority more than anything else. And no matter how hard corporations and other organizations strive to base social rank on "ability," they typically give in to pressure for

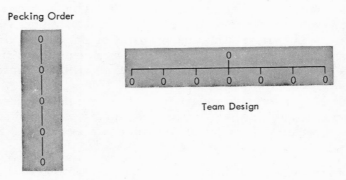

seniority. The organization that tries to merge social rank with job simply guarantees immersion in "monkey business," or dominance struggles. Seniority as the major determinant of job promotion never ensures that the right man will be placed in the right job, but corporations that weld social rank to job title will encounter persistent pressure to "promote by seniority." Objectivity in promotion in personal rank gives seniority its appeal, because seniority precludes human misjudgment.

## Role

The individual must have an identity and an accompanying status before he can have a role to play. But role need not be tied to status; indeed, it is far better that neither identity nor role have formal status, as in the natural social order. Then the individual can behave flexibly when it comes to his role, as he must if the group is to achieve team-work.

The social order must satisfy certain urges the individual has concerning his role. First, the role must be useful. Second, the individual must have a voice in how he plays it. Third, individual roles must not be compared invidiously to one another. Fourth, the individual must have an opportunity to try a variety of roles, for it can never be certain in advance who can do what best. Only trial and error can reliably place the round pegs in the round holes. Therefore the team must have its own reserve forces wherein role experimentation can occur without undue risk to actual performance. The ideal team has no such thing as a dead-end role, nor will it have fake roles designed merely to give people identity and status.

## Prestige and Alphaness

For the hominid, dominance was much attenuated in the interests of teamwork. Yet the hominid genes we have inherited incorporate a desire to rise to the top. The hominid solution to the problem created a sort of mountain range of many peaks where there had been a single height to be scaled. Each skill which contributed to the hunt and had to be developed by learning became an avenue of alpha achievement. In human society, alphaness can be thought of as the desire for prestige, the recognition we all crave from our fellows.

In pointing out the importance of bonding in achieving a clear identity, it was emphasized that achievement did not substitute satisfactorily for bonding. There is, however, a way in which achievement does contribute to identity. Once bonded, and having achieved a clear group identity, we need to establish our individuality within the group and to be recognized for new contributions to it. In the fraternal group, the prestige of achievement, of rising to the top of some specialized skill, sets us apart from others.

If there is no rank order of skills or jobs, individual strengths will be encouraged. Genetic inequality ensures that we will not all compete for the same type of alpha but will seek different avenues of achievement. We may all "try out" for each skill, but we can expect to be beaten out in some and to succeed in others.

If by genetic accident some individual stood out in nearly everything, while others were uniformly underendowed, a crisis of teamwork might follow. Should the well-endowed individual attempt to use his broad base of skills as an excuse to take over, teamwork would suffer. If, on the other hand, he chose to develop only one or two abilities and allowed others to rise in other areas, no harm would be done to teamwork, and he would still enjoy great prestige. Reticence would likely be the course of the well-endowed individual, because he would not, simply by virtue of being broadly talented, have less of an urge for fraternal association. His holding back would contribute both to teamwork and his own self-fulfillment. Thus teamwork depends in part on a reasonably distributed alphaness. Optimum achievement for the team is not dependent on continued maximum achievement by each individual on the team.

The opening of many avenues to achievement best defines the equality portion of "liberty, equality, and fraternity." Multiple routes to the top and equal opportunity to pursue the route of one's choice depend on genetic inequality. Genetic luck occasionally both underendows and overendows a few individuals, and each form of luck brings on its own problems.

The fraternal spirit of the hunting band was continually reinforced because the hunters completely depended on one another, to the extent that each might save the others from death. The weakest might fall behind to become food for the leopard or the hyena pack, but survival of the fittest by no means implies that the weakest or least able were done in by the tribe itself. The weak fell victim to other predators, accidents, or disease.

Tribal members competed for recognized special alphaness, not for survival. Leadership was a form of alphaness, but only one of many. By and large teamwork reduces the need for autocratic leadership. People instinctively resent bossiness, wherever they encounter it.

I suspect the fraternal instinct inhibits the urge for political dominance so long as the individual remains in his fraternal setting. Those with a strong primate lust for power may never experience the full sense of human fraternity. If they rise to the top, as they may, they could destroy themselves and their followers, in the manner of Hitler. The famous quotation of Lord Acton, "Power tends to corrupt and absolute power corrupts absolutely," intuitively recognizes a biological truth.

### Reward

Reward, devoid of implications of status and prestige, is last in importance in the list of social needs. Unless the rewards of our endeavors are sufficient to sustain life, however, nothing else matters. The object of the hunt centered on procurement of food, bones for weapons and tools, and skins for clothing and shelter. Because social rank grew with age and prestige came from teamwork, there was little motive to accumulate material possessions beyond the needs of survival. In a genetic sense, there is no such thing as a materialistic motive. We do strive for status and prestige, which some cultures achieve through material accumulation. In such cultures poverty degrades mainly because it deprives members of status and prestige.

In many primitive tribes no individual ownership existed for such things as hunting territory, food, or shelter. The extended family or clan usually practiced a sort of communalism in food and shelter similar to what we might expect in the modern Western nuclear family. But as Morgan's text on the North American Indian makes clear, nothing remotely approaching state ownership entered into such communal sharing, which primarily occurred on the family level. The Indian tribe shared much as a pack of hunting dogs would. The same sharing process is at work today in the nuclear family. Individuals within the family do not stake out claims on particular potatoes, slices of bread, or hamburger patties; the pantry or refrigerator serves as a communal larder.

Reward depended on how well the hunting band hunted. The product of the hunt was equally distributed, up to the point of subsistence. Only in the past few thousand years has there been any problem of distributing economic surplus; while the natural social order evolved, no consistent economic surplus could accrue. Since economic survival depended on teamwork, equal distribution best served the interest of each individual. The team performed better as a whole if every individual suffered slight hunger than if a few enjoyed satiety while others starved.

Thus the distribution of economic surplus must avoid divisiveness. Assuming everyone shares equally up to the point of subsistence, any method of distribution of surplus which avoids this will work. A distribution of surplus according to social rank probably risks the least amount of divisiveness. Of course, we refer to the surplus of an individual team or enterprise, not the whole economy.

## INTELLECT AND INSTINCT

It can be surmised that the natural social order had evolved more or less completely by the time of the last known hominids, the australopithecines. Otherwise, hominids would probably have failed as hunters. Once the form was perfected, the social order could be stabilized, and the forces of natural selection could turn to improving and enlarging the brain. Fossil evidence suggests that the big brain evolved quite rapidly by the standards of evolution, possibly in as little as half a million years. Most of this expansion occurred in the neocortex, the third and final stage of the modern human brain.

The neocortex accords humans their intellectual superiority over other animals, being the seat of foresight, conceptual and abstract thinking, symbolic language, and extended memory. But as Paul MacLean of the National Institute of Mental Health has shown, two older parts of the brain also exist.[19] One evolved in the age of reptiles. MacLean describes the other as a "lobe of primitive cortex surrounding in a ring the original reptilian brain." The primitive cortex has had 100 times as long to evolve as the neocortex. Consequently the reptilian and mammalian regions of our brain have good neural connections with each other, but not with the neocortex, our human intellect. The older parts of the brain, the limbic system and particularly the reptilian part, play, according to MacLean, "a primary role in instinctively determined functions such as establishing territory, finding shelter, hunting, homing, breeding. . . ."

The tenuous neural connections between our limbic or animal brain and the neocortex prevent these two from fully understanding each other. In Ardrey's words, "The new brain speaks a language the old brain does not understand. Through moods and emotions the old brain can communicate with the new. But only with greatest of difficulty can we talk back, for it is precisely the equivalent of talking to animals."[20] Our neocortex evolved so rapidly that nature did not have time to wire in our instincts with our intellect well enough to prevent their working at cross purposes. One result is observable when we engage in social experimentation and the intellect undertakes to design a social order. Our intellect can devise closed systems which may be triumphs of logic and can produce, on paper, a perfect social order and rational human relations. In practice, however, the system fails to work, because instincts collide with intellectual logic. It is easy for the intellect to make assumptions about human behavior which clash with instincts, because the neocortex has not been wired in adequately with the limbic system. Randomly, invented social orders may contain sound principle wed to nonsense. Classical economics is one such system, Marxism is another.

---

[19] Paul MacLean, "Man and His Animal Brain," in *Modern Medicine*, February 3, 1964.

[20] Ardrey, *The Social Contract*, p. 355.

# Appendix B:

# A Technical Note on Organization

## A MODEL FOR THE MATRIX ORGANIZATION

The text of this book deliberately avoided a technical discussion of how to organize work within the fraternal social order. For those interested in organization theory, this appendix will discuss, broadly, the type of organizational framework that would facilitate a fraternal social order in business or government.

Practically everything useful in modern organizations, bureaucratic or otherwise, has been worked out in the military. The concepts of line and staff, the general and special staff, divisionalization, chain of command, and task forces were first theoretically understood and applied in military terms. One technique of military organization that is vital to the proper application of fraternal concepts has seen only limited civilian use, however. This is the matrix form of organization typified by the U.S. Army's corps-unit system.

The soldier is provided with a broadly based career identity by the corps (such as infantry, artillery, or quartermaster) he is assigned to or recruited into, while the unit (such as the Second Infantry Division or Eighth Army Headquarters) gives him a more specialized identity. Thus the Army as a whole provides his primary identity, the corps comes next, and the unit, which must change frequently, comes last. The soldier wears the badges of all three identities simultaneously. The uniform of an Army captain of infantry serving in the Second Division would indicate his Army identity, the double bars on his shoulders would show his social rank of captain, the crossed rifles on his lapels would identify him as an infantry officer, and the Indianhead patch on his upper sleeve would identify his unit as the Second Division. His

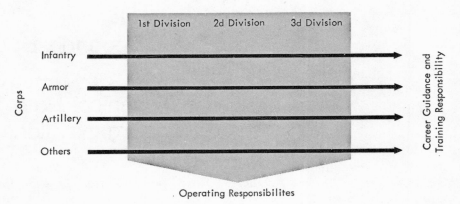

OPERATING UNITS

Operating Responsibilites

uniform will not normally change (except possibly purely in terms of changing fashion). His rank will rise in a reasonably predictable way, his corps could change but typically would not, and his unit identity might change every two or three years. If he were promoted to a general officer position, he would lose his special corps identity.

A simplified matrix of Army units and corps is shown in the accompanying illustration.

The U.S. Army grossly overdoes the corps concept by creating too many narrowly specialized corps, which hampers flexibility. But the concept is sound. The unit-corps matrix facilitates periodic rotation between units and training. Generally the corps run the training activities, while the units take care of combat and logistical operations. The matrix organization minimizes the trauma of transfer, because only the soldier's tertiary identity changes.

## THE MATRIX IN INDUSTRY

Industry would do well to adapt the matrix organization to its own needs. A three-axis matrix comprised of disciplines, functions, and units might be most suitable. The army corps combines function with discipline, in the sense of a body of knowledge. Separating function and discipline for industry has advantages in improving flexibility and lessening excessive attachment to either. A three-axis matrix would also provide for cross-fertilization of ideas. Each function might require several disciplines, while each unit requires several functions.

In the business world, the disciplines would consist of such basic fields of study as mathematics, the various basic sciences, or languages. The functions would include at least production, marketing, and finance, while the units would be comprised of the semiautonomous chapters of the fraternal conglomerate. Precise definitions of all three would depend on the particular business and would necessarily be arbitrary, at least in part.

The disciplines could well follow, in broad outline, typical academic definitions. Provision might also be made for some manual skills from the craft trades and a generalist jack-of-all-trades.

The functions, at least in a large conglomerate, would include such line activities marketing, production, finance, and perhaps engineering. Staff activities such as personnel, purchasing, legal affairs, research and development, and public relations could also be included as functions, but at some risk of matching the army's proliferation of specialized functions. An argument could be made for including such specialty functions under the most effective heading in the line groups, with a catchall category, perhaps administration, to take care of incidental functions. Under this scheme, production could include purchasing, engineering, and research and development. Marketing might include public relations, while administration could cover functions such as personnel, legal affairs, and other special functions.

The disciplines could be responsible for basic training in two senses —early training, and periodic reviews of new developments in the discipline. This training would usually occur completely outside the units, perhaps in colleges and universities (like the Navy's World War II V–12 program) or in trade school equivalents.

Functional training, however, would probably take place in the operating units themselves, close to the job and the needs of the unit. Such functional training would be similar to the combat division's goal of keeping about a third of its force in reserve for rest or retraining replacements. The existence of such training reserves does not mean recruiting additional people but redeploying existing personnel out of make-work, excessively narrow jobs, and bloated staff groups. This implies considerable job enrichment of the unit's operational assignments. The individual could variously find himself being a student, operator, or instructor.

The smaller the business, the less need would there be to separate the disciplines from the functions. The need to separate functions from units declines steadily with progressively smaller firms. On the level of the self-employed, disciplines, functions, and units combine in the person of the proprietor. The larger the business and the more varied its activities, the more useful are these formal distinctions. No matter how large and varied, however, a point of diminishing returns is reached where it does not pay to enlarge the number of functions or disciplines.

## THE MATRIX IN THE CIVIL SERVICE

The civil service might best use a two-axis matrix, because of the way our Constitution reads. The Constitution does not allow for integrated regional units of federal government, thus forcing a merger of units and functions. In a sense, of course, the states are integrated regional units, but they are politically separate from federal government.

The civil service could achieve most of its potential gain in efficiency by a two-axis matrix of disciplines and function-units, or more simply, units. The main breakthrough would be to deman the units (State, Defense, HEW) by putting 20 to 40 percent of their personnel in reserve as students or instructors and, as much as possible, outside Washington, D.C. This move would be facilitated by dismantling the "position classification" apparatus. Position classification more than anything else encourages overstaffing at all levels. As long as it is an accepted personnel policy, nothing will reliably or permanently impede the growth of the civil service.

It would be comparatively easy to do away with federal position classification because a well-developed, widely understood system of personal rank already exists. Those who practice the doubtful craft of position classification could turn their talents to assisting the units in job enlargement and make-work identification, which would free people for possible deployment to the reserves.

Civil servants coming out of reserve would not be assigned back to their original departments, except in special cases, to help diminish the parochial agency viewpoint. Indeed, civil servants should cease to have a primary agency identity. Rank could even be attached to the discipline—e.g., a GS–14 economist or a GS–9 engineer. The civil service also needs a "general officer" category of senior civil servants who lose their special career or departmental identities when they become the federal government's generalists.

Merely rearranging departments or combining seemingly related functions into "superagencies" does little to correct the fundamental problems of the civil service, which lie in the nature of bureaucracy itself. With a fraternal matrix organization, however, the problems of duplication would be much easier to handle. Note the ease, for example, with which the Army creates and disbands divisions. The Second Infantry Division has been in and out of active service many times in this century, and special-purpose units have come and gone by the thousands.

Because reform of government units or departments such as Defense and HEW will never occur without broad support from civil servants, their identity, rank, and pay must be detached from their departments so they can view them and their jobs in them objectively. Objectivity will never be achieved while personal identity and status derive from a classified position. If you attack the classified job you also attack the man holding it, and thus you guarantee his opposition while maximizing the difficulty of reform.

Because the work load of a government civil service is not expected to fluctuate much, outside of some seasonal or other norm, the average percentage of civil servants in reserve should fluctuate less than in industry. Over the long pull, the optimim percentage of people in reserve might be comparatively stable—say 20 percent. But in the transition period, 40 percent in reserve might be a better figure, pending an attritional decline in total government headcount. If no one died or quit, something like 2 to 4 percent of the present 2.5 million civil servants (50,000 to 100,000) would retire annually. By recruiting at half the retirement and quit rate, the federal government could be slimmed down by at least 500,000 people per decade and this process need not use the dreaded (and oft-sabatoged) RIF or "reduction in force."

Retaining more people in reserve than is really necessary for a decade or so would be a cheap price to pay for the quick uncluttering of actual operations. This is where the big savings are. Voluntary means such as attractive resignation bonuses and generous policies on early retirement could speed the slimming process.

## THE MATRIX IN THE MILITARY

The military already incorporates much of the fraternal social order and the matrix form of organization as has been noted. Military reform consists mainly of stripping away the bureaucratic overlay. A prime move would be to apply the theory of employed reserves to peace-time administration. The military, particularly the Army, would require a drastic deployment into reserve of its manpower, particularly senior manpower in top ranks.

Grade creep, the proliferation of senior people in high rank, has almost reached the crisis stage. The military has enough brass to staff a force seven times larger than its current strength of about 2.5 million. So long as so much brass is larded into operations (each general has his own retinue of aides, etc.), chaos is bound to ensue, while make-work will proliferate out of desperation for something to do.

The problem of grade creep is a true dilemma under existing ground rules. If the Army, for example, wants to attract normal people, a reasonably predictable rise in rank on a career basis must be more or less guaranteed. But if it does give this guarantee, it will inevitably overload the top ranks in any period comparable to the Cold War following World War II. Serious loss of morale would follow a purge of officers or the changing of career ground rules.

The problem is made far worse by the normal underutilization of any peacetime military force in garrison duty. Aside from proficiency training, the only real work it must perform is housekeeping, maintenance, and contingency planning. It cannot train 90 percent of the time without growing stale. What happens is a proliferation of Mickey Mouse regulations, spit and polish drills, and destructive concern over the privileges of rank, social protocol, and internal politics. This environment tends to become institutionalized, so that it is taken for granted and deemed both necessary and normal.

What any peacetime military organization needs is some kind of useful occupation for the bulk of its forces, outside the normal routines. Such an occupation should meet serveral criteria. It should be an activity that can be dropped at once in war or other emergency, but it should not be mere busy work, which tends to be dull and contrived. Ideally, such activities should include a fair component of physical labor, in the interests of physical fitness. Extramilitary duty would best occur in a semicivilian atmosphere providing for the wearing of civilian clothes. The aim is to inhibit the growth of exaggerated social distance between ranks.

Farming is an obvious candidate for such an occupation, as is construction and conservation work of various types aimed at improving the environment. None of this activity should bite deeply into standard civilian markets. Weapons manufacture would not be practical, since this activity would probably have to be expanded in case of war.

Farming could aim toward peacetime food self-sufficiency for the military. Highly mechanized types of farming, such as corn or wheat cultivation would probably be excluded. Truck garden farming, both labor and land intensive, might be more appropriate. Growing world food shortages and export demand for U.S. farm products should minimize any market losses to career farmers.

Construction should concentrate on the more labor-intensive forms, perhaps on projects that would normally not receive government or private funding. Environmental improvement, again on projects not otherwise deemed fundable by tax dollars, might be an acceptable area.

These ideas are merely suggestive, but some such extramilitary activity of useful social purpose could help solve the traditional dilemmas of peacetime garrison life. It could also enhance the military's image of being chiefly defensive in nature.

Reform of the Army would include reduction in the number of corps, or functions. I suggest only three—a Combat Corps, Corps of Engineers, and a Logistical Corps. A Medical Corps would be common to the Defense Department as a whole. The number of ranks should probably be trimmed slightly, particularly for enlisted men. Seniority pay increases could continue. It might also be useful to restudy the relationship between officers and enlisted men, which presently reflects an era when enlisted men were largely recruited from illiterate lower classes while officers came from the educated upper classes. So sharp a cleavage no longer applies, although the distinction has not entirely faded.

Under these reforms, a typical peacetime Army career might include 30 percent spent in training, about 30 percent in regular military operational duties, and the remaining 40 percent in socially useful extramilitary duties. While on extramilitary duty, the soldier should have a regular assignment to a combat unit. He would take proficiency training every fourth week or so, with occasionally longer stints.

Such a program would enable the Army to increase the number of combat units by eliminating most of the useless make-work now built into it. Combat units stationed in the States would need only to maintain a cadre on station. Fully trained reserves on extramilitary duty would be immediately available (say on 24-hour notice) to bring the unit up to desired strength in any emergency. This is rarely possible with scattered civilian reserves who resent call-ups short of declared war. The same principle could apply to combat support and logistical units. These too, if staffed to prescribed strength in peacetime (and often in war as well), are grossly overmanned.

The difference between war and peace is somewhat less pronounced for the Navy and Air Force, but both remain seriously overstaffed in peacetime. Both tend to institutionalize contrived peacetime make-work which then carries over into war.

The Israeli Army, as has been noted, has gone further toward putting these concepts into practice than any other army, if not on as formal a basis as suggested here. Of course, Israel's small size allows more informality. Kibbutz life is extramilitary duty for many Israeli officers of senior rank. Should we choose to adopt some of these concepts, America's military might achieve vastly greater defense efficiency, at much lower cost and with smaller forces.

### A CONCLUDING THOUGHT

Military doctrine has long stressed the importance of tactical mobility. This is sound doctrine, both in defense and offense. But more than that, it is a sound principle of organization in general, especially as applied to human resources. The organization which can shift its manpower flexibly to cope with new problems as they arise will always outperform the one that cannot. This mobility, however, requires esprit de corps and teamwork. The fraternal social order in the matrix organization provides the necessary motivation for both teamwork and mobility.

# Selected Bibliography

Abegglen, J. C. *The Japanese Factory: Aspects of its Social Organization.* Glencoe, Ill.: Free Press, 1958.

"Aerospace: End of the Gravy Years." *Time Magazine,* March 9, 1970.

"Akai Announces Japan's Fattest Bonus." *Bangkok Post,* December 8, 1969.

Alatas, S. H. *The Sociology of Corruption.* Singapore: Moore Press, 1968.

Albrook, R. C. "Those Boxed-in, Left-out Vice Presidents" *Fortune,* May 1, 1969.

Albrow, Martin. *Bureaucracy.* London: Macmillan & Co., 1970.

Allen, W. W. "Is Britain a Half Time Country, Getting Half-Pay for Half-Work under Half-Hearted Management?" *The Sunday Times* (London), March 1, 1964.

Ardrey, Robert. *African Genesis.* New York, Atheneum Publishers, 1961.

———. *The Social Contract.* New York: Atheneum Publishers and London: Collins, 1970.

———. *The Territorial Imperative.* New York: Atheneum Publishers and London: Collins, 1967.

Arensburg, Conrad M., et al. *Research in Industrial Human Relations.* New York: Harper Bros., 1957.

Barnard, Chester. *Organization and Management.* Cambridge, Mass.: Harvard University Press, 1956.

Bellah, R. N. *Tokugawa Religion: The Values of Pre-Industrial Japan.* Glencoe, Ill.: Free Press, 1957.

Benedict, Ruth. *The Chrysanthemum and the Sword.* Boston: Houghton Mifflin Co., 1946.

*The Budget of the United States Government, Fiscal Year 1974.* Washington, D.C.: U.S. Government Printing Office, 1973.

Bylinsky, Gene. "New Clues to the Causes of Violence." *Fortune,* January 1973.

266

Catt, Ivor. *The Catt Concept: The New Industrial Darwinism.* New York: G. P. Putnam's Sons, 1971.

Chandler, A. D., Jr. *Strategy and Structure.* Cambridge, Mass.: M.I.T. Press, 1962.

Clark, Alan. *Barbarossa.* New York: Signet, 1966.

Constable, George, et al. *The Neanderthals.* New York: Time-Life Books, 1973.

Coon, C. S. *The Hunting Peoples.* Boston: Little Brown & Co., 1971.

Crozier, Michel. *The Bureaucratic Phenomenon.* Chicago: University of Chicago Press, 1964.

Dahl, R. A. *After the Revolution.* New Haven: Yale University Press, 1970.

Dalton, J. W., and Thompson, P. H. "Accelerating Obsolescence of Older Engineers." *Harvard Business Review,* September/October 1971.

de Bary, W., Tsunoda, R., and Keene, D. *Sources of Japanese Tradition.* New York: Columbia University Press, 1960.

De Mente, Boye. "Can We Learn From Japan?" *Worldwide P & I Planning,* March/April 1970.

――――. "Japan's Unite to Win Philosophy." *Worldwide P & I Planning,* September/October 1968.

de Tocqueville, Alexis. *Democracy in America.* New York: Washington Square Press, 1964.

De Vore, Irvin, et al. *Primate Behavior.* New York, Holt, Rinehart & Winston, 1965.

――――. *The Primates.* New York: Time-Life Books, 1965.

Donovan, Robert V., et al. *Israel's Fight for Survival.* New York: Signet, 1967.

Drake, H. B. "Major D.O.D. Procurement at War with Reality." *Harvard Business Review,* January/February 1970.

Drucker, Peter F. *The Age of Discontinuity.* New York: Harper & Row, 1968.

――――. *Managing for Results.* London, Pan Books Ltd., 1964.

――――. *The Practice of Management.* New York: Harper Bros., 1954.

――――. "What We Can Learn from Japanese Management." *Harvard Business Review,* March/April 1971.

Eibl-Eibsfeldt, Irenäus. *Ethology: The Biology of Behavior.* New York: Holt, Rinehart & Winston, 1970.

Embree, J. F. *The Japanese Nation: A Social Survey.* New York, Farrar & Rinehart, 1945.

――――. *Suye Mura: A Japanese Village.* Chicago: University of Chicago Press, 1939.

Etzioni, Amitai. *Modern Organizations.* Englewood Cliffs, N. J.: Prentice-Hall, 1964.

Fair, Charles. *From the Jaws of Victory.* New York: Simon & Schuster, 1971.

Fei, V. C. H., and Ranis, Gustav. "Capital Accumulation and Economic Development." *The American Economic Review,* June 1963.

268

Financial Times Staff. *Japan, Miracle 1970.* London: Longmans, 1970.

Fitzgerald, A. Ernest. *The High Priests of Waste.* New York: W. W. Norton & Co., 1972.

Fitzgerald, T. H. "Why Motivation Theory Doesn't Work." *Harvard Business Review,* July/August 1971.

Flanders, Allan. *The Fawley Productivity Agreements.* London: Faber & Faber, 1964.

Fromm, Erich. *The Anatomy of Human Destructiveness.* New York: Holt, Rinehart & Winston, 1973.

Fromm, Erich. "Man Would as Soon Flee as Fight." *Psychology Today,* August 1973.

Fujihara, G. *The Spirit of Japanese Industry.* Tokyo: Hokuseido Press, 1936.

Galbraith, John Kenneth. *The Affluent Society.* Boston: Houghton Mifflin Co., 1959.

_____. *The New Industrial State.* Boston: Houghton Mifflin Co., 1967.

Gallese, Liz. "The Breaking Point." *Wall Street Journal,* November 30, 1971.

"General Dynamics." *Forbes,* October 15, 1971.

Gerth, H. H., and Mills, C. Wright, eds. & trans. *From Max Weber: Essays in Sociology.* New York: Oxford University Press, 1958.

Gooding, Judson. "The Engineers Are Redesigning Their Own Profession." *Fortune,* June 1971.

Goulder, Alvin. *Patterns of Industrial Bureaucracy.* New York: Free Press, 1964.

Haber, Gordon C. "The Social Lives of Wolves." *Seattle Post Intelligencer,* November 16, 1971.

Halloran, Richard. *Japan, Images and Realities.* New York: Alfred A. Knopf, 1969.

Hass, Hans. *The Human Animal: The Mystery of Man's Behavior.* New York, G. P. Putnam's Sons, 1970.

Heller, Robert. *The Great Executive Dream.* New York, Delacorte Press, 1972.

Hobsbawm, E. J. *Laboring Men: Studies in the History of Labour.* Garden City, N.Y.: Doubleday & Co., 1967.

Howell, F. C., et al. *Early Man.* New York: Time-Life Books, 1968.

Inami, E. "The Labor Movement in the Meiji Era." Unpublished research paper, University of Washington, 1959.

Jacobs, Erie. "Productivity Bubble Bursts." *The Sunday Times* (London), March 7, 1971.

Jay, Antony. *Corporation Man.* New York: Random House, 1971.

_____. *Management and Machiavelli.* London: Hodder and Staughton, 1967.

Kahn, Herman. *The Emerging Japanese Superstate: Challenge and Response.* Englewood Cliffs, N.J.: Prentice-Hall, 1970.

Kato, N. "Eastern Ideas and the Japanese Spirit." In *The Japan Society,* Vol. XIII. London: Transactions, 1914/15.

Kawasaki, Ichiro. *Japan Unmasked.* Tokyo: Tuttle & Co., 1969.

Kerwin, ed. *The Missing Link.* New York: Time-Life Books, 1973.

Kinoshita, Y. *The Past and Present of Japanese Commerce.* New York: Columbia University Press, 1902.

Klein, F. C. "Salaried Workers Find Cherished Job Security Is a Thing of the Past." *The Wall Street Journal,* June 23, 1971.

Kuhme, W. "Communal Food Distribution and Division of Labor in African Hunting Dogs." *Nature* (London), Vol. 205 (1965).

Kurten, Bjorn. *Not from the Apes.* New York: Pantheon Books, 1972.

Lee, Richard B., and DeVore, Irvin, eds. *Man the Hunter.* Chicago: Aldine Publishing Co., 1968.

Leibenstein, Harvey. *Economic Backwardness and Economic Growth.* New York; John Wiley & Sons, 1957.

Levinson, Harry. "Conflicts That Plague Family Businesses." *Harvard Business Review,* March/April 1971.

Lincoln, John. *The Restrictive Society.* London, Allen & Unwin, 1967.

Lockwood, W. W. *The Economic Development of Japan.* London: Oxford University Press, 1955.

Loomis, C. J. "Who Wants General Dyamics?" *Fortune,* June 1970.

Lorenz, Conrad. *On Aggression.* London: University Paperbacks, 1969.

McGregor, Douglas. *The Human Side of Enterprise.* New York: McGraw-Hill Book Co., 1960.

———. *The Professional Manager.* New York: McGraw-Hill Book Co., 1967.

Maas, Peter. *The Valachi Papers.* New York, G. P. Putnam's Sons, 1968.

MacLean, Paul. "Man and His Animal Brain." *Modern Medicine,* February 3, 1964.

Marshall, Samuel L. *Men against Fire: The Problem of Battle Command in Future War.* New York: Peter Smith.

Marx, Karl, and Engels, Friedrich. *Communist Manifesto.* London: Allen & Unwin, 1948.

Mendel, A. P., ed. *Essential Works of Marxism.* New York: Bantam Books, 1961.

Meyers, H. B. "The Salvage of Lockheed 1011." *Fortune,* June 1971.

Miller, P. C., and Form, W. H. *Industrial Sociology.* New York: Harper Brothers, 1951.

Mills, C. Wright. *White Collar.* New York: Galaxy Books, 1956.

Minear, Richard H. *Victors' Justice: The Tokyo War Crimes Trial.* Tokyo: C. E. Tuttle, 1972.

Mitsubishi Company. *An Outline of Mitsubishi Enterprises.* Tokyo, 1930.

Mitsui, House of. *A Record of Three Centuries.* Tokyo, 1937.

Modie, Neil. "Comments of Ex-Boeing Employees." *Seattle Post Intelligencer,* November 17, 1970.

Morgan, Lewis H. *Houses and House Life of American Aborigines.* Chicago: University of Chicago Press, 1965 (originally published 1881).

Morris, Desmond. *The Human Zoo.* London: Corgi Books, 1971.

———. *Intimate Behavior.* New York: Bantam Books, 1973.

———. *The Naked Ape.* New York: McGraw-Hill Book Co., 1967.

Morrison, S. E. *The Rising Sun in the Pacific, 1931–April 1942.* Vol. III, *History of U.S. Naval Operations in World War II.* Boston: Little Brown & Co., 1960.

Myrdal, Gunnar. *Asian Drama.* New York: Pantheon Books, 1968.

"Myrdal's Missing Message, Part I." *Bangkok World,* October 8, 1969.

"Myrdal's Missing Message, Part II: Teamwork, Japan's Secret Economic Weapon." *Bangkok World,* October 15, 1969.

"Myrdal's Missing Message, Part III: Zaibatsu, Engine of Japanese Industrial Expansion." *Bangkok World,* October 22, 1969.

Nance, John. "Lost Tribe Faces 20th Century" *Seattle Times,* July 19, 1971.

Nitobe, I. *Bushido.* Tokyo: Teibi Press, 1908.

Norman, E. H. *Japan's Emergence as a Modern State.* New York: Institute of Pacific Relations, 1940.

Nossiter, Bernard D. "F–111 Replacement Starts Row." *The Bangkok Post,* April 15, 1970.

———. "Records Shed Light on F–111 Procurement." *Pacific Stars and Stripes,* May 10, 1970.

Okakura, Y. *The Japanese Spirit.* London: Constable, 1905.

Parkinson, C. Northcote. *Law of Delay.* Boston: Houghton Mifflin Co., 1971.

———. *Parkinson's Law.* Boston, Houghton Mifflin Co., 1957.

Pavlov, I. P. *Conditioned Reflexes.* London: Oxford University Press, 1927.

Peter, Laurence J., and Hull, Raymond. *The Peter Principle.* New York: William Morrow & Co., 1969.

Pfeiffer, John E. *The Emergence of Man.* New York: Harper & Row, 1969.

Potter, J. D. *Yamamoto.* New York: Paperback Library, 1967.

"Prebendalism: Corruption Understood." *Bangkok World,* March 24, 1969.

"Prebendalism, Part II: Alarming Waste of the System." *Bangkok World,* October 8, 1969.

Presthus, Robert. *The Organization Society.* New York: Random House, 1962.

Randal, Jonathan C. "By Hard Work to the Skies." *Washington Post.,* April 1970.

Randall, C. B. *The Folklore of Management.* Boston: Little Brown & Co., 1959.

Reich, Charles A. *The Greening of America.* New York: Random House, 1970.

Reischauer, Edwin O. *Japan.* New York: Alfred A. Knopf, 1961.

Rice, Berkeley. "The B–1 Bomber: The Very Model of a Modern Major Misconception." *Saturday Review,* December 11, 1971.

Riesman, David, Glazer, Nathan, and Denny, Revel. *The Lonely Crowd.* Garden City, N.Y.: Doubleday & Co., 1955.

Riggs, F. W. *Thailand: The Modernization of a Bureaucratic Polity.* Honolulu: East-West Press, 1966.

Rostow, W. W. *The Stages of Economic Growth.* Cambridge, Mass.: Cambridge University Press, 1961.

Rothlesberger, F. J., and Dixon, W. J. *Management and the Worker.* Cambridge, Mass.: Harvard University Press, 1939.

Rukeyser, W. S. "The World's Fastest Growing Auto Company." *Fortune,* December 1969.

Samuelson, Paul. *Economics.* New York: McGraw Hill Book Co., 1964.

Sansom, G. B. *The Western World and Japan.* New York: Alfred A. Knopf, 1950.

Schaar, John H. *Escape from Authority: The Perspectives of Erich Fromm.* New York: Harper, 1964.

Sellman, R. R. *The First World War.* New York: Criterion Books, 1962.

Serrin, William. "The Assembly Line." *The Atlantic,* October 1971.

Shepard, Paul. *The Tender Carnivore & The Sacred Game.* New York: Charles Scribner's Sons, 1973.

Silberberg, Robert. *Home of the Red Man.* New York: Washington Square Press, 1971.

Skinner, B. F. *Beyond Freedom and Dignity.* New York: Alfred A. Knopf, 1971.

Sloan, Alfred P. *My Years with General Motors.* New York: McFadden, 1965.

Sloyan, P. J. "Fat Albert, The Nightmare of Lockheed's C–5." *Seattle Post Intelligencer,* December 19, 1971.

Smith, E. Owen. *Productivity Bargaining: A Case Study in the Steel Industry.* London: Pan Books Ltd., 1971.

Smith, T. P. *The Agrarian Origins of Modern Japan.* Stanford, Calif.: Stanford University Press, 1959.

―――. "Japan's Aristocratic Revolution." *The Yale Review,* Spring 1961.

―――. "Landlord's Sons in Business Elite." *Economic Development and Cultural Change,* October 1960.

Snow, Edgar. *Red Star over China.* New York: Grove Press, 1961.

"Sony's Akio Morita." *Time,* May 10, 1971.

Spiro, M. E. *Children of the Kibbutz.* Cambridge, Mass.: Harvard University Press, 1958.

―――. *Kibbutz: Venture in Utopia* (augmented edition). New York, Schocken Books, 1970.

*Statistical Handbook of Japan.* Bureau of Statistics, Office of the Prime Minister (Japan), 1970.

Storr, Anthony. *Human Aggression.* New York: Atheneum, 1968.

Storry, Richard. *A History of Modern Japan.* London: Penguin, 1960.

Taylor, A. J. P. *The First World War.* London: Penguin, 1967.

Tawney, R. H. *Religion and the Rise of Capitalism.* New York: Mentor Books, 1955.

Tiger, Lionel. *Men in Groups.* New York, Vintage Books, 1970.

Tiger, Lionel and Fox, Robin. *The Imperial Animal.* New York: Holt, Rinehart, and Winston, 1971.

Toffler, Alvin. *Future Shock*. New York, Bantam Books, 1971.

Toland, John. *But Not in Shame*. New York: Random House, 1961.

_____. *The Rising Sun, The Decline and Fall of the Japanese Empire*. New York: Random House, 1969.

Townsend, Robert. *Up the Organization*. New York, Alfred A. Knopf, 1970.

Van Lawick-Goodall, Jane. *In the Shadow of Man*. Boston: Houghton Mifflin Co., 1971.

Van Zandt, H. F. "How to Negotiate in Japan." *Harvard Business Review,* November/December 1971.

Wallace, William McDonald. "Are Layoffs Really Necessary?" *Seattle Post Intelligencer, Northwest Today,* September 27, 1970.

_____. "Cultural Values and Economic Development: A Case Study of Japan." Unpublished doctoral dissertation, University of Washington, 1963.

_____. The Institutional Environment and Cost Analysis in Developing Nations: A Conceptual Framework. Unpublished report to International Bank for Reconstruction and Development Djakarta, Indonesia, February, 1971.

_____. "Re: How to Negotiate in Japan." *Harvard Business Review,* March/April 1971.

_____. "The Secret Weapon of Japanese Business." *Columbia Journal of World Business,* November/December 1972.

_____. "Two Approaches to Human Labor" *The Wall Street Journal,* March 30, 1972.

Wallace, William McDonald and Comick, Thomas F. *Forecast of United States Domestic Airline Traffic,* 1961–1975. Document TSR–747. Renton, Washington: The Boeing Company, August 1961 (reprinted November 1963).

Wallace, William McDonald and Moore, James. "Calling the Turns." *Aeroplane* (London), October 9, 1968.

Washburn, S. L. "Tools and Human Evolution." *Scientific American,* September 1960.

Washburn and Lancaster. "The Evolution of Hunting." In Korn and Thomson, *Human Evolution*. New York: Holt, Rinehart, & Winston, 1967.

Weber, Max. *The Protestant Ethic and the Spirit of Capitalism*. Trans. Talcott Parsons. New York: Scribner's Sons, 1958.

White, Edmund, et al. *The First Man*. New York: Time-Life Books, 1973.

Whyte, William H., Jr. *The Organization Man*. New York: Simon & Schuster, 1956.

Wilsher, Peter. "Europe and the English Disease." *The Sunday Times* (London), March 7, 1971.

Wissler, Clark. *Indians of the United States*. Garden City, N.Y.: Doubleday & Co., 1966.

Wittfogel, Karl. *Oriental Despotism*. New Haven, Conn.: Yale University Press, 1963.

Wood, Peter, et al. *Life Before Man.* New York: Time-Life Books, 1972.

Yew, Lee Kuan. "The Twain Have Met." *The Sunday Times* (Singapore), November 15, 1970.

Yoshino, M. Y. *Japan's Managerial System.* Cambridge, Mass.: M.I.T. Press, 1968.

# INDEX

# Index

277

282